THE STORY OF
THE FENS

THE STORY OF
THE FENS

FRANK MEERES

Back cover image: Boston Stump by Walter Dexter. Image courtesy of King's Lynn Museums.

First published 2019

The History Press
The Mill, Brimscombe Port
Stroud, Gloucestershire, GL5 2QG
www.thehistorypress.co.uk

© Frank Meeres, 2019

British Library Cataloguing in Publication Data.
A catalogue record for this book is available from the British Library.

ISBN 978 1 8607 7697 7

Typesetting and origination by The History Press
Printed in Great Britain by TJ International Ltd, Padstow, Cornwall

CONTENTS

INTRODUCTION

'When you work with water, you have to know and respect it. When you labour to subdue it, you have to understand that one day it may rise up and turn all your labours to nothing.'

Graham Swift, *Waterland*

The Fens are perhaps the part of England most altered over the centuries: it is difficult now to imagine a time when the area was largely under water for much of the year, and the inhabitants lived by exploiting a watery environment. Today the Fens are fascinating in a different way, the skies dominating the flat landscape, while the drainage channels and sluices set the hand of man firmly upon the landscape. The area has been a favourite of mine for many years and I have tried to set out its history in this book. I am indebted to many friends with whom I have put up in Fenland homes, and also to Ayscoughfee Hall in Spalding – an amazing museum of Fenland heritage – uniquely for permission to see some of their images. I have worked for many years as an archivist at the Norfolk Record Office, which has also kindly allowed me to use some images from the archive.

Leisure craft on the Ouse near Ely.

Sheep graze in front of Ely Cathedral.

One

ORIGINS

Merrily sang they, the monks at Ely,
When Cnut the King he rowed thereby;
Row to the shore, men', said the King,
'And let us hear these monks to sing'.[1]

Landscape historians like to talk in terms of a *pays*, a distinctive countryside that is a product of physical differences in geology, soil, topography, and climate, and also of differences in settlement history and rural settlement, which give each *pays* its distinctive character. Few places today retain such individual character but Fenland certainly does. As the historian Mark Overton writes: 'the [last] remaining two types of *pays* are the fenlands and marshlands ... Fenlands were regularly drowned by overflowing rivers. They were therefore mainly pastoral economies, supplemented by fishing and fowling, but where arable land was available it was often very fertile. The Fens were inhospitable to outsiders, partly because of disease, and were typically peasant communities. The marshlands were also primarily grazing areas, but had more arable land than the fenlands and a more hierarchical social structure. They were also more accessible, less unhealthy and more fully exploited.' H.V. Morton was even more emphatic: 'You must not confuse the fens with the marshes of Lincolnshire. These two words have a meaning in Lincolnshire which does not correspond with the ordinary dictionary version. The marshes border the coast, and were once under the sea; the fen has been reclaimed from the swamp.'[2]

The watercourses that run through the Fens have frequently changed throughout the centuries. Ancient river networks can still be seen in aerial photographs, in the form of rodhams or roddons – high, silty levees of ancient watercourses left standing above the surrounding surface owing to wastage – and also to the sinking of the peat due mainly to modern drainage. Where the watercourse has been abandoned, whether because it has become choked or because an artificial diversion has been created, a central hollow forms the channel, which has normally become filled with peat. Sometimes the two banks still exist as distinct raised features, but very often, especially where the stream was relatively small, they will have merged into one bank of silt. John Clarke, in 1852, was one of the first to draw attention to the feature, correctly suggesting that they were 'veins of silt' but regarding them as tidal deposits rather than freshwater silt: he called them rodhams. Gordon Fowler drew wider attention to their significance in the 1920s and '30s, using the spelling roddon. Both spellings are in use today, with rodham the more common among Fenmen themselves. These 'silt river skeletons in the soil' (as A.K. Astbury calls them) have been used since Roman times as solid foundations on which to build houses.

The outstanding feature of the ancient water system is that almost all the rivers that now run into the Wash at King's Lynn formerly made their way into a great estuary beginning immediately north of Wisbech: this must be the Metaris described by the Roman geographer Ptolemy. The diversion of the River Ouse to run through Lynn rather than Wisbech is a man-made feature, as we shall see.

The Fens are a large natural depression, inland of the Wash, that was not quite deep enough to be permanently flooded by the North Sea. About 10,000 years ago, at the end of the last Ice Age, the climate grew milder and melt-water from the glaciers caused the sea level to rise. River valleys flooded and became bays, such as the Wash itself. The vast, flat landscape of the Fens was dominated by forest. The lowest lying valleys began to get wetter about 7000 BC: the forest was flooded, the trees died and fell into swamps, which became the fertile peat soils that are so distinctive of the Fens today. Trunks known as 'bog oaks' are often found in the ground by farmers when ploughing: by no means always oaks, these are trees that were drowned when the Fens began to form, or else trees growing in the fen deposits during a dry spell. They have been preserved in the airless waterlogged conditions. When William Dugdale visited the Fens in 1657, he saw for himself oaks that had been taken up near Thorney, and heard stories of many other finds. Local history and archaeology were much more primitive disciplines than they are today, but he was able to draw the correct conclusion: there had been a time in the distant past when the Fens were dry land on which large numbers of trees were growing.

Many bog oaks have been found in the Whittlesey Mere area: these are indeed oaks, and they were growing there around 6,000 years ago. When Alan

'Plan and Description of the Fenns', based on a 1604 survey (Norfolk Record Office, BL 7a/14)

Bloom ploughed up 18 acres of fen in the Second World War, he found enough bog oaks to make a stack 200 yards long, 5 yards wide and up to 8ft high: one monster was 108ft long!

William Edwards, Sybil Marshall's father, recalled that the Fenland ploughman used to carry a bundle of reeds with him: when he struck a tree, he would mark the spot with a reed, and they would be taken out of the ground in winter: 'The wood o' the trees is carted into heaps where it lays for years, till somebody gets sick on it and burns it out o' the way ... They used to be begged for nothing, and hacked up for fuel. Fen folks say as black oak has one advantage over all other fuel. It warms you twice, once getting it a-pieces, and again on the fire.'

In September 2012, a huge oak was found at Southery after a field of Chinese cabbage had been harvested: it was 44ft long and its age was estimated at 5,000 years: the black soil of the Fens had preserved this relic of the past. It was announced that a table would be made from the wood and donated to the 'Queen of the Fens' – Ely Cathedral.[3]

First Inhabitants

There is some evidence of men living in the Fenland areas from the Stone Age. One Mesolithic site is at Peacock's Farm at Shippea Hill. People were still nomadic, following herds from one clearing to another as grazing became exhausted. The Neolithic period began about 4,500 BC, marked by the development of farming: this could be a new group of people bringing new ideas, or just a natural development by the resident population. The writer and archaeologist Francis Pryor thinks that that the fields uncovered at Fengate are around 2930–2560 BC and are the earliest fields in Britain, apart from some in Ireland. These fields were not for arable uses, but to contain and manage livestock. He thinks there was no great gap between Neolithic ritual sites and Bronze Age landscape here, both running down to the wetland. Track ways ran through the Fengate landscape – ribbons of land with ditches on both sides, along which livestock were driven. At least one of the track ways was overlain by a Roman road and was therefore pre-Roman in date. Cereal crops would be grown in gardens close to the farmstead, rather than in fields. Three or four Bronze Age houses were found – circular, with an internal ring of posts, probably because the roofs were NOT reed or straw (which would not have been so heavy as to require them) but were covered with turf.

Main communications were by boat, making use of river routes into the Midlands and East Anglia. There would have been land routes around the fen edge or across it on islands rising out of the marsh. The later Fen Causeway originates from the Bronze Age droveways at Fengate through the two islands of Whittlesey: hordes of bronze axes have been found at Whittlesey and Eldernell (the point where the Fen Causeway heads off the island across the wet fen to March 'island'); a log boat was found at the junction between the two islands, suggesting a ferry crossing. Gravel digging in the Fenland in the early twentieth century exposed sections of the Fen Causeway with brushwood foundations – probably Bronze Age in origin.

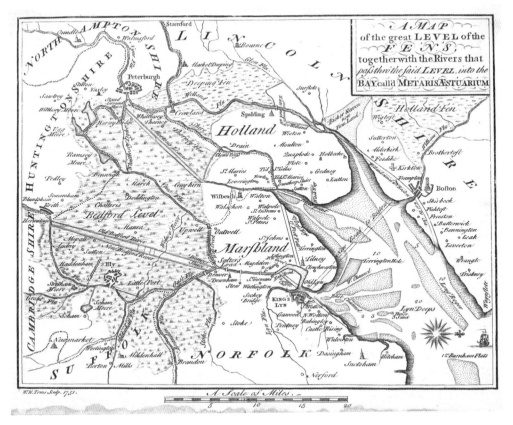

Map of the Great level of the Fens, and the rivers flowing into the Wash, 1751. (Norfolk Record Office, BOL 4/5)

The place to visit to understand Fenland in the later Bronze Age is Flag Fen, discovered in 1982. The finds included large quantities of worked wood – also the earliest piece of fine string – and the earliest dog poo in the country! Flag Fen, at first seen as a Lakeland village, is now understood to be a timber platform, with a boardwalk all round it. Francis Pryor writes:

It was not until we had completed most of the post-excavation analyses, by 1996, that we were able to plot the types of wood used at Flag Fen. The main conclusion was that fenland species, such as alder and willow, occurred most frequently in the earlier phases of the structure. It was not until later that oak began to be used at all frequently. The preponderance of fenland species lower down in the sequence doubtless reflects the fact that the alder carr woods around the edges of the Flag

Fen basin had to be cleared, before construction of the post alignment and the platform could begin.[4]

Flag Fen is more than just a settlement. Broken swords from the later Bronze Age and from the Iron Age indicate a ritual purpose, as Pryor makes clear: 'The withdrawing of metal from circulation may have helped keep prices high, and the public act of destroying something valuable like a sword is itself a sign of wealth. My current "best bet" is that the platform may possibly represent a miniature symbolic dryland within a wetland – in effect, a "tamed area intended for ritual purposes".'

Discoveries at Must Farm, Whittlesey, in 2015 and 2016 have enhanced our knowledge of Fenland life in the Bronze Age. Houses have been found that were built on stilts over a river: they date from 1000 to 800 BC. There was a fire and the houses and their contents collapsed into the river, where they were gradually covered with river silt, and thus preserved. The contents of this Fenland Pompeii include pottery, metal objects, fragments of clothing made from plant fibres – and even two wooden wheels!

The Iron Age

The best example of an Iron Age fort in Fenland is Stonea Camp, one of the few large earthworks in the area. It was scheduled as an ancient monument in the 1920s, but the outer circuit of defences was completely obliterated by aggressive farming techniques in the 1960s. The archaeologist Tim Potter raises the possibility that Stonea could be the very first site in England with a written history as well as an archaeological one: it *might* be the scene of a battle between the Iceni and the Romans, which, Tacitus tells us, took place in a site enclosed by a rough earthwork and with an entrance narrow enough to prevent the Roman cavalry getting in. The Roman soldiers stormed the earthworks and the defenders were then obstructed by their own defences.

Iron Age sites are found on the western fen edge, on a strip of land immediately to the east of the gravel on which lies the long run of modern villages stretching from the Kymes in the north to Bourne in the south. These Iron Age sites appear to reflect the later course of the Roman Car Dyke. There are other minor but important groupings of occupation deep into the Fens, principally in

Wrangle, Whaplode and Cowbit. As in the succeeding Roman period, there is no evidence of land use or settlement in the peat fens.

In such a low-lying marshy area, the smallest upland would act as an island emerging from the wetland – the word 'ey' is a common place name element that means island. These were natural places for defences. A good example is at Wardy Hill in Coveney, on a spur on the north side of the Isle of Ely, where a double-ditched ring-work has been excavated: it was created in the Middle/Later Iron Age and used until the first century AD – a nearby pillbox from the Second World War shows that the ground was being used for the same purpose in the twentieth century as the ditches fulfilled 2,000 years earlier!

The Romans

It was during the time of the Roman Empire that major changes took place in Fenland, with man asserting a permanent influence upon the landscape for the first time. The traditional view is that the area was under direct control from Rome. Helen Clarke wrote:

> Some settlement appears to have taken place in the fens during the second half of the first century, but it was not until the beginning of the following century that full exploitation of the area began. After the Boudiccan revolt we know that a proportion of the East Anglian population was transported, and it may have been then that the original settlement began. At least the western part of the fenland was Icenian territory and it may be that after the revolt the land was confiscated from the Iceni and turned into an Imperial estate. If the whole area had been owned by a single authority it would account for the elaborate system of drainage and communications which grew up.[5]

Oliver Rackham calls the work of the Romans the first draining of the Fens, but does not support the planning idea:

> Falling sea-level at the end of the Iron Age coincided with the coming of the Romans. They had the most elaborate fen-engineering technology that Europe has ever seen, the fruit of centuries of Mediterranean experience. For the first time, by nature and art, the surface of the silt fens was made habitable. The pattern of farms, fields and lanes was haphazard; it looks like piecemeal native settlement rather than

MARCH · FIRST CENTURY
ROMAN OCCUPATION

Roman 'March' as visualised by artist John Moray Smith. (Norfolk Record Office, ACC 2009/161)

the rural planning which would be expected of a Roman colony. The Fens were probably not especially attractive to the Romano-Britons, but were an overflow of population from what was already, by the second century, a rather crowded upland. As in the Middle Ages, livestock may have been important, the peat fens being used for summer and autumn grazing.[6]

Roman Stonea

The Iron Age settlement at Stonea became a Roman town, and perhaps the centre of a government estate. The town appears to have been created about AD 125, and the main buildings seem to have become disused just a century later. However, it continued as a settlement with buildings suggesting it was a farm – and this continued into post-Roman times, the farm probably based on sheep farming. The main artery of the town ran roughly west–east, with a regular pattern of streets crossing it. Tim Malim sums up the evidence:

> The majority of the structures appear to have been timber-framed houses and ancillary buildings with wattle and daub walls, but there were also some more substantial buildings in timber, Roman concrete and stone. Among the latter was the showpiece of the Roman town, the administrative complex, which may have included a tower building rising up from major foundations for perhaps four storeys in height. In an essentially flat landscape such a structure would have been a significant landmark, similar to that provided by the medieval cathedral at Ely in later times.[7]

There was also a temple some 250m north-east of the administrative core of the town with walls of limestone and a double colonnaded frontage. Votive objects included five busts of Minerva, suggesting that the temple was dedicated to her.

Stonea may have been the centre of a government estate, probably for the manufacture of salt, often a state monopoly. Two inscriptions have been found that might confirm this. A limestone block was found at Tort Field at Sawtry on the edge of the Fens: it was inscribed 'PVBLIC', which according to Peter Salway 'leaves little doubt that this was imperial domain'. A boundary stone at Titchmarsh in Northamptonshire bore the letters 'PP', which has been taken to mean '[TERMINUS] P[UBLICE] P[OSITUS]'.

However, this is far from proved and Michael Green has an alternative interpretation: 'I have been suspicious of the interpretation of this structure as an administrative centre from the outset. My architectural thesis many years ago was on Romano–Celtic temples and I recognised that this was a badly damaged example of this class of building.' Green sees the site as a market/fair site centred on a sacred complex: 'It may be significant that the small temple at Stonea had a tree-pit in the centre of the *cella*, 1m wide and deep. A contemporary fresco shows how such "sacred" trees were accommodated in shrines when they became old.'[8]

Whether temple or government office, the buildings were demolished and levelled in the third century: it is presumably the stone of these buildings that have given the area the name it has today, Stonea meaning 'stone island'.

The Car Dyke

The Car Dyke runs around much of Fenland, an artificial waterway that has influenced the landscape for 2,000 years: that great Fenland engineer John Rennie said of it: 'a more judicious and well laid-out work I have never seen.'[9]

The antiquarian William Stukeley, writing in the eighteenth century, was the first writer to suggest that it was Roman: he thought that its purpose was to supply the northern garrisons with wheat from East Anglia. It appears to have been built in a series of sections, most probably in the years AD 140–180.

What was the Car Dyke actually for? It was probably both a drain and a canal, but, as Donald Mackreth suggests, served a third and perhaps most important purpose: as a territorial boundary marker between the presumed Imperial estate and the well-populated upland of mixed ownership on the fen edge.[10]

The Romans made several other canals in the Fens: many of the short canals known as 'lodes' are thought to be Roman. Reach Lode runs for 4km from Reach to Upware on the River Cam: there have been many Roman finds, and the Anglo–Saxon Devil's Dyke was built to end at Reach, so the lode must already have existed. The purpose may have been to provide transport from the clunch quarries at Reach, as well as of grain. Other lodes, such as those at Burwell, Swaffham and Bottisham, are also probably Roman. Three other examples of canals are the Bourne–Morton canal, linking the Roman town at Bourne with a natural watercourse in Pinchbeck North Fen, and shorter canals at Rippingdale and at Deeping St James: all three provided communication with local salt-making works.

Salt

The mainstay of the economy of the Roman Fen is no longer thought to be corn, as Stukeley once supposed, but sheep and salt: indeed, as Tim Malim points out, the latter two went together. The export of sheep as carcasses during the second and third centuries can be demonstrated at Stonea, and salt was essential to preserve the carcasses on their journey. Related products included sheep-gut for the springings to power the army's artillery; leather and hides for shoes, clothing, tents; wool and textile manufacture – the unusual frequency of loom-weights found in the Fens and the fen edge suggests cloth production.

Dairy production – shown in finds of cheese presses, with the milk no doubt coming from ewes rather than cows – made another use of the local salt.

Salt had been produced in the Fens from the Iron Age. The evaporation of sea water to produce salt was practised at Wolferton on the east coast of the Wash and at Denver Sluice on the River Great Ouse. The industry peaked in the early Roman period, declining in the later Roman era, perhaps because of changing environmental conditions. How was salt made? 'Fenland salt was constructed during the Roman period by allowing tidal waters to flow into channels and settling tanks at high tide, and then the brackish water was removed into coarse, baked-clay troughs supported on clay bars above hearts (salterns), which evaporated the water to leave salt.'[11]

Alongside the salt and the sheep, there would have been supporting industries, such as peat cutting for fuel for the salt-makers and local pottery, made on the fen margins.

In the later Roman period a long cool spell gave way to a warmer period: the sea level rose and reclaimed land was lost to marshland and sea. Many Roman sites were abandoned during the third century: these sites show evidence of flooding, with deposition of silts covering earlier features. Peter Hunter Blair writes:

> Evidence of one such catastrophe comes from a small group of huts which have been excavated in the Welney Washes. Here a period of occupation which began in the first century came to an end in the third when a belt of tidal silt six feet thick was deposited in the bed of the stream by which they stood. A further occupation began late in the third century and continued into the fourth, although it was then proving necessary for the farmers to embank their fields, as if to give protection against incursions of water. This was probably the beginning of the process which by the fifth century, if not earlier, had turned the whole of the Fens into a watery waste, fit only for those who sought to earn a living by fishing or fowling.[12]

Saxons and Vikings

The difficulties of the Fens could be advantages, the isolation of the settlements in the area keeping out invaders:

> At a time when most of the smaller kingdoms were losing their identities as they merged in Wessex or Mercia, the kingdom of East Anglia was able to retain a large

measure of independence before its ultimate destruction during the Danish invasions of the ninth century. This was largely because the great belt of fenland reaching southward from the Wash as far as Cambridge served as a protective moat of such width along its inland boundary that the kingdom could enjoy security against aggressive neighbours in the midlands ... In Guthlac's age there were small groups of people, the Gywre for example, whose name means 'fen-dwellers', living along the margins of the fens and on island sites where they could support themselves by the abundance of fish and fowl, but in the age of invasion the fens were avoided in preference for drier sites further inland.[13]

Place names can help us to picture the pre-Conquest landscape of Fenland. The word 'fen' itself is an Old English word referring to marshy land. The Wash is also Old English, meaning 'washing, flood'. Many place names end in 'ey', a Saxon word for dry ground surrounded by marsh, and a very early formation, most commonly before the eighth century. The first part of a place name ending in 'ey' can have various origins. Some are personal names such as Whittlesey and Torksey, others are descriptive of the island such as Stonea, already discussed, and Stuntney ('steep').

A few names refer to the vegetation, like Thorney, or to animals, like the almost unpronounceable Quy, which means 'cow island'. The word Lindsey means 'island of the people of Lincoln'. Place names are not always as straightforward as they sound, and it takes an expert to explain them. Margaret Gelling tells us that Ely does not mean 'island with eels' as one might expect, and as very many books claim, but 'district of eels' and that the final element in Welney is not island at all, but ea, which is a word for river. This word is common in Fenland even today. It is often spelled 'eau' as though it came from the French word for water, and some people pronounce it in that way: really it should be pronounced 'ee'.

Gelling has also explained the word 'beach' found in several quite large places in Fenland such as Wisbech, Holbeach, Waterbeach and Landbeach. Nobody supposed that these referred to beach in the sense of seashore: older books such as Ekwall's *Concise Oxford Dictionary of English Place Names* relate them to the Old Norse word 'beck', meaning a stream. However, Gelling has a different, and, to my mind, more likely explanation of these names, writing:

> The two settlements called Waterbeach and Landbeach are named from the same feature, whether it be a stream (as stated in previous reference features) or a low

Holbeach records its history.

ridge in the fens. They occupy slightly raised ground on the edge of North Fen, the height rising from three feet in the Fen to 20 feet in Waterbeach village. Wisbech occupies a slighter elevation in deep fenland, and Long Beach is near Wisbech. Holbeach has a raised site from which many streams fall away. Ekwall translates Holbeach as 'hollow, i.e. deep brook', but a slightly concave ridge seems a more likely topographical feature. If *hol* is a noun not an adjective, the meaning might be 'ridge in a hollow place'.[14]

The whole district became known as Holland, NOT meaning hollow land as might be thought, but high land – high relative to the low lands around, of course. The word 'lode' is also fairly common, meaning a water channel in a fenny district. Gelling takes one example:

Whaplode lies between Moulton and Holbeach on the slight ridge from which Holbeach is named, with fen on either side. The first element is thought to be an

Old English word *cwappa*, 'eel-pout' [a type of fish], and the 'lode' may have been a partly artificial water-channel in which these creatures were found or were bred. The name 'Spalding' is also an ancient one, preserving the name of another of the tribes of the early Saxon period.[15]

In the time before the Norman Conquest, Viking influence was especially strong in the western Fens. The Lincolnshire Fens came under the rule of Stamford, the nearest of the five Danish Boroughs. Because of this, the divisions of the county are known as 'Wapentakes': in the Cambridgeshire and Norfolk Fens they are called by the English word 'Hundreds'.

Early Christianity

Some of the Roman inhabitants of Fenland were Christians. Archaeological evidence includes lead baptismal vats at Burwell and Willingham, associated with villas; and a pewter plate with a chi-ro found at Earith Road, Willingham. Similar plates have been found at Ely and Welney. The Saxon incomers of the fifth century were originally pagans. They converted to Christianity in the seventh century, and this led to the development of the many monasteries that became such an important feature of medieval Fenland. The monasteries were literally islands in the Fen, they were also islands of Christianity in a world of paganism. The seed spread from these monastic houses: graves have been found as early as the sixth century of people buried with crucifixes: one, of a young girl, was found at Ely itself in 2008, and another, also a young female, was found at Trumpington in 2012: there were links between Trumpington and Ely at this time (Cambridge had not yet come into existence).

Most of the monasteries began very simply, as hermitages, such as Thorney, founded in the seventh century, staring as a community of anchorites: it was sometimes known as 'Anchorites' Island'. One famous name was St Botolph. Born in East Anglia, he founded a monastery in AD 654, on land given by the king of East Anglia. This was almost certainly at Iken in Suffolk, but is sometimes thought to be at Boston, where the town that rose around a church dedicated to him has taken on his name – originally Botolph's stone. Little is actually known about his life, but he was highly venerated, with more than sixty churches dedicated to him.

Etheldreda

Etheldreda was one of four daughters of King Anna of East Anglia, all of whom were to become saints! In about 652, she married Tondberht, a leader of the South Gyrwas, and is said to have received the Isle of Ely as her dowry (although Bede, writing in the eighth century, says nothing about this dowry). She remained a virgin, and on her husband's death retired to a life of seclusion there. Political considerations demanded that she marry Egfrith, the young son of Oswy, the king of Northumbria: at 15 he was her junior by eight years. Oswy died in 670 and Egfrith became king, which led Etheldreda to take up the religious life, at first at Coldingham. She then founded a new monastic house at Ely in 673. It was a double monastery (that is, for both men and women), centred round a restored church said to have been built by Augustine of Canterbury and later destroyed by Penda, the pagan king of Mercia. Etheldreda spent seven years in penitence and prayer before she died in 679 of a plague that also killed several other monks and nuns. The immediate cause of her death was an ugly tumour on her neck, supposed by Etheldreda to have been atonement for her vanity in wearing necklaces when she was a young woman. She was buried in a plain wooden coffin in the monastic cemetery. Sixteen years later, her sister Sexburga, then the ruling abbess, had her exhumed: her body was as uncorrupted as if she had been buried the previous day. The corpse was later moved to within the church and her shrine was much visited by pilgrims. Her name lived on in the Isle: 1,000 years later, in 1657, a young Walpole woman brought a case against her master, who had beaten her black and blue: the woman's name was Etheldreda Moryinson. Another form of the name has lived even into the present day: an alternative spelling was Audrey, and St Audrey's Fair was held every year at Ely. The poor quality of the goods on offer has given us the word 'tawdry'.

Guthlac

Guthlac was born in about 674, the son of Penwalh, who was related to the Mercian royal family, had an estate in what is now Leicestershire and was a Christian. At the age of 15, Guthlac became the leader of a gang who robbed and looted: unusually, he returned to its owners a third part of the booty that he collected. After nine years of this way of life, he had a vision of the fleeting

The story of Ely. (Norfolk Record Office, UPC 313)

Guthlac sailing through the Fens.

riches of the world. He told his gang to find another leader and went to Ripon, where he spent two years learning monastic discipline. Then he travelled to the Fens, to a place described by his biographer Felix, writing within forty years of Guthlac's death:

There is in the middle of Britain a most terrible fen of immense size, which begins at the banks of the river Granta not far from the little fort which is called Gronte [now Cambridge]; now in fens, now in flashes, sometimes in black oozes swirl-ing with mist, but also with many islands and reeds and hillocks and thickets, and interrupted by the braising of meandering streams ... up to the sea ... When [Guthlac] was questioning the nearest inhabitants as to their experience of their solitude ... a certain Tatwine declared that he knew another island in the more remote and hidden parts of this desert [heremi]; many had tried to live there but had rejected it because of the unknown monsters of the desert and the divers kind of terrors. Guthlac, the man of blessed memory, heard this and besought his informant to show him the place ... It is called Crugland [now Crowland, the word means 'barrow-land'], an island sited in the middle of the fen ... no settler had been able to live there before ... because of the fantastic demons living there. Here Guthlac, the man of God ... began to dwell alone among the shady groves of the solitude ... he loved the remoteness of the place which God had given him ... There was in the said island a barrow ... which greedy visitors to the solitude had dug and excavated in order to find treasure there; in the side of this there appeared to be a kind of tank; in which Guthlac ... began to live, building a shanty over it.

However, God did not leave Guthlac without a protector. One night the demons carried him through cloud and mist into the caverns of hell. They were about to thrust him in, when God sent Saint Bartholomew, who appeared in a sudden splendour of light: the demons could not stand the light and Guthlac was saved.

Guthlac moved to Crowland in about 700: he made it famous and attracted many visitors. Perhaps the most important was Aethelbald, a relative of Ceolred, the King of Mercia. Seen as a rival, he was exiled when a mere teenager and spent several years with Guthlac at Crowland. By 730, he had become King of Mercia and, according to Bede, overlord of all the kingdoms south of the Humber. Of two refugees in Crowland, one became a king, the other a saint.

Guthlac died in about 715. Even after his death he worked miracles: when the Archbishop of Canterbury was cured of ague in 851 he attributed the cure to Guthlac, most appropriate for a Fenland hermit. Guthlac's story can still be seen told in stone in the roundels on the west front of Crowland Abbey.

Other early Anglo–Saxon monastic foundations were by royal families of East Anglia and Mercia – Ely, Soham and Medeshamstede (Peterborough). However, early Saxon monasticism in Fenland came to a sudden halt in the late ninth century: Viking raiders brought devastation to Christian communities. Thorney Abbey was destroyed by the Danish raid of 870, Abbot Theodore

The west front of Crowland Abbey. (Norfolk Record Office, BOL 4/34)

being murdered at his own altar: his skull still survives, a grim reminder of those times. Thorney was still an island of hermits: three were also murdered by the Danes at Thorney in 870, two men, Tancred and Torthred, and a woman, Tova. They were venerated as saints there by the year 1000. Crowland was also burnt in 870 and local legend says it was saved from a second raid when friendly people in Cowbit used lanterns to signal the monks of the approach of a Danish raiding party.

The monastic houses were refounded in the following century. Great impulse came from the monastic house at Abingdon: the first abbots of Peterborough, founded 966, Ely, 970, and Thorney, 972, had all previously been monks there. Crowland was also refounded in about 966. When Bishop Oswald met Aethelwine, son of King Athelstan, at a funeral at Glastonbury, the latter offered him the fertile island of Ramsey and a new house was founded there in about 971, originally staffed by monks from an earlier foundation of Oswald's at Westbury-on-Trim, near Bristol.

The monastery at Ely was refounded by Ethelwold, but this time for male monks only. It became the second wealthiest abbey in England (after Glastonbury). As one example, Emma, wife of Canute, presented the shrine

Crowland in the nineteenth century. (Norfolk Record Office, BL/BG 3/9/89)

with a purple cloth covered with gold and jewels. The Liberty of Ely dates to Edgar's charters for the refounded monastery: he gave the abbot the soke over the two hundreds of Ely, comprising the entire Cambridgeshire Fens: by the mid-eleventh century the abbot was holding courts and the Liberty was a county in its own right. These rights passed to the bishop in 1109 when it became a diocese.

H.V. Morton suggests that 'the hill of Ely was so windy and exposed that the monks obtained special licence from the Pope to wear head-coverings which were known as wilkoks', and which has passed down in English as 'billycock' – so that the phrase 'billycock hat' recalls the tough conditions in Fenland and the headgear worn as protection![16]

In the early eleventh century, King Canute, who was a devout Christian, was a frequent visitor to Fenland. He is said by legend to have been rowed to Ely to attend services: on one occasion when he wanted to attend the Feast of Purification there (2 February) he had to go by sledge over frozen waters. He is also supposed to have been caught in a storm on Whittlesey Mere when crossing from Ramsey to Peterborough, as a result of which he caused a channel to be constructed north-east of the Mere. It became known as King's Delph; the name and the story were known to William Dugdale, visiting the Fens in 1657. In truth, King's Delph is mentioned by name in a royal charter of 963, recorded in the *Anglo–Saxon Chronicle*, half a century before Canute's time. However, Matthew Paris, writing in about 1250, said that Canute *erudaverit* (cleared of rubbish) the dyke, so that it was older in origin, perhaps monastic or even Roman: however, no Roman remains have been found, and the dyke is unusual for a Roman waterway as it drives straight across peat fen.

It is very possible that the dyke was a monastic creation: late-Saxon monks took a great interest in drainage, and had the money to get things done. When St Ethelwold refounded Thorney Abbey in 972, he gave three pounds for improvements at Yaxley, and another three pounds of gold, one of which was used for dyking at Farcet. Charters of the 1070s and 1080s refer to a fishery at Westlode as being in an aqueduct, clearly an artificial channel that must have been pre-Conquest, and could be Roman or a later creation.

The stone to build grand monastic houses came from Barnack, a very durable limestone: the quarries were owned by the monks of Peterborough: Peterborough and Ely cathedrals are built principally of Barnack stone. Many abbeys, including at different times Ramsey, Crowland and Thorney, were granted quarrying rights at Barnack, for which they had to pay. As rent for their stone, the monks of Ramsey in the reign of Edward the Confessor undertook to provide their brethren at Peterborough with 4,000 eels every year during Lent.

The Sea Bank

Fenland society was capable of working together to create substantial engineering works: the great sea bank, often known as the Roman bank (a name apparently given to it by Dugdale in the seventeenth century), is now generally accepted as being late Saxon. It is a major achievement. As Oliver Rackham says: 'To construct a seabank and a fenbank, each 50 miles long, is not something which even in the twentieth century we do every year.'

The Sea Bank stretched for 45 miles from Wainfleet to north of King's Lynn, making large loops inland towards Spalding and Wisbech. Much of it still exists, in some places 10ft high – and as much as 10 miles from the present seashore. The surface on the seaward side is considerably higher than that on the landward: this is because of deposition of silt by the tides through the medieval period. Near Wisbech the difference is as much as 2m.

It is not clear if there was parallel expansion inland towards the peat Fens – Hallam thought at least one bank that protected intakes in each of the Lincolnshire silt land wapentakes, and possibly a succession of fen banks at Wrangle in the extreme north, dated from this period.

Some authorities think that the Bank has led to the Norfolk place names Walton, Walpole and Walsoken, the 'wal' element meaning the bank, behind which they all stand. However, other experts in place names think that their names come from the word 'walh' (the same word as Welsh), the Old English word for foreigner, and suggest continuation of British settlement when the rest of Fenland had been inhabited by Saxon incomers.

One monument to those times is the Elloe Stone in Whaplode, of the tenth or eleventh century, and said to have marked the site where the men of Elloe Wapentake held their Hundred Court: it was probably at such meetings that decisions as to drainage and reclamation were made. The stone was removed from its original position sometime before 1889, but was re-erected on a new base to commemorate the coronation of King George V in 1911.

Tom Hickathrift, Fenland's First Hero

Every child in the Fens knows – or should know – the legend of Tom Hickathrift. Hickathrift was the son of a Cambridgeshire labourer, born, in some versions of his story at least, about the time of the Norman Conquest. He was a giant of a

The Elloe Stone.

man, already 6ft tall when he was just 10 years of age. A Lynn brewer asked him to carry beer from that town to Wisbech: the problem was that an ogre lived in the marshes between the towns, who cut off the heads of any traveller trying to pass by! Tom took his cart full of beer barrels and, on meeting the ogre, turned the cart upside down, using the wheel for a shield and the axle-tree for his sword. The ogre had an enormous club and battle was joined. Tom was victorious and cut off the head of the ogre. Entering his cave, he found a vast quantity of gold and silver, which he gave to the delighted brewer, building himself a house on the site of the cave.

Hickathrift's other exploits included defeating an army of 2,000 men and killing a giant that had landed in Thanet riding on a dragon and accompanied by bears and lions: the giant had a head like the root of an oak tree, his hair hung down like snakes, his beard resembled rusty wire and he had one eye as big as a barber's basin in the middle of his forehead. Hickathrift stood his ground and cut off the head of the giant, whereupon a fountain of blood spouted out from the neck reaching up as high as heaven, and the lions and bears vanished in smoke.

The story of Tom Hickathrift goes back many centuries, being told to Dugdale when he visited Fenland in the 1640s:

Tom Hickathrift, the first Fenland superhero.

Now in Marshland there is a famous plain called the Smeeth, which being common to all the towns thereon maintaineth at least at thirty thousand sheep; and yet it is not of a larger extent, in the widest part, than two English miles. Of this plain I may not omit to mention a tradition, which the common people thereabouts have, viz: that in old times the inhabitants of the neighbouring villages had a fierce conflict with Hickafric (then owner of it) touching the bounds thereof; which grew so hot that at length it came to blows; and that Hickafric, being a person of extraordinary stature and courage, took an axletree from a cart, instead of a sword; and being so armed most stoutly repelled those bold invaders.

The story continued to be told in Fenland oral tradition, eighteenth- and nineteenth-century chapbooks and children's stories. Three hundred years after Dugdale, in the early years of the twentieth century, similar tales were still being told, as Arthur Randell recalled:

The person we most loved to hear stories about was Hickathrift, the Fenland giant who lived hundreds of years ago in Marshland, and was, my father always said, a 'civilised' giant and a very good man … We heard how Hickathrift was playing ball one day. After a while, getting bored with the game, he picked up the ball and said to his friends; 'Look, I'm going to throw this ball as far as I can and wherever it lands that's the place where I want to be buried when I die.' Going to the top of a bank of a nearby stream, he hurled the ball with all his giant's strength and it went soaring through the air to hit a church nine miles away, bounced off and fell to the ground just by the south wall. If you go there today you see his grave, just where he wanted to lie after his death.

Hickathrift Farm and House at Emneth commemorate the traditional site of his axle battle, his castle and of his grave. Another tradition connects him with a large grave in Tilney All Saints, while broken columns of memorial crosses in both Tilney All Saints and Terrington St John are known as 'Hickathrift's candlesticks'. A small stone figure on the outside north wall of the chancel wall at Walpole St Peter, supporting a rood stair-turret, is said by locals to be him.

SAINT IVES – THE MAN AND THE TOWN

The settlement now called St Ives was called Slepe in Saxon times: the change illustrates how Christianity worked in Saxon Fenland.

The village of Slepe was owned by Ramsey Abbey. One way in which an abbey made money was from pilgrims – but pilgrims would only come if there was something worthwhile to see. Ramsey did possess relics of a couple of martyred members of a Saxon royal family, but they were not much of a draw. Then the abbey struck lucky. In the first years of the last millennium (1001 or 1002) some fields were being ploughed in Slepe when the plough struck something hard. It turned out to be a coffin, which contained bones and a silver chalice: the village people promptly broke up the chalice to divide among themselves! The bones were no doubt from a holy man, but who? Fortunately the dead man identified himself, coming to a local peasant in a dream. He was St Ivo, a travelling bishop from Eastern Europe who had come to the area to convert the locals to Christianity. There were some doubters, including the village bailiff who said that the bones were just as likely to be those of a local cobbler! However, the monks of Ramsey convinced themselves that the bones were indeed those of St Ivo, and took them to Ramsey Abbey. The village of Slepe was renamed after the saint and a fair was held every year in his honour. The fair was a profitable venture – as can be seen from the stone bridge that was built to enable travellers to cross the river to reach it – and all the profits went to the abbey. The wealth of today's St Ives rests on the 'godsend' of the discovery of the saint's bones one millennium ago!

Two

THE FENS DROWNED

The toyling Fisher here is tewing of his Net:
The Fowler is imployed his lymed twigs to set.
One underneath his Horse, to get a shoote doth stalke;
Another over Dykes upon his Stilts doth walke:
There other with their Spades, the Peats are squaring out,
And others from their Carres, are busily about,
To draw out Sedge and Reed, for Thatch and Stover fit.[17]

Hugo Candidus, a monk at Peterborough in about 1150, gives a vivid description of early medieval Fenland:

> From the flooding of the rivers, or from their overflow, the water, standing on un-level ground, makes a deep marsh and so renders the land uninhabitable, save on some raised spots of ground, which I think that God set there for the special purpose that they should be the inhabitations of his servants, who have chosen to live there. The marsh, however, is very useful for men; for there are found wood and twigs for fires, hay for the fodder of cattle, thatch for covering houses, and many other useful things. It is moreover productive of birds and fishes. For there are various rivers, and very many waters and ponds abounding in fish. In all these things the district is most fertile.

People knew how to make the best of their environment. As Wheeler says:

> So wild a country naturally reared up a people as wild as the fen, and many of the Fenmen were as destitute of all the comforts and amenities of civilised life as their isolated huts could make them. Their occupation consisted in dairying and haymaking, looking after the beasts and sheep which grazed in the fen in summer; and in winter, gaining a living by fishing or fowling.

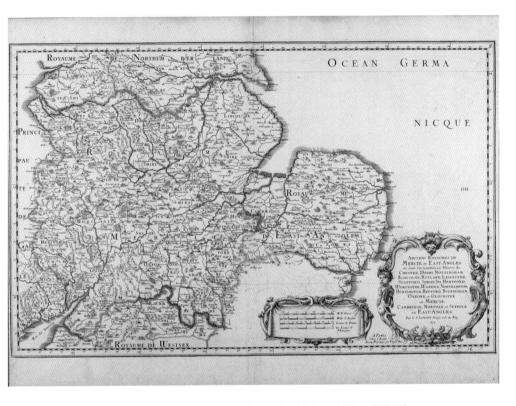

The Fens in context: A French map of Eastern England, 1654 (Norfolk Record Office, RFM 2/5)

The most characteristic sound in Fenland was probably the croaking of the many frogs – they were known as 'fen nightingales'.

The 'drowned fens' seemed a wasteland to some, but there were many 'products' available for harvesting, some of very great value.

Fish were a vital part of the diet in the Middle Ages: even those who could afford a meat diet had to eat fish in Lent, on Fridays and on the many other fast days imposed by the Church. In the Fens, they were abundant. Every authority notes the great importance of the Fenland fisheries. In about 1125, William of Malmesbury wrote: 'here is such a quantity of fish as to cause astonishment to strangers, while the natives laugh at their surprise'. The fish were caught at weirs, the *Liber Eliensis* noting: 'In the eddy at the sluices of those waters, there are netted innumerable eels, large water-wolves [pike], even pickerels, perch, roach, burbots and lampreys which we call water-snakes.'

Even a millennium ago, you could not just take a boat or a net and fish where and when you liked. Regulations, including rules to prevent the overuse of resources, are nothing new: for example, the number of boats on Whittlesey Mere was limited by a rule made in the mid-eleventh century! The Domesday Book informs us that:

> The abbot of Ramsey has one boat, and the abbot of Peterborough one boat, and the abbot of Thorney two boats. One of these two boats, and two fisheries and two fishermen, and one virgate of land, the abbot of Peterborough holds of the abbot of Thorney, and for these he gives pasture sufficient for 120 pigs, and if pasture fails he feeds and fattens 60 pigs with corn. Moreover he finds timber for one house of 60 feet and rods for the enclosure round the house. He also repairs the house and the enclosure when they are in decay. This agreement was made between them in King Edward's time.

In some areas, the benefits of nature seemed almost limitless. Ramsey Abbey had seven fishermen with seven little ships and seven assistants on Ramsey Mere, 'in the deeps of which mere there are frequently taken, with several kinds of nets, as well as with baited hooks, and other fishing instruments, pike of extraordinary great size, called Hakedes by the country folk: and though both fishers and fowlers cease neither day nor night to frequent it, yet is there always no little store of fish.' Communities outside Fenland shared in the demand: in the early thirteenth century, Ralph de Warren gave the priory at Castle Acre near Swaffham in Norfolk two fishing boats on Soham Mere. These fishermen took risks, of course: John Sabyn, a young man, drowned in Wisbech Marsh in 1387 while 'carelessly steering his little boat', and in 1398 John Browham and Thomas Atlane were caught by the sea and drowned at Walpole Ford. These must have been common incidents. They are remembered, the first because the coroner viewing the body was the Cambridgeshire one, setting a legal precedent that the area was in Cambridgeshire (rather than Lincolnshire), which was still being cited two centuries later; the second because it is recorded on a map of the area.

The rules to be followed by the fishermen were determined by local officials. At Wainfleet in 1234, the lord of the manor/port had priority: he could spread his nets to catch eels before anyone else. He was followed by the heirs of another local lord, Ranulf of Praeres, and, only after them, anyone else from Wainfleet who wished. Byelaws for Spalding and Pinchbeck (the earliest series surviving date from 1422) forbade anyone to have more than six weirs. Those who had fishing rights had to cut back bushes and reeds from the dykes at regular times.

Disagreements might result in court cases. In 1290, there was a dispute about fishing rights between Crowland Abbey and Thomas Wake, the manorial lord of Deeping. Wake accused the abbot and his monks of fishing at East Deeping, which was in 'his' area, and claimed that the monks had thrown down a bank that he had made to safeguard the Fen from being flooded. The abbot agreed that he had fished there, but claimed it came within the area to which he was entitled to fish as lord of the manor of Crowland. The bank raised by Thomas was, the abbot claimed, also in the manor of Crowland 'in a certain place where none had ever been before, by which bank the course of those fresh waters being stopt, the fen called Goukesland [within his manor] and other Fens adjoyning thereto were overflown; and the Abbey and Town of Crowland in danger to be thereby drowned; he, the said abbot, perceiving that the above-specified bank was so raised to the end that the said Abbey and town might be drowned, did cause several parts thereof to be thrown down.' The jury decided against the abbey's claims: they found the abbot guilty both of fishing in Wake's property and of damaging Wake's bank, and he was heavily fined for it.

Fishermen might obstruct navigation and the free passage of water by erecting weirs, and also deliberately creating artificial shallows. Orders for Cottenham made at Crowland in 1550 laid down: 'That no fisher put in any mud or sand in mere, dyke or high lake'. In a set of Orders for 1639, 'it is ordered that no person using fishing shall neither lay nor set any engine or net within the fen side of the banks to take any fish nor within ten poles of any lakes end or in or upon any gull or Breach that shall or may happen upon any man's banks Common place or stopping, in or about the bounds of Cottenham, except they first hire them of the town Officers.'

A detailed set of Orders for the Norfolk Fens survive, dating in their present form from 1614 but no doubt merely setting down rules that had been in force for many years, perhaps many centuries. No stamps or weirs were to be set in any lode or sewer unless it was the full width of the channel, and no stamps were to be made in any lakes that were notable drains, unless they were of sufficient width. No nets were to be set in any tunnel or clowes, and no nets were to be used unless their 'mascles' were large enough to allow the spawn and frie [young fish] through – once again, people of old Fenland were just as aware of the dangers of over-fishing as people are today. There was to be no stinging of fish with glaves or pilgars [forms of spear with three or four prongs]: fish killed with these might prove impossible to retrieve, and their decaying bodies in the stream could 'corrupt the waters to the hurt of men's cattle'. A Wisbech court in 1587 ruled that nets, drags, trammels and bunnets were to have meshes of 2½in to allow the fry through.

Individual fish naturally varied enormously in size. Fenland was noted for the size of its pike: Camden quotes an already-old saying, 'Witham pike: England hath none the like', and Sir Joseph Banks recorded taking a pike of 31½lb in the river. In contrast, there would occasionally be immense shoals of sticklebacks in the Witham and the East and West Fens. In the eighteenth century, one man was reported to be earning four shillings a day by gathering sticklebacks from West Fen and selling them at a half penny a bushel. They were spread on the fields as a manure.

Fishing was often a part-time occupation for people who were also small farmers, like William Pardye, waterman of Willingham, on the edge of the Fens. When he made his will in 1593, he left to his only son John two cows, 'all my lodge as it standith ... with the fodder that is upon the same lodge, my boat in the fen, my boots and a pair of high shoes'. There was a drop-off in the number of fishing people leaving wills after 1650, as increasing areas were drained. Fishing might be a common right or private property: the Boston Level Corporation claimed fishing rights and rights of fodder from reeds in their drains. In 1669, the town of St Ives claimed that navigation was inhibited by a fishing weir at Sutton, and there were other complaints that these weirs led to flooding.

Eels were the most abundant commodity of all: they were so much a part of local life in Fenland that rents were frequently paid in eels rather than in cash! At Wells (as the area now called Upwell/Outwell was originally known), twenty fishermen gave Ramsey Abbey 60,000 eels every year, while Castle Acre priory received 2,000 eels a year from fen-edge Methwold. There are many similar examples. Debts might be settled in terms of 'sticks' of eels, a stick being twenty-five. Eels might even be swapped for other desirable products: in the middle of the eleventh century, Ramsey agreed to pay Peterborough 4,000 eels a year in return for building stone from Barnack. These payments were usually made in Lent, when the eating of eels was especially important because it was forbidden to eat meat. By the twelfth century, as the cash economy took over, some of these rents were commuted to cash known as fish-silver, still paid in Lent.

Eels remained an important food source through the following centuries; they could be caught between March and October, especially in September and October when the eels make their annual migration to the sea. They were caught in various ways. One way was with the three- or four- pronged spear, called a gleeve or glave, already mentioned: this could be thrown from the bank or from a punt and had serrated edges so that the eels would not slide off: special scissors were used to cut the eels off the glave. Another method was 'babbing' – threading worms onto lengths of worsted, attaching to a string and dangling into the bottom of the ditches: the eel would try to eat the worm and its teeth would get stuck in the wool, allowing the fisherman to pull the string up. The babber might be in a boat, or fishing from the shore, in which case a bucket, or, in later centuries, an inverted umbrella, would make an ideal 'keep-net'.

An easier way to catch large quantities was to lay traps. There were two kinds of these, both made from willow osier, which gave thin shoots, or withies, also used in basket-making. A hive was a small trap anchored to the bank of the river, which was baited with flesh to attract the eel in: it then found it impossible to turn around and escape. The hive had a bung at the far end that could be taken out when the eelman wanted to remove the trapped eels. The grig was much larger, 5 or 6ft in length with a fan-like entrance. It was not baited: it would be laid in a dyke or a drain in a place where the eel would naturally swim in – and once again it would be unable to turn around and escape. These eel traps would be checked once a day and any trapped eels transferred into a tank or keeping box, a perforated box that would be sunk close to the river bank in which to keep the eels alive until the catcher had a sufficient crop. C.E. Hennels makes a distinction between trapping in fresh water and in sea water: a fresh-water trap was baited with worms, threaded on thin copper wire, a salt-water trap with tiny fish fry that had been caught with a net on the previous tide.[18]

Nets might also be used, as Ernest James of Welney recalled in a letter to James Wentworth Day: 'When there's a summer flood we get a lot of eels down the Delph river, so I set nets right across the river with long tails on called the "cod". Then we put a lot of eel griggs in front, so when the "cod" gets full the griggs fill up. I have had them all full sometimes, about 40 stone in all … We caught a ton once in a few weeks.' The 1587 Wisbech Court recognised that eel nets were different to fishing nets: they were exempt from the rules about mesh size 'for they be small in the meshes for the taking of eels for which they

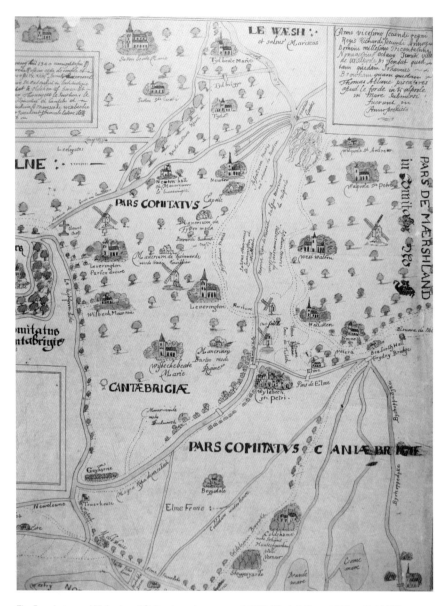

The Fens between Wisbech and Sutton based on a map of 1597. (Norfolk Record Office, BL 14/68)

are principally made'. It decreed that 'setting nets and greggs' were only to be used at night, and that any small fish caught in the nets were to be thrown back into the water.

As always, there might be clashes of interests between different groups. In 1717, the Wisbech Court of Sewers ordered that the sluice at Bevis Hall be

locked: local people were in the habit of opening it up to let the tide water in when young eels were running in the spring!

For coastal settlements, there was also sea fishing on the shores of the Wash, of course, demonstrated by a dispute between fishermen of Moulton, Holbeach and Whaplode in the mid-fourteenth century. The fishermen on the beach were legally obliged to take their fish to the vills and markets of their lords, who of course would have to pay a fee, in practice, it was claimed, many fishermen simply sold their fish on the sand to strangers.[19]

Shellfish were also gathered along the shore, a practice not without its dangers: the tide on such flat shores can come in faster than a man can run. William, son of Nicholas Baly of Spalding, aged 12, was washed out to sea while collecting cockles at Moulton in March 1367.

Wild birds were also a great delicacy, and as the church's prohibition on meat only applied to four-footed beasts, could be eaten during the frequent periods of fast. The twelfth-century monk Thomas of Ely recorded that fens held numberless geese, coot, dabchicks, water crows and herons. He had seen these taken in nets and snares in their hundreds. Monarchs appreciated the taste: in 1249, the abbots of Peterborough, Thorney and Ramsey, and the priors of St Neots, Barnwell, Spalding and Ely, were asked to supply swans, herons, cranes and bitterns for the King's use, and a similar request followed for the feast of St Edward in 1251. The monks, of course, ate the birds at their own table, either making their own catches or buying in. Just one account roll survives for the little priory at Wereham, covering the single year of 1251–52: the monks bought wildfowl on two occasions, once on Christmas Eve, no doubt for a pleasant Christmas treat for this isolated fen edge house.[20]

The birds included now-lost species. Cranes, bred in the Fens, and were a treat for royal and aristocratic households – King Henry III had 115 cranes among the many delicacies for his Christmas feast in 1251. In 1534, when many edible birds were protected by statute, taking of cranes' eggs incurred the heaviest penalty – 20 pence per egg – so they were already becoming rare: the crane apparently ceased to breed in the Fens soon after. Drayton described the lifestyle of the crane and the heron in verse:

There stalks the stately Crane, as though he marched in war,
By him that hath the Hern, which (by the fishy carr)
Can fetch with their long necks, out of the rush and reed,
Snigs, fry, and yellow frogs, whereon they often feed.[21]

The great Fenland writers all talk about the wildfowl. William Camden, in his *Britannia*, first appearing in 1586, wrote that:

> Amazing flights of fowl are found all over this part of the country ... the delicacies of
> the tables and the food of heroes, fit for the palates of the great – puittes, godwits,
> knots, which I take to mean Canute's birds for they are supposed to come from
> Denmark, dotterell, so called from their extravagant doltishness, which occasions
> these imitative birds to be caught by candle light; if the fowler only puts out his arm
> they put out a wing, and if his leg they do the same; in short, whatever the fowler
> does, the bird does the same, till the net is drawn over it.

Camden also noted the vast numbers of birds on the Fens near Boston: 'the fen called the West Fen is the place where the ruffs and reeves resort in greatest numbers; and many other sorts of water fowl, which do not require the shelter of reeds and rushes, migrate hither to breed; for this fen is bare'. He also recorded that the heron was very common, but in his day man was already beginning to have an effect. Camden describes 'a vast heronry at Cressy Hall. The herons resort hither in February to repair their nests, settle there in spring to breed, and quit the place during the winter. They are as numerous as rooks, and their nests so crowded together that Mr Pennant counted 80 in one tree ... They have been considerably reduced on account of the mischief which they do to the land.'

Wheeler quotes a description of the Fens by a Mr Cox:

> As to the fowl this shire, as Dr Fuller says, may be termed the aviary of England, for
> the wildfowl thereof being remarkable for their:

> 1. **Plenty**, which is so great that sometimes in the month of August, 3,000 mallards
> and other birds of that kind have been caught at one draft (as it is here said)
> 2. **Variety**, there being scarce names enough for the several kinds
> 3. **Deliciousness**, wild fowl being more dainty than some, because of their continual
> motion.

Wheeler also quotes the value of the various birds in 1512, as given in Lord Percy's *Household Book*: stints [dunlins] six for a penny; pigeons, terns and snipes three for a penny; lapwings, knots and dotterels, one penny each; bitterns, curlews, sea gulls, plovers, woodcocks and redshanks 1½d each; ruffs,

Fen slodgers.

reeves and partridges two pence each. Wheeler notes that the bittern used to be called the butter-bump, and that its melancholy booming was heard for long distances over the Fens.

Fowl could be driven into nets: this was done when the birds were moulting their feathers and so were unable to fly away: in 1432, a mob seized the nets of the Abbot of Crowland and carried off 600 birds. A late seventeenth-century work describes the 'day of fowling' as the occasion for 'a great concourse of men and boats. To one Fowling sometimes you shall have four hundred boats meet. We have heard that there have been four thousand Mallards taken at one Driving in Deeping Fen.'[22]

Fowlers needed controlling. The Spalding and Pinchbeck byelaws decreed that no one could watch or search cranes' nests, catch fowl in breeding time with nets or engines, or snare swans without the permission of the reeve. An entry in the 1514 Crowland Court Roll reads:

that Thomas Rogers broke the banks or shores of the river, by which the water came into the common marsh lying there and submerged it so that the lord's tenants lost their use of the marsh, to the damage of those tenants, and further they say that the same Thomas placed in the said marsh a certain engine or instrument for catching fowls. And lest his engine be destroyed he would not permit the tenants' animals to be depastured there, but drove them away from thence, to the damage of the said tenants.

At the Waterbeach leet court in 1522, it was ordered that 'none take any fowl viz cranes, butters [bitterns], bustards and herons haws within the commons, and sell the same out of the Lordship unless he first offer them to the lord of the manor to buy'. Also at Waterbeach in 1580–81, it was ordered 'that no stranger hunt or fowl within the manor without licence'. The 1548 Fen Laws said that no one was allowed to use any sort of net or 'engine' to catch fowl before Midsummer Day. The 1614 Norfolk Orders said that fowlers who laid their nets on the fen must fill up and close the grass again.

Fenland was one of the two areas of England most noted for its swans (the other being the Thames). The Crown set up commissions in the two areas in the 1460s and 1470s examining how swans were kept, and at the ways they were caught, by hooks, nets and other 'engines'. They also looked into the taking of eggs. The commissions led to the Act for Swans of 1482. This confirmed the swan as a royal bird. The Crown could lease out swans to individuals or monastic houses: these would mark 'their' swans on the beak so they could identify the ones that they were entitled to catch.

Just one community in England was exempted from the Act: Crowland. This was because the swan was so important there. The inhabitants had exploited great games of swans since time out of mind 'by which the great part of their relief and living hath been sustained'. If they lost these rights, it would lead to the community's 'utter poverty and destruction' so they were exempted from the terms of the Act within the bounds of the parish.

Naturally, the laws were continually ignored and having to be reissued. A swan mote (court) at Wisbech in 1587 ordered that people were to be punished for breaking or taking eggs, for damaging swans' nests, or 'aries', for chasing swans with dogs, or pulling the feathers off a swan's back – 'none but the owner may do it'.

One valued creature to be found in Saxon and early medieval Fenland was the beaver, because of its aquatic habits it was not regarded as meat and so could be eaten in Lent! Its tail was a special treat and other parts also had medical qualities – the testicles and the secretion that gives the musky smell with which the beaver marks its territory. The beaver was highly esteemed by the nobility in the Anglo–Saxon kingdoms: fragments of fur have been found at the royal Sutton Hoo burial site in Suffolk, and beaver teeth have been found used as jewellery – sometimes even encased in gold. These may have been imported, but the beaver whose two mandibles were found in a food refuse dump at Castle Acre castle, dating from the 1140s at the latest, was no doubt caught in Fenland, only a few miles away. Giraldus Cambrensis, writing in the late twelfth century, thought that the beaver was not found in England in his time, only in a few places in Wales and Scotland. They had probably become fairly recently extinct, so that the animal enjoyed by the nobles at Castle Acre may have been one of the last survivors in England.

The cutting of reeds and sedge was another source of profit. Thatch for houses used reed in Norfolk, Hunts and the Isle of Ely; while sedge roofs were found elsewhere in Fen country, where it was once used extensively: it can still be seen at Stretham, Wicken and Fordham, all between Ely and Newmarket. Sedge and reed are very different plants. Alec Clifton-Taylor describes sedge as 'this coarse, grass-like, water-loving plant, which is distinguished from the true grasses by having a stem devoid of joints, offers an excellent material to the thatcher'. It was cut every fourth year. Its leaves are like hacksaws, as recorded in an Anglo–Saxon poem: 'blood draweth from any man that maketh any grasp at it': in America it is aptly called sawgrass. Sedge was tied in bundles, and carried from the fen, on a litter made of two poles, to barges.

Reed was cut each year in shallow water and was very profitable: in the seventeenth century Camden thought that a stack of reeds well harvested was worth from £200 to £300. In the 1880s, Wheeler wrote: 'reed grew naturally in all the unenclosed fens, and before the introduction of tiles and slates, were used very generally for thatching house roofs. They are still occasionally used for this purpose.' A roof of sedge was said to last about thirty years, while one of reed should last eighty years, although it had to be protected from sparrows and starlings by small-mesh netting. Before Whittlesea Fen was drained in 1850, the reed border was worth £5 an acre, while the area of sedge growing outside the reed was worth £1 an acre.[23]

Starlings, known locally as stares, were a menace as they would roost in the reed beds in their tens of thousands, their weight breaking the stems. However, they were a crop in themselves – in the nineteenth century they were being sold in local villages at a penny a dozen. Wentworth Day was told that starlings should be killed by pulling off their heads – this was supposed to prevent them tasting bitter.

Gathering in the harvest of sedge.

Reed cutting was regulated like everything else: it was only allowed in certain places and at certain times of year: at Doddington, for example, turf digging was permitted on the common pasture of Echenesmoor but forbidden on another common pasture, that of Weremere Moor. The Fen Laws drawn up in 1548 said that reed was not to be mown until it was of two years' growth.

The 1614 Norfolk Orders strictly controlled reed cutting. It could only be done by those entitled to do so as tenants of the manor: it was never a freely available resource. Reeds could only be cut between Saint Andrew's Day and 27 March. Each commoner could gather 1,000 sheaves and no more, and each sheaf was to be no more than 4 spans (40in) in diameter where it was tied. The sheaves were not to be left loose on the stubble for more than a fortnight after cutting, and not to be stacked upon 'any heading or leggat in the fen with any gripple or ditch made about the same'. No scythes were to be used in a frost. Any offences against these regulations would result in forfeiture of the reeds by the fen reeves of the manor, whose job it was to police the system.

Personal tragedies recorded in medieval inquests capture the risks of daily life in Fenland. A 6-year-old boy who was drowned while gathering reeds in a Cambridgeshire marsh was probably working with his mother: the incident shows that even young children were expected to help play their part in the family economy.

Thatched roofs look romantic, but were full of insect life, as Charles Lucas points out: 'One morning about five o'clock when some sedge-cutters were going to work (this work had to be done when the dew was on the sedge) they saw one Tom P leaning against his house, "propping up the wall", they called it. They said to him: "Hullo Tom, you are up betimes this morning." "Yes," he answered, "I could not rest a-bed, there is too much company there." He was referring to the flea *pulex irritanae*, "always to be found where sedge is used for thatching".[24]

In the tidal areas, salt-making continued to be a major industry. The salt was vital for preserving fish: 'Ships laden with salt would leave Wainfleet or Saltfleet for the fisheries at Great Yarmouth, and return laden with salted fish. Merchants from Scandinavia came to medieval Boston to buy salt for the Baltic fishing industry.'[25]

The Customs of Wainfleet of 1234 ordered that every man boiling salt there had to give a 'funding' of salt to the lord, defined as one 'satemel', which ought to be 18in in length: there were certain exemptions. Salt-making produces mounds, which can still be seen at Holbeach, Gedney Dyke, and at Wainfleet Tofts, where massive crescent-shaped mounds represent waste from the medieval salt industry, in which Revesby Abbey was involved. The great abbey of Bury St Edmunds in Suffolk also obtained salt from Wainfleet, having an estate at Sailholme: the salt was presumably conveyed by boat via Lynn.

Wheeler says that the salty water was run through three pits. In the first, the mud and silt was allowed to sink to the bottom. The clean water was run into a second pit, where it gradually became brine. It was then run into the third pit to evaporate in the sunlight, leaving behind the crystals of salt.

Salt preserved food in the days before refrigeration, and also provided flavour. The link between a boiled egg and salt – remembered in the Victorian saying that 'kissing a man without a moustache is like eating an egg without salt' – is ancient, as illustrated in a tragic case in medieval Lincolnshire: an 18-month-old boy tried to dip his egg into a salt pan, lost it when it slipped out of his hand and was drowned in the pan trying to retrieve it.

Willows were also valued, arguably the most valuable crop in Fenland: a local proverb says 'the profit of willows will buy the owner a horse before any other crop will pay for his saddle'. J.R. Ravensdale saw osiers growing at the boundary between waste marsh and the fen proper.

The 1548 Regulations allowed 'wythes' [the growth on pollarded trees] to be cut only between Michaelmas and May Day. Camden, writing in 1586, wrote about the Cambridgeshire Fens: 'chiefly it bringeth forth exceeding store of willowes both naturally, and also planted by man's hand': apart from their value as a crop, they helped secure and protect the banks. In 1655, Samuel Hartlib saw immense quantities of willows around Whittlesey, 'which in those vast and vacant grounds being always very moist doth soon produce an incredible profit, and increase of fire-wood and Timber for many Country uses'. The crop was still being harvested in the twentieth century by a few Fenmen. H.V. Morton, writing in 1928, described basket-making from osiers as an 'ancient British industry ... perhaps prehistoric'. He saw it still being practised 'at Ely, Somersham and many Fenland villages'. However, Ernest James, writing in the 1940s, recalled: 'Grandfather ... used to have a lot of women peeling rods [osiers] for him in the spring. There's none of that now. I should think a lot of young people have never seen it done. We sell a lot of our willows to the catchment board.'

Beyond the areas that were almost permanently flooded came 'the half lands' as they were known, land flooded in the winter but usually drying out in the summer months. They were used for hay, for livestock grazing, and also for turf cutting, the basic form of fuel for Fenlanders, and many people further away. Turf cutting was another key fen 'industry', and one that continued into the twentieth century in a very few areas. Charles Lucas wrote in 1930:

Working with wicker.

Turf-digging was also a prosperous industry and carried on up to quite recent times. In the earlier time sods or hassocks were dug with a moorland spade, heart-shaped, but about 1856 a tool eighteen inches long and four inches wide, with an iron flange, called a becket was used, which enabled the work to be done more systematically and laid up in rows to dry properly. The becket was first used in Isleham Fen, and was of smaller dimensions than that used in Burwell Fen, being fourteen inches long and two and a half inches wide. It cut a thousand turf blocks to the ton, whilst the Burwell becket cut only sixty to the hundred. Therefore, if a hundred of Burwell turf were asked for only sixty would be supplied … Nearly all the village people burned turf in their houses.[26]

The 1614 Norfolk Orders show how turf cutting was organised. The fen reeves gathered together in May or June, when they decided if the fen was dry enough to 'grave' turves. They went onto the fen and marked out the areas from which the turves were to be taken. The turves could only be taken up on two days in a year, which would be announced in the local churches. The fen reeves watched as the turves were dug, making sure that the diggers did not use scythes more than 2ft long, and did not dig any pit more than 6ft wide and 2ft deep, and that no pits were made on the 'heading' of the area being dug. Each commoner could employ up to two men on the said two days, and no more. No turves were to be cut at night or on Sunday, and no carts were to be taken onto the fen in the evening or before sunrise.

Digging peat.

Peat working: carrying the turves across a Fenland river.

Peat working, young men and women of the Fens.

There were many fines for breaking regulations about turves. At Landbeach, John Frerer, the lord's reeve himself, broke the rules. He was perhaps blinded by love, the jurors reporting in 1330: 'They say that the same man kept a foreign woman in the lord's bakehouse at the lord's expense, for how long they know not; the same John sent a cartload of the lord's turves, value 6 pence, to the house of John de Waldeseef at Westwyk where Milsent his concubine was staying.' Milsent may not have been as exotic as she sounds: 'foreign' in this context merely means that she was not from Landbeach!

There were many accusations of digging in the wrong places, of over-digging and of selling turves to people from outside the manor for profit. At Waterbeach in 1426–27 it was forbidden to sell turves without licence: in 1558, the fine for doing this was set at 3s for every 1,000 turves and in the following year the penalty was raised to 10s. However, any inhabitant of the manor could give or sell his first 1,000 turves, which shows on what a large scale turf-digging was being carried out on. People's fines were often for digging more than 1,000 turves illegally, and cases of over-digging by 6,000 turves were not uncommon.[27]

The Spalding and Pinchbeck byelaws echo these cases: they forbade the selling of turf, except to fellow commoners. Anyone who dug more peat turves than he could carry away between Mayday and Martinmass had to surrender the excess to other commoners.

The industry continued, on a small scale, into the twentieth century. The last peat digger in the Fens may well have been Bertram Bailey of Wicken, who left school at 12 to join his father in the industry: he stopped digging in 1939 when it was prohibited because every inch of land was required for food production in the war effort.

As we have seen, the tool of the trade was the becket, a word still part of several pub names in the Fens: at first glance it looked like an elongated spade but one could see after closer inspection the angled metal cutter, forming half the end shape of a peat block. The wood part of the becket was made from red willow, while the metal cutter blade was made from such things as worn out rasps forged together by fire, hammer and anvil, the completed implement taking up the time of a blacksmith and his mate from morning to night. Bailey demonstrated the technique:

Bertie took up his position, then drew a marker line with the edge of the cutter on what would then be the wet oozy mass beneath his feet. He marked four widths of the becket to the left, then thrusting and penetrating for fully 18 inches into the soggy peat, withdrawing and twisting the becket, completing the final thrusting on the back run. Then the first oblong-shaped peat product was dug and laid, that is brought up with a squelch and thrown to the side on a predetermined spot, followed by its successors until they looked like a row of black notes on a piano and just as straight. Each block of peat weighed approximately seven pounds when dug ... For three weeks after digging and laying the peat blocks were left to drain and partly dry, then turned and left for another three weeks.

Adders could be a problem. William Edwards noticed how the turf-digger would often tease them with his spade, which had been worn to silver by constant use: 'when the adder was penned it would show fight, and strike at the bright blade glistening before it. Wherever it discharged its deadly poison, the silver would turn to brilliant blue-green in an instant.' The Fenmen knew how to catch them: they would take off their neckerchiefs and shake them in front of the adder, who would strike out at it. The snake's fangs would penetrate the silk, and it would be unable to disengage them. The locals had a dodge to deal with the constant flies and mosquitoes, too: they would tie a bit of rag to a long pole and stick it in the ground: 'the silly, deluded flies buzzed round a bit of rag all day, instead of bothering the sweating men'.

The peat was used for fuel by the local inhabitants. W. Martin Lane recalled:

As a boy I well remember the man with the horse and cart delivering to our cottage the hard, dry, rooty, fibrous black blocks which, before they performed their intended function, were utilised with boyish ingenuity to make our toy brick houses, forts and, I am sorry to say, bird traps. These were constructed with three turfs (as we called them), a small twig to support the centre one in a half-elevated position, a good length of cotton and some corn sprinkled in the right place.[28]

Mary Coe recalled its domestic use in the years before the First World War: 'They used to dig a lot of turf, down the fen, for fires ... The turfs were cut and we used to collect them and put them into the brick oven and stand them up like a cone, not flat, stood up, and they would burn clear till there was nothing much. There was no cinders with it, they burnt to a powder.'[29]

What impact did so much peat extraction have on the Fenland landscape? It is interesting to compare the Norfolk Broads, where it is estimated that some

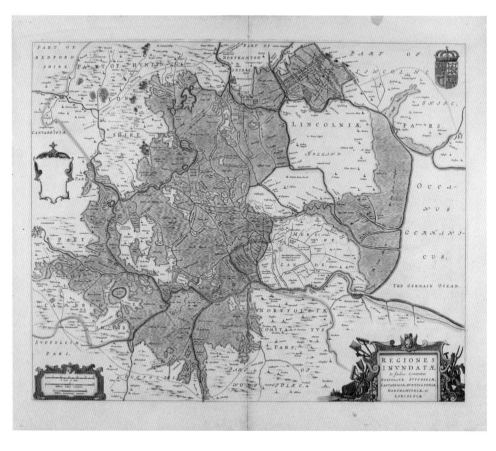

Map of 'fens drowned' showing the areas usually flooded in winter, 1646. (Norfolk Record Office, RFM 2/1)

60 to 70 per cent of the peat was stripped for fuel: flooding then created the lakes that now make up the Broads. Of course, the nearby city of Norwich, the second city in England, was making enormous demands for fuel, not matched in the Fens despite the proximity of Cambridge. However, the Deeps in Lincolnshire are much the same as the Norfolk Broads: it may be that the landscape of the meres of South Cambridgeshire was modified by peat extraction – perhaps the 'Fens' also had 'Broads'? The question is an academic one as the lakes of Fenland have long been drained.

MEN ON STILTS: 'CAMBRIDGESHIRE CAMELS'

In the early fourteenth century, the Assize rolls record the case of a boy who went on *ligni pedes* into the marsh to look for ducks' eggs and was drowned. The Latin translates as 'feet of wood', which could just be some form of clog, but this would hardly seem worth noting in an inquest report: surely stilts must be meant? Camden talked of 'a kind of people according to the nature of the place where they dwell, rude uncivill and envious to all others whom they call Upland-men; who stalking on high upon stilts, applying their minds to grassing [grazing], fishing and fowling'. The peat fen was even worse, 'foule and flabby quavemires, yea and most troublesome Fennes, which the very Inhabitants themselves, for all their stilts, cannot stalke through'. When England was fighting Spain in Holland in the late sixteenth century, the Privy Council asked for a dozen stilt-men from the Fens to be sent to the English army there! In 1611, the traveller Isaac Casaubon saw men driving cattle through the Fens while on stilts: one man was driving 400 head to pasture, with the help only of a little boy!

People on stilts, or the stilts themselves, were often known as 'fen camels', as recorded in a nostalgic article in *The Times* of 21 November 1861: '[the fen country] was long given up to the "Fen Slodgers:", or "yellow bellies" as they were desig-nated, who probably got from their elevation the name of "Cambridgeshire camels".'

Three

FENLAND IN THE MIDDLE AGES

Far to the left he saw the huts of men
Half hid in mist, that hung upon the fen;
Before him swallows, gathering for the sea,
Took their short flights and twittered on the lea[30]

One lasting legacy of the wealth of medieval Fenland is its magnificent parish churches. As Nikolaus Pevsner puts it:

> The churches are always of prodigious scale, from the rich Norman fragment at Bicker to the major buildings of the medieval years that followed, at Long Sutton, Gedney, Gosberton, Crowland and elsewhere. Their silhouettes are always memorable, and this indeed is the key to the landscape of Lincolnshire: whatever is put on the ground by mankind pales into insignificance in a view that is at least two-thirds sky.

Simon Jenkins writes, 'From Cambridge to the Wash, the Fenland churches ride the landscape like galleons on the Spanish main.'[31]

Of Jenkins' 1,000 best parish churches in England, many are in the Fens, the number depending on your exact definition of that area: I make it thirty-four, so that if you add the cathedrals at Ely and Peterborough you have a round three dozen stunning monuments to man's aspirations towards heaven. Some are cathedral-like in size, such as Gedney, 'the cathedral of the Fens' and Walpole St Peter, 'the queen of the Marshlands'. Terrington St Clements is often called 'the cathedral of the marshes': 'we see before us an amazing display of pinnacles and spirelets and these together with numerous windows suggest that the whole of this glorious apparition will float away'. Although Boston has never acquired any similar nickname, it is the biggest of all, the largest unaltered medieval church in Britain.

Churches of Fenland: Long Sutton Church spire.

In such a low-lying landscape, towers can be seen for many miles. The most well-known is Boston Stump, crowned by an octagon – perhaps influenced by the marvelous octagon at Ely Cathedral described later. There are many others. The towers are often detached from the main body of the church –

Churches of Fenland: Fleet Church with its detached tower.

and a few have a distinct lean, the Fenland equivalents to the Leaning Tower of Pisa! Detached towers include those at West Walton and Fleet, while that at Long Sutton was originally detached but has since been incorporated into the church: the early thirteenth-century tower here is roofed in lead, one of the earliest surviving in England. At Donington, the tower acts as the porch. Terrington St John has a detached tower, with a small two-storey 'house' in between said to have served as a temporary lodging for visiting clergy in the event of foul weather and floods.

Gedney displays the start of a stone spire that was never completed: its intended height is estimated at 40 to 50ft. Other prominent towers include Moulton, Spalding, Gosberton and Lutton. Leaning towers include that at Surfleet – the west tower leans considerably. Emneth tower is held together by an encircling chain hidden within the thickness of its walls, the stairway exposing a link-coupling that is periodically tightened to prevent the tower from falling outwards. The curious castellated porch at Holbeach Church is said to have been salvaged from a castle, that of Thomas de Moulton.

There are many wonderful interiors, and some excellent internal features. Gedney, uniquely, has nave arcades on massive timber posts, (but the outside,

Churches of Fenland: Boston Stump.

according to Pevsner, is ruined by 'the hideous N porch of 1931'). The splendid
roof at March, with 118 angels and eight saints and martyrs is 'worth cycling
40 miles into a headwind to see', according to John Betjeman. Other treas-
ures include the stone rood screen at Bottisham, lecterns at Leverington and

Croft, fonts at Leverington and Tydd St Mary, and a fourteenth-century wall painting at Willingham. Wisbech St Mary has a wooden lectern carved from a figurehead from a Tudor warship. The churches of Norfolk Fenland include marvelous sets of pews at Walpole St Peter, Wiggenhall St Germans and, above all, Wiggenhall St Mary.

The spirit of the hermit that had inspired the founders of Crowland and Thorney in the Saxon era had not entirely passed away from medieval Fenland. In 1348 the 'master of the hermits of the hermitage of Saint Christopher' in Outwell and his fellow hermits were pardoned for having erected their chapel in Outwell without royal permission. They were allowed to enclose and build upon an adjoining piece of land. A small room or cell beside the tower at Walpole St Andrew was probably inhabited by 'an anchorite who, according to his own desires, was shut away from the outside world and fed by parishioners until he died'.

The parish church was one centre of the social life of the Fenlander. Another was the pattern of markets and fairs that dotted the area; 'the diversification of the agricultural economy of the fens of south Lincolnshire led to the establish-

Churches of Fenland: Gedney Church.

Churches of Fenland: the porch of Holbeach Church.

ment of markets and fairs in almost every town or village in that part of the Holland division of the county as well as in the settlements which skirted the fens'. The oldest known market is Spalding, mentioned in the Domesday Book of 1086. Most villages had a weekly market, a few towns might have two a week as at Boston and at Lynn, where the Saturday and Tuesday Market Places are still a key part of the urban landscape.

Fairs were even more of an occasion, held just once a year but sometimes lasting several days. The great medieval fairs, such as those Boston and St Ives, might attract traders from across Britain and even Europe. There was a regular circuit of these great fairs, as a thirteenth-century legal case demonstrates. In 1273, a merchant from Bordeaux in France sold wine to some Norwich merchants at Boston fair, but was cheated of his money. He searched for them at fairs at Norwich and Boston in the following year and finally caught up with them at the St Ives fair in 1275! Smaller fairs would draw in people from nearby villages, and be about socialising and entertainment as much as trade, and

A Fenland fair as portrayed by John Moray Smith (Norfolk Record Office, ACC 2009/161)

Fenland Markets: the Market Place, Boston.

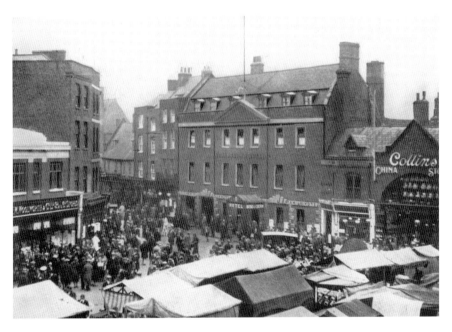

Fenland Markets: Wisbech Market in 1932 (Norfolk Record Office, BR 184/2309)

Fenland Markets: Market Day in Spalding.

gradually developed into the 'funfair' of the nineteenth century, with mechanical rides such as those made by Savages of King's Lynn.[32]

Monasteries

The hermitages had developed into monastic houses, and many others had been founded, attracted to the isolation of Fenland. A well-known verse sums up six of them:

Ramsey the rich of gold and of fee,
Thorney the bane of many fair tree;
Crowland the courteous of their meat and their drink,
Spalding the gluttons as all men do think;
Peterborough, the Proud, as all men do say,
Sawtrey by the way – that old Abbaye
Gave more alms in one day than all they.

The compiler of Ramsey Abbey's *Book of Benefactors* explains in about 1170 that the abbey had lost almost everything in the 'dark and gloomy days' of King Stephen, a generation earlier, both from attacks from enemies and domestic disputes, 'and so we have collected together in one volume our chirographs and the charters of our privileges … as a warning for future ages and to instruct our readers'. The compiler also translated the abbey's pre-Conquest documents from English into Latin to make them more acceptable, describing the Anglo–Saxon language as 'barbarous'. Interestingly, two of the royal charters he includes were undoubtedly forgeries, though we can be charitable and assume that the compiler himself did not know this![33]

William of Malmesbury wrote about Thorney in 1135:

A little paradise, delightful as heaven itself, fen-circled yet rich in loftiest trees, where water-meadows delight the eye with rich green, where streamlets glide unchecked through each field. Scarce a spot of ground lies there waste; here are orchards, there vineyards … A vast solitude is here the monks' lot, that they may the more closely cling to things above. If a woman is there seen, she is accounted a monster, but strangers, if men, are greeted as angels unawares. Yet there none speaketh, save for the moment: all is holy silence.

Crowland Abbey burnt down in 1091, not because of a raid but due to the care-lessness of a plumber working on the lead of the roof of the tower: it is said that a library of 700 volumes was lost in the fire. The fire also destroyed the abbey's Anglo–Saxon royal charters and other muniments numbering nearly 400 docu-ments. Luckily, Ingulf had removed several documents from the archive some years earlier in order to instruct the younger monks in Old English. The present building is that rebuilt after the fire, begun under Abbot Joffrid in 1109 and taking sixty years to complete: it is constructed of stone from Barnack.

Spalding Priory was founded in the late eleventh century. Two buildings in Spalding traditionally associated with the priory still survive – the fifteenth-century range known as Abbey Buildings and the Prior's Oven in Sheepmarket, sometimes said to be the priory prison! Wykeham Chapel in Weston was built in 1312 by Prior Hatfield of Spalding as the private chapel of his country house.

Norfolk also had monastic houses in the Fens. They tended to be much smaller than those in Lincolnshire and Cambridgeshire, and also included the only female monasteries in Fenland. Slevesholm Priory in Methwold, a cell of Castle Acre, was on an island in the Fens – Blomefield says it was known as 'Slush-holm', no doubt because of the marshy nature of the ground. Crabhouse, a female religious house in Wiggenhall St Mary Magdalene, was founded on the bank of the Ouse at a place called Bustard's Dole, which according to the monastic cartulary, was 'all wild and far around on every side was no human habitation'. The site was subject to flooding: the cartulary shows that some of the monastic property had been newly recovered from water.

It was the dedication and hard work of the monastic houses that turned these unpromising sites into profitable farming estates, and this sometimes shows in the surviving records, such as this example of draining from Blackborough, another female religious house in Middleton on the edge of the Fens. The nuns were given a piece of marsh in Tilney by a clergyman called Samson. A ditch or drain was then built around it by William Bek and its agricultural improvement began. However, a monastic house needed capital to invest in its estates and some of these monasteries were simply too small, especially that at Molycourt in Outwell, apparently a Saxon foundation. By the mid-fifteenth century, or so it was claimed, continual flooding had so ruined its estates that there was barely enough produce to feed a single monk! Molycourt was relegated to a cell of the large monastic house at Ely.

The Red Book of Thorney shows how that abbey engaged in drainage work. A lease of about 1200 mentions a toft in Whittlesey 'which Lord Roger, some-

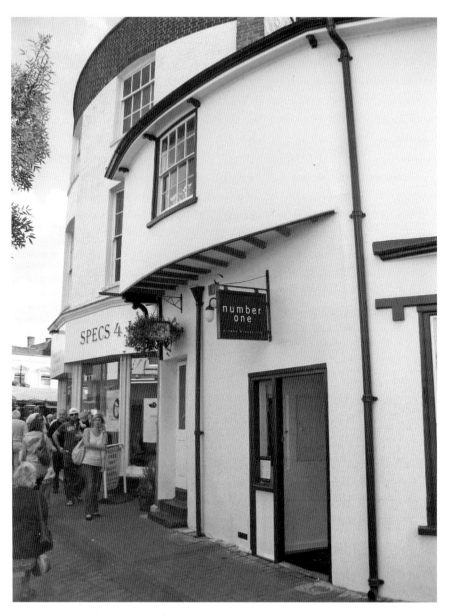

Spalding, the Prior's Oven.

time our prior, raised from the fen'. William Clopton, abbot between 1305 and 1322, built a house and offices in the midst of Thorney Fens and enclosed 'a large part of the fen to have as arable land or meadow with the lapse of time, if fortune should prove gracious'.

As well as drainage, the ecclesiastical authorities in Fenland led the way in the use of a new technology, the windmill. The use of windmills for grinding corn spread very rapidly in the last two or three decades of the twelfth century. No mills are mentioned in Ramsey Abbey estate surveys of the 1160s, but things changed in the next twenty years. In the 1190s, Pope Celestine issued a decretal saying that windmills had to pay tithes: the papal order was addressed to the Abbot of Ramsey and the Archdeacon of Ely, suggesting that it was in Fenland that this question had first come up. By 1222, windmills on the Ely estates were providing an income of £37 a year to their owner, and by 1298 this had risen enormously to £192. By this time, Ely and Ramsey had windmills in thirteen Fenland parishes.[34]

Townships could also act together to reclaim land: village communities between Spalding and Tydd St Mary worked together to build a series of banks enclosing land and reclaiming it from the marsh. H.E. Hallam has worked through the documents. The first line of dykes to the south known as Austen Dyke, Hurdletree and Fen Dyke were probably built before the Norman Conquest. Between 1160 and 1240, five more lines of defensive banks pushed the frontier between land and marsh further and further south. As Hallam says: 'In less than eighty years, some

Hurdletree Bank, a pre-Conquest dyke preserved as a feature today.

50 square miles of new arable and pasture land were added to these townships.'
After those years, however, the impetus to reclaim land appears to have declined.

The Friars

There was a new religious fervor in the early thirteenth century, brought by friars, who dedicated their lives to serving the poor, preaching, hearing confessions and burying the dead. They were very much an urban phenomenon, and it is a sign of the wealth of Boston and Lynn that both attracted all four main orders of friars: the only other friary in Fenland was a short-lived house of Crutched Friars at Whaplode.

Boston Dominican Priory first appears in recorded history when it was burned down in 1288 during St Botolph's Fair. Local people rallied round, making many grants of land after the fire. Typical benefactors were John of Sutton and his wife, and Peter son of William Gode. The new priory church was probably finished about 1309 when the altars were licensed. We know that the friary had a bell tower because in 1376 the friars stood on it with heavy stones threatening to drop them on the Bishop of Lincoln when he wanted to go into the choir to say a Mass for the funeral of a local squire: the friars thought the offerings from local gentlemen at the funeral would go to the bishop rather than to the friars! Most of the buildings have completely disappeared, but William Hinnebusch describes what can still be seen:

> At Boston there still stands a long, low building built of rather uneven stones and surmounted by a waving red-tiled roof. On the upper floor, formerly reached by a circular staircase, is a long, low room lighted by five or six windows. The building formed the southern range of the main cloister, if we may judge from the existence of a ledge and several corbels on the exterior of the northern wall just below the windows. The corbels evidently supported the roof of the cloister alley. The use of the building is uncertain, but the presence of three thirteenth-century fireplaces suggests that it may have been the guest house.[35]

Friars were noted for their large and up-to-date libraries. One highly educated Fenland friar achieved an important position with the royal family: Nicholas Wisbech, Dominican friar and confessor to the Duchess of Brabant, daughter of King Edward I, presumably came from the town of his name.[36]

Boston Blackfriars.

Another friar of some importance was a man known as Nicholas of Lynn, a Carmelite friar in that town. He was a keen astronomer and also a traveller – he is said to have visited the Arctic regions – and even the islands off Labrador, Canada: this was in or before 1350, well over century before Columbus 'discovered' America! He wrote a book about his travels, which unfortunately does not survive, but was known to Hakluyt, the great chronicler of sea voyages, writing in the time of Queen Elizabeth I. The tower of the Carmelite friary still survives, and I like to imagine Nicholas using it to observe the stars above Fenland almost 700 years ago.

Ely Priory and Cathedral

Ely was a house of Benedictine monks, but it was also a cathedral. Ely became a diocese in 1109, almost the only new one in England created between the Norman Conquest and the Reformation: it was carved out of the enormous

Horses near Ely Cathedral.

diocese of Lincoln. From then on, the bishop and the monastic house were in effect two separate landowners, each administering their own estates in the Fens and elsewhere. The bishop was an important royal official: when he was not serving his king he was staying at one of his many houses on his estate, whether the palaces at Ely or Downham, the castle at Wisbech or elsewhere. Most of these journeys were made by boat.

There was a priory at Ely from the seventh century, as we have seen. The present Ely Cathedral was begun by Abbot Simeon in 1082, the nave and transepts are Romanesque, as are the carvings of the Prior's and Monks' doorways from the cloister into the church. This church had a central tower, which collapsed in 1322. The sacrist in charge of building work at the time was Alan of Walsingham. Pevsner records his initial reaction:

When the tower fell, the archives tell us, Alan was so overwhelmed that he did not know 'where to turn and what to do'. He collected himself, had the stone and timber rubble cleared out of the church and then 'he had the place excavated where the new tower was to be constructed, measuring it out with architectural skill in eight parts, in which eight stone columns were to be erected to support the whole building'.

Alec Clifton-Taylor takes up the story:

> The opportunity was taken to widen considerably the space at the crossing and, with great daring on the part both of the master-mason and of the master-carpenter, to erect what might be described as the Gothic equivalent of the Classical dome. Aesthetically, the chief delights of the octagon are a sudden sensation of space for which the long Norman nave has left us quite unprepared, and especially, when looking up, the contrast between the shadowy vaulting of the wide area and the bright light flooding on to the eight-pointed star of the octagon.[37]

Each of the eight posts weighs about 10 tons and had to be raised almost 100ft above the floor to be positioned on to the octagonal sill above the lantern: completed in 1334, the total weight of the lantern is about 400 tons.

Historians of architecture love what Walsingham created. According to Pevsner, 'it is a delight from beginning to end for anyone who feels for space as strongly as for construction'. John Harvey is equally ecstatic: 'It must also reflect some knowledge of the central plan abroad, and probably of the great buildings of Persia, through the medium of travellers' tales. It is at any rate an astonishing achievement, with no direct parentage and no immediate progeny.'[38]

Like any cathedral, Ely has seen some changes over the centuries: the flying buttresses were removed in the eighteenth century by James Essex, only to be reinstated 100 years later by Sir George Gilbert Scott when he restored the original Gothic outline of the lantern. The front has a lopsided look because the north-west tower collapsed in the late Middle Ages and was never replaced. The Lady Chapel has beautiful carved details, surprisingly disliked by Alec Clifton-Taylor, who commented: 'It is in truth, with its multitude of small piercing, a little too reminiscent of the parsley bed.'

Ely Cathedral, standing on its hill, can be seen for many miles in all directions: it has often been likened to a ship in full sail across a golden sea. In days gone by, a light burned in the great west tower, guiding the traveller through the treacherous marsh. It is one of Fenland's greatest glories.

Although the bishop was technically the abbot of the monastery, he did not live there, having his own bishop's palace. The present palace was originally

Ely Cathedral: the west tower.

built by Bishop Alcock (1486–1501) but has been rebuilt many times since, lastly in 1771. There is still a medieval gatehouse, inside which is the monks' room, supposedly haunted. Later features include the Georgian sitting room and the Victorian chapel. The bishops stopped using the house in 1840, and in recent years it has been a Sue Ryder hospice.

Crime and Punishment

Most forms of ancient document record the activities of the rich – landowners and taxpayers. The great majority of people lived largely unrecorded lives, showing up perhaps in the records of their local manor – and also in criminal records if they were deemed to have broken one of the many national and local laws that regulated their lives. In the Middle Ages, the system of justice was simple: if you were found guilty of a crime, you were hanged. There were prisons, but they were only for people awaiting their trials: people were never sentenced to a term in prison as a punishment.

The Bishop's Palace, Ely.

The Fens had a reputation for lawlessness and violence, and the documents suggest this reputation was justified. In 1189, fearing loss of common grazing because of drainage works by Crowland Abbey, more than 3,000 men of Holland invaded Crowland Fen, cutting peat and using the pasture. The abbot took legal action, which was settled in his favour in 1193. In 1329, a later Abbot of Crowland said that he had constructed walls, gutters and trenches to defend the abbey against flooding, strengthening the walls with transverse bars of wood. Men from seven nearby villages (Spalding, Weston, Moulton, Whaplode, Holbeach, Pinchbeck and Surfleet) had cut the bars in pieces, broken down the walls by frequent passage of men and horses, displaced the gutters, carried off the timber of the gutters and bars, and filled up the trenches with turves.

The towns could be just as violent. More than forty men (and one woman, Juetta, wife of John de Claymont, himself one of the men involved) were pardoned by the King for 'disturbance, to the terror of the King's people' in Boston in 1348. One of those pardoned, John de Glenteworth of Fylyngham, was said to have been one of those who had stirred up the riot in the first place. Another man, John de Themelby, was pardoned in November 1351.

H.E. Hallam wrote of medieval Fenland:

> It was a progressive and grasping society which practised violence so frequently that the prior of Spalding had to get permission from Edward III in 1333 to strengthen and crenellate the great wall around the curia [monastic court] against severe raids of the men of Deeping, who habitually attacked the town of Spalding across the fens and rustled the cattle of the men of Holland whenever they thought they might get it.[39]

Spalding men were also violent: 'John son of John of Spalding' was charged with murdering three men in Lynn in 1316, while Simon Bird of Spalding was the leader of a six-man gang that held up Harford Bridge near Norwich and robbed everyone who tried to cross.

In the days before a police force, it was difficult to catch criminals. The victim or a relative might prosecute but many cases were brought by 'approvers', criminals who 'shopped' other people in return for postponement of their own death sentence. Thomas de Losenham was such a man. He was originally accused by an accomplice, Peter le Suter of Cambridge, of killing and robbing a man. The jury found Thomas not guilty – which meant that Peter was hanged for bringing a false prosecution! Thomas then turned approver and accused several people in Fenland of crime, the cases continuing after Thomas himself was hanged in the summer of 1315. On his evidence, William and Hugh Spirling were charged with stealing linen from Wisbech Hospital, Agnes Moody with robbing and murdering a man at Whittlesford Bridge, Margaret of Ashwicken with murder and theft, Martin Frere of Setchey with stealing two colts, worth 100*s*, at Raveley in Huntingdonshire, and with killing a man near Anstey in Hertfordshire.

Crime, as in the twenty-first century, could run in families. When William Bird was hanged for homicide at Warboys in 1348, he and four relatives with the same surname – Simon, Richard, Michael and Christine Bird – all had long records of theft and assault. Robert Carless of St Ives was charged with homicide in 1339 – he and his family had been committing assaults for four decades. Two brothers in Ramsey both called John Porthos were frequently in court for assaults against each other: in 1333 the case ended in the death of one brother at the hands of the other. John White had been in court for assaults five times before he was killed in a fight in a tavern – which he had started. However, young criminals might reform, just like Guthlac centuries before. One such was John, the son of Hugh de London, who was a bailiff of Ramsey Manor. John was a frequent petty offender in the 1350s, including a burglary, but had become a respected pillar of the local community himself by 1380.

Records do not give motives, so we shall never know the background to a dramatic fourteenth-century murder. In 1332, John Revely, a parson of Huntingdon, was murdered by a large band of men from Godmanchester: two men, William Colyon and Andrew Bonis, were accused of the actual murder and the other eighteen of aiding and abetting.

Most crimes were of theft, usually of grain or animals, and the people involved may have been in desperate need in some cases: in at least one case this was explicitly recognised. In June 1316, Peter le Synekere was charged with burgling a house in Lynn and stealing fourteen pence worth of grain and some clothing. He was found guilty but the jury said that he 'did this because of hunger and destitution': this was at the height of the great famine of 1315–17, which affected Fenland and everywhere else in England. If a man was brave or desperate enough, he could easily round up a number of sheep from a marshland common, like John Wyryng, who made off with four, and Richard Spirling, who took eight sheep from the prior of Well in 1314, and on another occasion stole a horse.

Other cases illustrate the dangers of simply travelling through Fenland. In 1309, Geoffrey le Marchaunt, a Great Yarmouth man and no doubt a merchant as his name suggests, was murdered at Walsoken and the goods he was carrying, worth the very large sum of £30, stolen. In 1316, three Terrington men killed a merchant between Wisbech and Walton, robbing him of his cash,

2s, and of the cloth in which he was trading, valued at 40s. No doubt there were many similar incidents.

The maritime equivalent to highway robbery was piracy. Ships were naturally at greater risk in wartime, when enemy vessels would regard them as

Statue on Crowland Bridge.

Transporting hay on a Fenland river.

legitimate targets. In 1350, a ship called *La Katherine* of Boston, William Drove master, loaded up at Bruges with merchandise for England. It was attacked off Blakeney, on the Norfolk coast, by armed French ships: some of the English mariners managed to escape in small boats and others were thrown overboard. The merchandise, the property of Andrew Aubyn, a London merchant and valued (by him!) at the enormous sum of £2,000, was taken to France. The French ship must have been a large one: there were 140 of the French pirates, led by Mikelet de Boleyn and John Fage.

Robbery was not the only danger: as the well-known legend of King John illustrates, the elements themselves could cause tragedy. John left Lynn on 11 October 1216 and rode to Wisbech, where he stayed at the castle. His enormous baggage train – said to be a mile long – set out from Lynn the following morning, but in attempting to cross the Wash it was caught by the rising tide: the drivers panicked and set off southwards, coming off the 'road' and being trapped in the quicksands. The wagons, including a great deal of treasure, was never seen again. The train is traditionally said to have followed the Wash-Way between Cross Keys and Long Sutton. In the 1930s an organisation known as the Fen Research Committee made a serious attempt to find it. They decided that the crossing point had probably been further south, from Walpole St Andrew to Tydd St Mary. However, despite their best efforts nothing was found: Fenland holds this secret still.

Universal application of the death penalty meant there were an enormous number of hangings, which, of course, took place in public to act as a deterrent. A list survives of the number of thieves on the Spalding Priory estate hanged at Spalding by the priory officials between 1256 and 1501: there are eighty hangings, sixty-two of them between 1256 and 1300, after which they become much rarer, with 'only' about one hanging a decade in the fifteenth century. Details of the procedure as it was in the fifteenth century are recorded: the bailiff of Spalding would lead the prisoner from the priory to the gallows, the bailiff of Weston would carry the ladder needed to raise the victim up, the bailiff of Pinchbeck would provide the rope, and the bailiff of Mouton would 'turn the criminal off', as Victorian newspapers loved to say, that is, perform the actual act of hanging.[40]

Church courts were also watching you, keeping an eye out for crimes such as sex outside marriage, which was against church law, and would normally result in some form of public penance such as standing in church with a hood over one's head. These cases can provide fascinating details of Fenland life. To take just one example, Thomas Barbo and Joan Seustere were lovers. In March 1376, Joan claimed that they had got married at Stourbridge Fair – fairs were clearly an opportunity for socialising as well as for trade, the couple perhaps being inebriated. Thomas had a different story. He said that he had told Joan that their affair was over, but found that he could not live without her: he promised Joan that, if she stayed, he would be true to her, and they then had sex. Thomas insisted he did not mean to marry her but just have her as his mistress, but Joan eventually won the case. The courts then lost interest in them, and we do not know whether the marriage turned out happily.

The strict morality that church courts tried to impose ran against a natural cycle of the seasons, and against ancient customs that may well have existed before Christianity. Robert Mannyng of Bourne was just one Christian writer railing against lechery. In his poem 'Handling Sin', written in 1303, he wrote:

Dancing, carols, summer games
Of many such come many shames

Even an innocent-sounding activity such as gathering of spring flowers might lead on to carnal activity, and was therefore to be avoided – especially on Sunday! Some of the traditional celebrations of Plough Monday, the traditional start of the ploughing season, were tamed – a plough was set up in Holbeach Church as the centre of Christian worship for example – but wilder aspects continued: the Straw Bear festival held today in Whittlesey represents a revival of ancient Plough Monday junketings.

The Peasants' Revolt

We have seen protests against the activities of landlords could lead to violence in medieval Fenland. This reached its peak in the so-called Peasants' Revolt of 1381, a national protest in which Fen people played their part.

Some Fenmen took part in national events. John Greyston of Bottisham was present in London and Kent at the time the rebels murdered the Archbishop

Shodfriars' Hall, Boston.

Hussey's Tower, Boston.

of Canterbury and Robert Hales: he then returned to his home village and destroyed property there. George de Dunsby went to Bury St Edmunds to rouse the local men to rebel. In a phrase still relevant in the early twenty-first century, he called himself 'a messenger of the Big Society' and urged the commoners of the town to rise up.

There were also local troubles. On 15 June a band of men led by John Saffrey and Peter le Eyr attacked and wrecked the houses of Thomas de Swaffham and

Thomas Torel at Reach: Swaffham's house at Burwell was also attacked. On the same day, riots began in Ely itself that lasted for several days: a local Justice of the Peace, Edmund de Walsingham, and a local lawyer, Edmund Galon, were murdered; Walsingham's head was placed on the town pillory. The leaders included local men Richard de Leycester, John Buk and Adam Clymme, all of Ely. However, one of the leaders was an outsider, Robert Tavell: he and his men had earlier taken part in riots in Bury St Edmunds. A group of rebels, led by William Combe, took control of the bridge and causeway at Stuntney: they allowed Tavell to enter the city but prevented men loyal to the King and the bishop from crossing.

On 7 June, Tavell and two local men, Robert Plumer and John the son of Nicholas Gunneld, led a marauding expedition out of Ely, reaching Ramsey, where they forced the abbot to send supplies of food and wine to their camp. There they were defeated by men of the Bishop of Norwich (Henry Despencer, known to history as 'the fighting bishop'). Twenty-four rebels were killed, and others caught as they fled: their heads were placed on high trees as a grim warning. The bishop found himself in possession of the goods left by the rebels as they fled, including seventeen horses and nineteen saddles and bridles.

In Norfolk, there were riots at Southery, where the land was owned by the abbey of Bury St Edmunds, everywhere a target of the rebels, while a man taken by the rebels to Littleport to be executed was rescued at the last minute by men of the Bishop of Ely. A house belonging to the Duchy of Lancaster was destroyed at the fen-edge settlement of Methwold. A gang of Lynn tradesmen, led by John Spanye, took advantage of the situation to demand money from everyone they could, and also to kill any Flemings that they met. There seems to have been little trouble in the Lincolnshire Fens apart from a riot at Dunsby, home of the George de Dunsby already mentioned, where tenants protested against labour services.

After the riots were suppressed, came trials and executions wherever trouble had occurred. For example, Greyston was executed at Bottisham, Leycester, Buk and Clymme at Ely, Tavell at Ramsey and Dunsby at Bury. Despite the name 'Peasants' Revolt', few of these men were peasants. Greyston owned a house, 3 acres and 3 roods of land in Bottisham worth 5s a year, Leycester owned a tenement in Ely with a dovecot, two shops in Sadler's Row and goods worth 40 marks, while Buk had a messuage at Castle Path, four shops and other property in Walpole Lane, and Clymme's goods were valued at almost £11. Saffrey had land at Stow, Quy and Walpole, only worth 5s a year in total, but his other goods were valued at £20 2*s* 6*d*. He was a lucky man: managing to remain hidden at the time, he was later part of a general pardon issued by the King. His property, which had been seized by royal officials, was restored to him.

Downham Market: clock tower, the Swan behind.

The Fens and the Monarchy

In 1460, King Henry VI was at Coventry but the armies of his rival, Edward IV, were massing against him. One plan was for him to retreat to the Isle of Ely, where it was thought he would be safe. His opponents raced to cut him off, and met him at Northampton, where he was heavily defeated and taken into captivity. Had he made it to the Fens, this phase of English history might have been very different!

Almost two centuries later another English king found – brief – sanctuary in the Fens. In April 1626, King Charles I was under siege at Oxford. Determined to escape, he had his long hair cut by a friend and fled disguised as a servant, with just two companions. They reached Downham Market on 29 April, staying at the White Swan. In Downham, the King bought a hat and went to a barber's, illustrating the facilities available at a market town. This barber was so sarcastic about the way Charles' hair had been cut that he suspected he would be betrayed. He fled, going to Southery where he crossed the Ouse by ferry, and rode through Littleport, Ely, Earith and Huntingdon: eventually he gave himself up to Scottish leaders then at Southwell. This was the start of his long imprisonment and eventual execution three years later.

AYSCOUGHFEE HALL, SPALDING

Ayscoughfee Hall was probably built in about 1450 by Richard Alwyn, a Fenland wool merchant who made his money exporting wool along the Welland from Spalding: the central part of the building, with its two wings and tower, date from his time. The roof timbers have been dated by dendrochronology (it is this that fixes the date: there is no documentary evidence). It was briefly owned by the Ayscoughs in the sixteenth century: presumably it was in their *fee* (a form of feudal landholding), hence its name. The hall then passed through various hands until it was inherited by Maurice Johnson in 1685. It descended through many generations of the Johnson family, who made various changes over the centuries: Maurice Johnson, the son of the first owner of that name and the founder of the well-known Spalding Gentleman's Society, brought in the stained glass in the large window at the rear of the building, a later owner of the same name put in the plaster ceiling and the balcony in 1794, and yet another Maurice Johnson added the front porch in the Victorian period.

Ayscoughfee Hall.

The hall was acquired by a committee of Spalding citizens from Isobella Johnson in 1898 and presented to the Urban District Council in 1902. The citizens had intended the building to be used as a museum and this finally happened in 1986, when the hall opened as the Museum of South Holland life. It was closed for refurbishment for three years in the early twenty-first century, reopening in 2006.

Ayscoughfee Hall is a fantastic museum in a wonderful building with lovely gardens – and it is free to visit! It is a must-see attraction for all residents and visitors of Fenland.

Four

THE GREAT DRAINING

See Deeping Fens
And the long lawns of Bourn. 'Tis art and toil
Gives Nature value, multiplies her stores,
Varies, improves, creates.[41]

'*The Air nebulous, gross and full of rotten bars; the Water putrid and muddy, yea full*
of loathsome vermin; the earth spewing unfast, and boggy; the Fire noisome turf and
bassocks; such are the inconveniences of the Drownings.'[42]

William Camden toured pre-drained Fenland in 1587. His impression of
Crowland is memorable:

> [It] lies among the deepest fens and waters stagnating off muddy lands, so shut in and
> environed as to be inaccessible on all sides except the north and east and that only by
> narrow causeys. Its situation, if we compare small things with great, is not unlike that
> of Venice, consisting of three streets, divided by canals of water, planted with willows,
> and built on piles driven into the bottom of the fen … Except where the town stands,
> it is so moory that you may run a pole into the ground a depth of 30 feet, and nothing
> is to be seen on every side but beds of rushes and near the church a grove of alders. It
> is, notwithstanding, full of inhabitants, who keep their cattle at a good distance from
> the town, and go to milk them in little boats, called skerries, which will hold but two
> persons: but their chief profit arises from the catching of fish and wild fowl, which
> they do in such quantities that in the month of August they drive 3000 ducks into one
> net, and call their pools their fields. No corn grows within five miles of them.

He was pleasantly surprised by Spalding: 'surrounded on all sides with rivulets
and canals, a handsomer town than one would expect in this tract among stag-
nated waters'. All this was about to change.

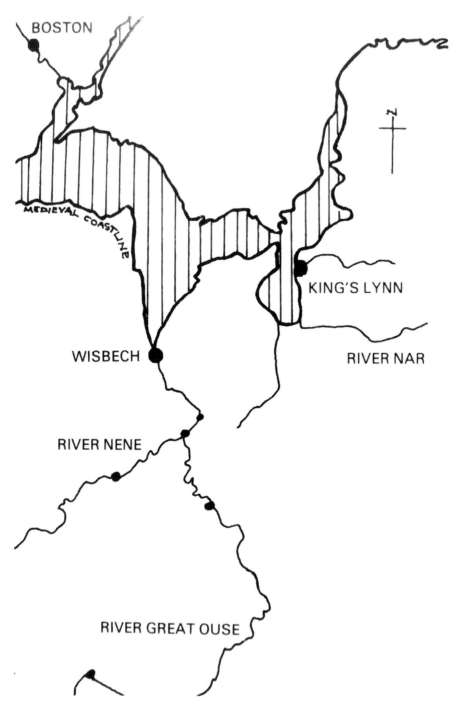

The natural flow of Fenland rivers.

People had been improving the drainage of the Fenland rivers for centuries, but on a relatively small scale, and often facing reverses as floods broke through. One of the largest engineering changes had been to divert the main river system, the Great Ouse, so that it ran through Lynn rather than Wisbech. The date of this is uncertain: the archaeologist Kenneth Penn thinks it was done as early as the late eleventh century, by Bishop Herbert Losinga, connected with the founding of his new town at Bishop's (now King's) Lynn. In the 1470s, Bishop Morton constructed Morton's Leam, carrying the waters of the Nene in a straight channel between Peterborough and Wisbech.

The seventeenth century saw large-scale drainage plans, creating man-made monuments of enormous size – and changing the face of the Fens forever. Rackham calls it the 'end of the era when men worked with the environment, rather than against it'. This may be connected with a major change in land ownership in the Fens, as elsewhere in the country. We have seen that much of Fenland was owned by monastic houses, and that it was the monks who drove forward many of the drainage schemes of the Middle Ages. Between 1536 and 1538, all the monasteries were dissolved: their estates passed into the hands of the King, and from him to new lay landowners. These seem at first to have struggled with large-scale drainage enterprises and conditions in the Fens deteriorated for a time. It has even been said that 'the dissolution of the monasteries brought about the dissolution of the Fenlands'.[43]

However, eventually the new owners adapted, and were able to put into place the dramatic changes of the first half of the seventeenth century. In 1568, the Maud Foster drain was cut north of Boston to help drain the West Fen, described as 'imperfectly drained by narrow canals which intersect it for many miles'. Although imperfect, this represented real progress compared with the East Fen, described as in 'quite a state of nature, and exhibiting a specimen of what the county was like before the introduction of drainage. It is a morass, intermixed with a number of lakes, from half to two or three miles in circuit, communicating with each other by narrow ready straits. They are shallow none above four or five feet deep but abound with pike, perch, ruff, bream, tench, dace, eels etc.'

A survey of Over made in 1575 records that in one moist summer and hard winter following, townsmen lost more than their year's profits by the drowning of their cattle: they got together and formed a common fund for maintaining their banks and dykes. In 1577, Sir Edward Montagu cut a ditch from Whittlesey Mere westwards to a point between Caldecote and Stilton. In the same year, according to Eric Kerridge, the draining of fens to the south of Gedney Hill was commissioned. Foreign expertise was called upon. In 1590, that great landowner, the Earl of Bedford – he owned 20,000 acres at Thorney – brought over three Dutchmen to advise about draining Thorney Fen. Three years later, Humphrey Bradley, from Brabant, submitted a scheme to drain the Fens. It would cost £5,000 – and give the Crown a profit of £60,000. It sounded too good to be true – and probably was. Certainly, Queen Elizabeth refused to invest.

In 1596, Fenmen appealed to the Privy Council for help, claiming they had suffered great loss 'by the outragious inundations and overflowinge of waters descendinge from the higher parts … in so muche that a great number of the said inhabitants of those countis togeather with their families are verie greatly impoverished and like to be overthrowne and utterly undone, to the great hinderance of the State, yf some speedy remedy be not had and provided'. There were further floods throughout the Fens in November 1598.

In 1599 Captain Thomas Lovell spent the £12,000 rates allocated for a project to drain land in Deeping, Spalding, Pinchbeck South, Thurlby, Bourne South and Crowland – only to see his banks destroyed by rioters. He was given three years to make good his works, or else the commoners would re-enter. His account of his experience differed hardly at all from that of his successors a generation later. Opposition was of two kinds. It began with 'cavills and exceptions' – disputes by the commoners on points of law – about boundaries and common rights. These delayed, but did not halt, operations. When once they were settled, opposition took the sharper form of 'open tumults and violence', often encouraged, or at least not hindered, by the local justices of the peace. In the early summer of 1602, men and women living in the neighbourhood of Deeping Fen took up arms against Lovell and threw down dikes, finding an unexpected friend in Mr Lacy, a justice of the peace living at Deeping St James, who refused to assist in indicting the rioters.[44]

The most important of the early statutes concerning drainage was the General Drainage Act 'for the recovering of many hundred thousand Acres of Marshes' of 1600. This was significant in the history of drainage for it established a legal mechanism for financing drainage works. Until that time few landlords, small farmers, or even communities could find the capital for anything but small-scale drainage and reclamation. The 1600 Act sanctioned the granting of a proportion of any area of newly drained land to outsiders in return for their providing finance. So appeared the Adventurers, individuals who adventured their

capital, and the Undertakers, who undertook to carry out drainage work: both would receive a portion of the newly drained land, so the phrases Adventurers' Fen and Undertakers' Fen begin to appear in Fenland for the first time as a direct consequence of the 1600 Act. Many of the seventeenth-century and later drainage schemes were only possible because of this system: for the first time it was recognised that outside finance could improve the Fens – and make money for the investor. Nothing, however, was undertaken at once. Another Dutchman, Cornelius Liens, did submit a plan to drain the Fens, but nothing came of it: however, Liens was employed in less ambitious schemes elsewhere in England.[45]

Relatively small improvements continued. In 1601, an individual from Outwell left money to build a sluice at the end of Ship Lode and to buy lands producing an income of £8 a year for its maintenance. In 1609 Lord Chief Justice Popham created Popham's Eau, a straight cut from the Nene into Well Creek: it drained some 5,000 acres at Waldersea and Coldham.

One of best documented of failed drainage schemes, which had the support of the King and the Privy Council, was that of Sir William Ayloffe and Sir Anthony Thomas, resuming Lovell's unsuccessful attempts in Kesteven in 1619–20. The promoters of the scheme promised to drain lands in return for between half and two-thirds of the lands drained! Landowners would be giving up a large proportion of their land in return for the benefits of drainage: many local landowners did not want to do this. The Commissioners of Sewers for Cambridge and Ely told the Privy Council that they could undertake the drainage themselves better than any outsiders, and commissioners from other counties also refused to co-operate. The promoters wanted their lands marked off before the drainage began, so as to encourage other people to invest. In February 1620, both Undertakers and commissioners of sewers petitioned the King and the Privy Council: the latter decided that promoters could claim between a half and two-thirds of reclaimed land and this later became more or less the standard amount claimed.

In May 1620, the Privy Council decreed that the plan should go ahead, but made concessions to the commissioners – lands already worth more than 8s an acre would not have to contribute. The commissioners were the only people who could value the land, and they nominated four men in each parish to value the Fens and surrounding grounds in but their parishes – the surveys vary from a couple of lines to very detailed surveys. Ten of the nineteen parishes surveyed claimed that all, or nearly all, their lands were worth more than 8s an acre.

There were many variations. At Tydd St Giles, most land was found to be worth 2s an acre or less. However, at Leverington, the document has seven pages of landholdings worth more than 8s; at Sutton a first survey valued *all* land at more than 8s shillings an acre, but a second surveyor put a lot of the land at below this magic figure. At Haddenham, the survey said 'all fens worth eight shillings an acre or better'.

The total exclusions, that is the land declared already to be worth 8s or more an acre, came to well over half the land involved. The Undertakers complained to the Privy Council that they were not allowed to see the valuations. They asked that the matter be referred to Parliament and said that, if the land was really as valuable as was being claimed, it should be taxed accordingly! However, the plan fizzled out. King James then claimed himself as sole Undertaker, but he soon lost interest in the improvement scheme. No ground was ever broken in this project – local officials had triumphed over the royal will. By the 1630s conditions had changed; the King and Undertakers had independent surveyors they could bring in: the drainers and the Crown managed to take possession of their common for a few years before the Civil War broke out.

The first real attempt at large-scale drainage of the Lincolnshire Fens followed as Adventurers under Sir Anthony Thomas began to drain the East and West Fens between the River Witham and the coast in return for 1,600 acres of reclaimed land, of which 400 acres were to be given to the poor. New drains were cut in the West and Wildmore Fens to the natural outfalls to the sea at Wainfleet and Friskney and to the River Witham at Anton's Gowt and New Gote. The Maud Foster drain was also enlarged and improved. The cost of upkeep was to be paid by the granting to the Corporation of Boston of the rents of 2,500 acres.

The next block of marsh to the north, between Morton and South Kyme, was drained between 1635 and 1636 by the Earl of Lindsey, for which he received a payment of land: Lindsey had been promised 14,000 acres when the drainage was complete. He drained 30,000 acres of common land in Kesteven with the South Forty Foot Drain (1635–38). The area has been known ever since as the Lindsey Level, but at the time the changes met violent opposition. The local population threw down banks and destroyed crops and even the houses of the drainers.

When the Civil War broke out, this private war was still in progress, and the peasants living in the Lindsey Level found themselves the leaders of a much wider and yet spontaneous movement to eject the drainers and their tenants from every fen in Lincolnshire. The inhabitants of Little Hale and Horbling took possession of their common in March 1642. By May 1642 the Earl of Lindsey and other participants had been completely driven out of the Level. The Crown was dispossessed of its share at the same time. The drained lands were turned once more into common pastures and remained so at least until the Restoration in 1660. Most of them, indeed, remained common until the second half of the seventeenth century, when drainage schemes on an entirely new and more acceptable basis were introduced hand in hand with enclosure by Parliamentary act.

The fen north of South Kyme was not drained, but had to contribute to schemes for improvement of the River Witham that they adjoined.[46]

Sir Philip Vernatti undertook the drainage of Deeping and Crowland Fens in 1631 for the Earl of Bedford. The drains converged on Pode Hole and the water ran on from there by Vernatti's Drain to the Welland. 'Washes', that is, natural overflow reservoirs, were created alongside the Welland and Glen.

These various schemes were overshadowed by Vermuyden's enormous project, but they had their effect on Fenland, as Eric Kerridge points out:

One single document, hitherto neglected, is fatal to the argument that peat-fen drainage was merely nebulous and indeterminate until Vermuyden came on the scene. The survey made of the fens in 1619 clearly shows that although only a third of the fenland around Peterborough was dry, and only half that south of Holland and Marshland, very little remained drowned south or east of the Ouse, south-east of Ely or about Somersham. Deeping Fen was perhaps deteriorating. The survey originally declared it mostly well drained by the Earl of Exeter's undertaking, but a later hand denied this was any longer so. Even the drained fens, however, were mostly only summer-ground, or wet meadow overflowed in winter. At Cottenham, some fens, said the surveyors, 'upon extraordinary flood are sometimes overflowed and upon the fall of the river doth forthwith drain again, as the upland meadows do; but unless the said flood happen to overflow them in the summer season (which is very seldom), we do find that the said grounds receive more benefit than hurt thereby and are thereby much bettered and enriched; for those grounds which lie lowest and are oftenest and longest overflown in the winter season are the most fertile grounds and yield the best yearly value ... unless it be some dry year when they are not overflown, for the white fodder is decayed and the grounds turn much to a kind of small hammer-sedge which the cattle like not so well.[47]

King James I declared in 1620 that 'the Honour of the Kingdom would not suffer the said Land to be absorbed to the Will of the Waters, nor let it keep Waste and unprofitable'. He would himself be responsible for the reclamation of the Fen lands. He invited Cornelius Vermuyden to England, initially to drain marshes in Essex. Vermuyden was a Dutchman, then only 26 years old but probably already widely renowned for his drainage works in the Low Countries. His drainage works in England included Hatfield Chase, near Doncaster, in 1626, which was a royal estate. He was knighted in 1629.

King Charles I also planned to drain the Fens – in 1638, he declared he would do this and create an eminent new town there – which would be called Charlemont in his honour. He planned to build himself a house at Manea, more than two centuries before the royal family did purchase a property on the fen edge, at Sandringham. Charles had a direct hand in the cutting of

Oliver Cromwell, another hero from Fenland.

the South Forty Foot Drain, which also provided a 24-mile navigable river from Bourne to Boston: the drain was not popular and was destroyed by the locals. Fenmen claimed that they made their living by gathering 'reeds, fodder, thacks, turves, flaggs, hassocks, segg, fleggweed for flegeren, collors, matt-weede for churches, chambers, beddes and many other fenn commodytes of greate use in both towne and countreye'. The opposition of Fenland people to drainage proposals focused around a fensman from Huntingdonshire – Oliver Cromwell.

Cromwell's story is part of the history of England. He was born at Huntingdon in 1599 and later inherited property in Ely from his uncle. He was MP for Huntingdon in 1628–29, and subsequently MP for Cambridge. He became Lord Protector of England in 1653, and remained in power until his death in 1658. There are museums about him at his school in Huntingdon and his house in Ely, and a statue of him in St Ives.

Vermuyden in the Fens: First Stage

In 1630, King Charles I appointed Francis, 4th Earl of Bedford, to lead a team of thirteen other 'Gentlemen Adventurers' to develop drainage schemes in the Fens: he at once engaged Sir Cornelius Vermuyden. Vermuyden designed and supervised the construction of a new straight channel from Earith to Salters Lode on the tidal reach of the River Ouse. This cut off the great loop of the river through Ely and shortened by 10 miles the distance to the Wash. This cut was more than 60ft wide and 21 miles long, and had a sluice at each end, the upper to regulate the amount of water diverted from the river, the lower to inhibit the flow of tidal water from the lower reaches. It was the first of the great cuts across the Fens, and was begun in 1631 and completed in 1637 in spite of fierce opposition from many Fenmen. It was named the Bedford River (now of course the Old Bedford River).

A party of travellers in August 1634 saw the actual process of draining in action: close to Wisbech 'we spent best part of an houre in viewing a little Army of Artificers, venting, contriving, and acting outlandish devises about the same'. Perhaps this was the same bank Dugdale saw some years later: 'passing up towards Wisbeche, rode by the side of a large and high bank, lately made by the said Adventurers on the west side of the river, for defence of the Marshes lying on the west side of it, from inundation'. When the 1634 party reached Spalding, the bridge had been pulled down and they were afraid they would not be able to cross the river, but in fact 'the river had not so much water in it as would drowne a Mouse … At this we perceived that the Towne and Country thereabouts much murmur'd, but let them content themselves, since the Fendrayners have undertaken to make their River navigable, 50 feet broad and 6 foot deepe, from Frostick Slough to Deeping, which they need not long be about, having 600 men daily at work in't.'

To administer the scheme and maintain 95,000 acres for ever, the Bedford Level Corporation, a private company, was founded by the drainers in the 1630s. The Commissioners of Sewers were now all board members of the company. The Corporation competed with inhabitants for resources such as fishing, and inhabitants competed with each other. The Corporation would prosecute men for putting cattle or pigs on the banks – they would do damage to them – and for acts such as putting straw on the banks to feed cattle. The Fen Office was in the Temple in London: some archives were destroyed in the Great Fire of London. The Office moved to Ely in 1845: the side door still has its coat of arms. Bedford Level Drainage records are now at the Cambridgeshire Record Office: they include 850 volumes running continuously from the 1650s down to 1920, and about 200 maps. About 2,000 petitions to the Corporation are also available online.

Vermuyden and the Fens – Second Stage

After a pause because of the Civil War, work began again. Various plans were put forward, as R.L. Hills makes plain:

> There were two main schools of thought which put forward conflicting suggestions. There were those who thought it required only a thorough cleansing and embanking of the rivers to once more secure the Fens in their former pristine condition. The greatest proponent of these ideas was the Dutchman Jan Barents Westerdyke. His original plans for draining the whole of the fens were defeated in 1630 by another Dutchman, his great rival Vermuyden. In 1649 he was asked again to consider alternatives to Vermuyden's plans, but Vermuyden triumphed a second time.[48]

In 1649, the fifth Earl of Bedford and his associates were declared Undertakers of a second scheme. The Act's preamble declares:

Whereas the said Great Level, by reason of the frequent overflowing of the Rivers of Welland, Neane, Grant, Ouse, Brandon, Mildenhall and Stoke, have been of small and uncertain profit, but (if drained) may be improved and made profitable and of great Advantage to the Commonwealth, and to the particular Owners, Commoners, and Inhabitants, and be fit to bear Cole Seed and Rape Seed in great abundance, which is of singular Use to make Soap and Oils within this Nation, to the Advancement of the Trade of Clothing and spinning Wool, and much of it will be improved into good Pasture for feeding and breeding of Cattle, and for Tillage to be sown with Corn and Grain, and for Hemp and Flax in great Quantity, for making all Sorts of Linen Cloth, and Cordage for Shipping within this Nation, which will increase manufactories, Commerce and Trading at Home and Abroad, will relieve the Poor by setting them on Work, and will many other Ways redound to the great Advantage and Strengthening of the Nation.

The work included the building of the New Bedford River beginning in 1651, again under the direction of Vermuyden, which was parallel to the old and half a mile east of it: between the two was a vast storage area for flood water that became known as the Washes and covers 5,600 acres – as it still does, almost four centuries later: train passengers between Ely and Manea cross a long bridge over fertile fields or an enormous lake, depending upon the season. The work was finished by 1652, and blocks of land were finally allotted to the Adventurers. In 1663, the Bedford Level Corporation was set up: this maintained the drainage works and levied taxes on local landowners.

The change in the landscape seemed almost miraculous: when Dugdale visited in 1657, he saw new farmsteads, rich grazing and many new crops such as onions, peas and hemp being grown. The area drained by Vermuyden's project was greater than all the land reclaimed in the Netherlands between 1540 and 1690. However, there was a flaw in the arrangements: as water was removed from the Fens, the peat soil dried out and sank. Rivers and watercourses became perched high above the level of the fields, so it was impossible to get excess water into them – and, if the banks burst, the fields flooded. Much of the area was flooded once more by the end of the seventeenth century. The situation was saved by the introduction of windmills, which could lift the water in scoop wheels up from the level of the fields into the drainage channels.

As B.A. Holderness saw it:

… not even Vermuyden understood the problems of successful drainage in a 'saucer', with the outfalls constantly at risk of silting up. The Bedford level, for example, was well engineered as far as realignment of the Ouse and its feeders down to Denver was concerned, but the flow proved too sluggish to prevent internal silting, and all the black fen channels were subject to backwash from the tidal outfalls. The use of windmills assisted the flow but was inadequate to overcome the shrinkage of the peat that followed upon the drainage. Accordingly, much work had to be repeated after 1630, and it was often necessary to cut new channels to relieve particular pressure points. Some drainage works were so badly damaged by riots, as at Mildenhall or Deeping Fen before 1670, that the reclamation broke down. At Deeping a running fight between drainage projectors and fenmen lasted for more than a century, and the work was not completed till well after 1750. Other projects, notably that in the east Lindsey fens, were seriously underfinanced from the start.[49]

The shrinkage could even lead to houses leaning over, as can be seen, for example, at Benwick: according to Alan Bloom, 'walls that lean and crack, foundations that gape, calling for underpinning concrete or buttresses and the levelling of floors, are accepted as quite usual in Benwick'.

Skertchly comments:

Vermuyden began badly, progressed ignorantly, and finished disastrously. These are strong words, but they are the honest outcome of long and practical acquaintance with the subject. If there was one fact more prominent than the rest it was that the interests of the whole Level were one and inseparable; but he put asunder that which Nature had joined, and divided the Bedford Level into three portions, North, Middle, and South, whose common interests were thus made to clash to a degree which none but the hereditary occupiers can adequately estimate.

The Times commented two centuries later: '[Vermuyden] having sunk therein the moneys of the Duke of Bedford and his own, sustained and survived the hostility of Cromwell, reclaimed the Fenmen as well as the bogs, got a grant of 1,000 Scottish prisoners after Dunbar, and 500 Dutch prisoners when Blake beat Van Tromp, with these instruments he eventually conquered the morass.' At a public thanksgiving service at Ely, Vermuyden boasted that 'the present or former age had done nothing like it for the good of the nation'.

William Dugdale was commissioned in 1657 to write a history of fen drainage: he spent a fortnight in the Fens on research! He received £150 for the work

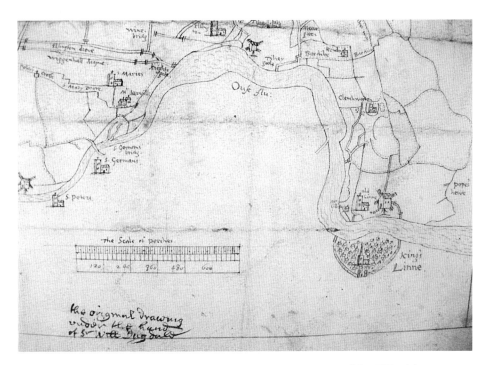

Hand-drawn map by William Dugdale: the river Ouse near Lynn. (Norfolk Record Office, RYE 17/6)

between 1657 and 1660 (which did not include printing costs). Five hundred copies of the book were destroyed in a fire at his lodgings in 1666. Dugdale visited Earith, where he saw a sasse 'to let Boats pass down towards Ely'. At the far end of the [Old] Bedford river was 'a strong Sasse built of good freestone'. The word sasse, meaning a lock or sluice gate to aid navigation, comes from the Dutch word 'sas' with the same meaning. The earliest use known to the Oxford English Dictionary is 1642. The word is used by Pepys in his diary. Dugdale also visited Thorney – the island where the abbey stood was about 300 acres in extent, but the fens surrounding it had been made so dry by the Adventurers that here were 'all sorts of corn and grass now growing thereon, the greatest plenty imaginable'. He saw that some sluices had a short life: one built by the Earl of Bedford at a cost of at least £7,000 had become useless because of more recent work by the Adventurers: it was pulled down and the stone used by Mr Thurlow in building his new house on the site of Wisbech Castle. He noted two cuts near Chatteris designed by Vermuyden whom he calls 'an eminent man

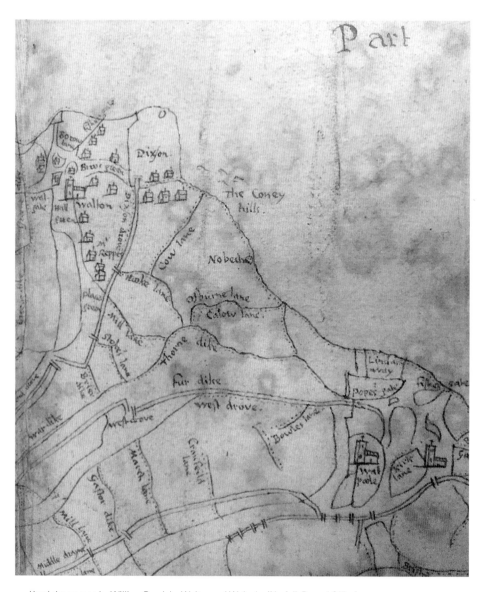

Hand-drawn map by William Dugdale: Walton and Walpole. (Norfolk Record Office)

for his drayning worke'. They were 30 and 40ft wide and 9 miles long, but by 1657 were already 'wholly useless' because there was no current to scour them.

Dugdale recorded that the water passed through the old Sea Bank at a place called the Four Goats. A Goat, sometimes spelled Gote, is a Fenland word for a drainage channel, especially one carrying fresh water out into the sea. It was used in 1602 in connection with a proposal to drain water out of the South

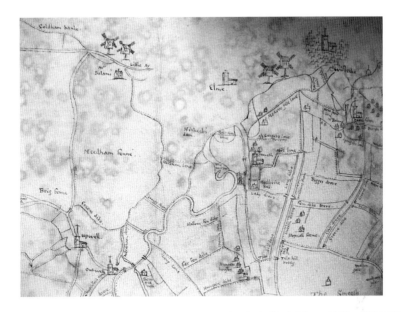

Hand-drawn map by William Dugdale: Upwell, Outwell and Wisbech. (Norfolk Record Office, RYE 17/6)

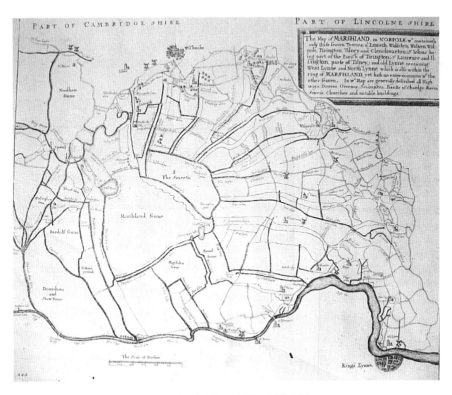

Dugdale's map of the Norfolk Marshland. (Norfolk Record Office, RYE 17/6)

Wisbech Castle.

Holland Fens by building two new goats into Boston Haven. More than two centuries later, Samuel Wells in 1830 writes about the charge on landowners of using spades to 'keep your goats and sluces open into the salt marsh or washes' because 'the sea of late years hath lodged its silt and sand some feet above your sluces or goats to sea'. The soil was already shrinking noticeably: land near Crowland had sunk by almost 2ft and alders growing there now had 'a very shallow footing in the earth'.

Cobbett, in his *Rural Rides*, also approved of the drained landscape:

The whole country as level as the table on which I am now writing. The horizon like the sea in a dead calm ... the land covered with beautiful grass, with sheep lying about upon it as fat as hogs stretched out sleeping in a stye ... Everything grows well here: earth without a stone so big as a pin's head; grass as thick as it can grow on the ground; immense bowling greens separated by ditches; and not a sign of a dock or thistle or other weed to be seen.

Mrs Alfred Berlin was especially scornful about the old Fenlanders: 'The haggard, half savage, stunted little "yellow bellies", amphibious creatures, who dragged out a miserable existence by damming up the waters and catching the fish and fowl with which they abounded ... and rather resented than otherwise any attempts to retrieve the swampy land from the waters, whence they derived their subsistence and a liberal supply of rheumatism, ague, and low fever.'[50]

Flooding

Floods in the seventeenth century were at least as common as in the Middle Ages, and, because better documentation survives, we know more about them. On 1 April 1607, 'a mighty tide broke through the defensive bank called Catts Banke and drowned Clenchwarton'. There was a very severe flood in November 1613. Dugdale saw an inscription on the east wall of the south aisle in Wisbech Church:

> To the immortal praise of God almighty, that saveth his people in all adversities, be it kept in perpetual memory, that on the feast day of All Saints, being the first of November in the year of Our Lord 1613, late in the night the sea broke in, through the violence of a north-east wind, meeting with a spring tide, and overflowed all marshland, with this town of Wisbeche, both on the north side and the south; and almost the whole Hundred round about; to the great danger of men's lives and the loss of some; besides the exceeding great losse which these Counties sustained, through the breach of banks, and spoil of Corn, Cattel and Howsing, which could not be estimated.

Details of the devastation wrought at Terrington survive. On the night of 1–2 November 1613:

> The people of the town fled to the Church for refuge, some to hay-stacks, some to the baulks in the houses, till they were neer famished; poor women leaving their children swimming in their beds, till good people adventuring their lives, went up to the breast in the waves to fetch them out at the windows; whereof Mr Browne the minister did fetch divers to the church upon his back: And had it not pleased God to move the hearts of the Mayor and aldermen of King's Lynne, with compassion; who sent beer and victual thither by boat, many had perished; which boats came the direct way over the soil from Lynn to Terrington.

A presentment made by a jury for Freebridge Marshland at Lynn on 9 December summed up the damage:

We present and say that there is belonging to the town of Terrington, a sea-dyke, containing 1100 rods in length, or thereabouts, which was in good repair before the first and second of November last; wherof 420 rods were ruinated by the rage of the sea that then happened; and also one bridge, called St John's Bridge, was then broken up. There were at that time lost by the rage of the sea etc 1876 sheep, amounting to the sum of £58 and more; in great Beasts, lost 120, valued at £322; in corn sowed in the fields, 480 acres valued at 30 shillings the acre, amounting to £720; hay lost in the fields and barns, to the value of £200; corn in the barns lost, to the value of £700; grass in the fields lost, to the value of £500. Thirteen dwelling houses were utterly ruinated and wasted, and 142 dwelling houses damaged, to the value of £1,000.

Bedding and other household stuff was lost, to the value of £40: this small sum reflects the fact that people in sixteenth-century Fenland had very few possessions to lose.

Flooded Fenland, early seventeenth century.

The jury blamed inadequate precautions. They found:

that the Creek, which now runneth under Terrington bank, and underneath them, hath within four or five years last past, run half a mile off; and that about 20 years since it did run about a mile off. We think, that the approach of the said Creek, is the greatest cause of the decay and overthrow of the said banks, and that at this present, the said Creek runneth where Banks have lately stood, being 23 foot deep or more, at a low water. And that by the said outrage, there are four other great Creeks, worn in the whole ground, to the town-ward, where there was corn reaped the last Harvest; whereof two of the said Creeks are fourscore foot broad a piece, and neer 30 foot deep; and are worn to the town-ward, within ten rods of the In-dyke, by the reflowing and ebbing of the waters, from out of the Town to the seaward, and that these creeks were so worn within the space of 48 hours.

They concluded: 'We say that in our opinions it were very convenient that the Marshes of Terrington, Tilney and Clenchwarton were imbanked, and made Inmarsh, for the better preservation of the said Towns.'

The same flood had breached a sea bank in Walpole in twenty places 'and the residue so rent and torn as the making up and repairing of them hath and will cost a thousand pounds'. Six hundred acres of corn had been lost, to the value of £900, eight messuages or cottages were lost or damaged – some were 'carryed away clean' – to the value of £100. The floods demonstrated how a single community could not rely on its own defences – the damage at Walton was caused not by breaches in the banks there: 'the waters which came in at the breaches in Walsoken did drown us more than the waters which ran over our banks'.

As so often happens, disaster followed upon disaster:

To add to these losses, such were the Snows that fell in January and February ensuing, which occasioned mighty floods from the Upland Countries upon their going away, that a great part of this country was overflowed with the Fresh waters; viz from their bank called the Edge, between their Towns and the Smeeth, unto the new PoDike, through divers breaches between Salters Lode and Downham Bridge.

A board in the church at West Walton reads:

To the immortal praise of God Almighty that saveth his people in all adversities be it kept in perpetual memory that on the first day of November 1613 the sea broke in and overflowed all marshland, to the great danger of men's lives and loss of goods. On the three and 20th day of March 1614 this country was overflowed and on the 12th and 13th of September 1670 all Marshland was again overflowed by the violence of the sea.

A report survives on a flood in 1673: 'many cattle are drowned, stacks of hay and grain are swimming or standing a yard deep in water, all the cattle are driven to small banks, the poor people's houses are full of water, and they are forced to save themselves in boats. All their cole-seed lost, and all they have besides, in and about Thorney Fen, where were many farmhouses.' Fields were flooded all round Crowland, Spalding, Wisbech and Ely – houses were damaged, many cattle drowned, and the colza crop totally lost.

People in Fenland were thought to have their own unique character, often condemned by outsiders, and associated with the untamed countryside in which they lived. William Camden (1587) wrote of 'a kind of people according to the Nature of the Place where they shall dwell, rude, uncivil and envious to all others they call Upland men'. William Dugdale (1662) refers to the Fenmen as 'barbarous, sort of lazy and beggarly people'. It was thought that drainage would change their moral character: as a poet put it in 1685, 'New legs shall learn to Work, forget to Steal.'

The locals became known as 'Fen tigers', although it is not clear when this phrase first came into use. Wentworth Day thought it originated in the seventeenth century 'when the fenmen fought the imported Dutch drainers of Cornelius Vermuyden with shot-gun and bludgeon'. It puzzled Sybil Marshall's father in the early twentieth century: 'I don't know why some old fensmen were allus called tigers unless it were because they used to act so wild and shy, not being used to seeing many folks, or whether the strangers thought he looked a bit fierce.'

DENVER SLUICE AND THE BEDFORD RIVERS

Denver Sluice is the keystone of the whole drainage scheme of Fenland. It was first built by Vermuyden in 1651. The success of Vermuyden's grand design for the drainage of the Fens depended on a means of preventing the ingress of tidal water into the River Great Ouse system and the retention of sufficient water for navigation. This was achieved in 1652 by the construction of a sluice at Denver where the waters of his Old and New Bedford rivers rejoined the Ouse. The great sluice, coupled with the

The sluice at Denver.

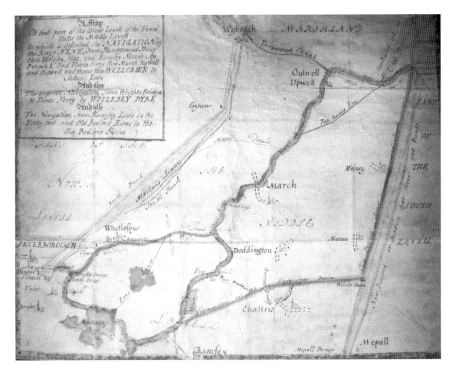

The Middle Level, 17th century map (Norfolk Record Office, BL 6/3)

sluice up the river at Earith, now named Hermitage Lock, effectively separated the flows originating in Bedfordshire from those of Cambridgeshire.[51]

Inevitably, there were complaints that the sluice blocked the river. The men of Lynn and Cambridge complained that ships that used to make eighteen voyages a year to Cambridge carrying coal could now only make ten or twelve – as a result the cost of fuel in Cambridge had risen by half. The sluice was 'blown up' by the tide in 1713, but built up once more in 1752. In 1867 it was guarded by soldiers because it was thought Irish nationalists might try to blow it up, in the traditional use of those words. The contrast between one side of the sluice and the other is described by Conybeare: 'it is a striking thing to be on the Sluice at high water and gaze at the sea waves ridging up the old river with force that seems illimitable … Still more striking is it to be on the Sluice when the spring tides are on, and see the sea on the north of the Sluice standing fifteen or twenty feet higher than the fresh waters on the south. One realises what widespread disaster would ensue if the Sluice were to give way.'

Conybeare says that the New Bedford River was used in the mid-nineteenth century in an experiment to see whether the earth was flat or spherical. Three boats, each with a cross-tree of identical height, were moored 3 miles apart. If the earth were flat, an observer in the end boat would see the other two cross-trees as one; if it were spherical, the central cross-tree would appear above the other. The judges decided that the earth was indeed round.

Together the sluice and the rivers make up one of the great man-made landscapes. In their own way, they are as much a demonstration of man's technical achievements as Ely Cathedral, 14 miles away – and visible from Denver Sluice on a clear day. They should be boosted as a tourist attraction.

Five

THE FENS HALF-DRAINED

The sheep and cows were free to range as then
Where change might prompt nor felt the bonds of men
Cows went and came with evening morn and night
To the wild pasture as their common right
And sheep unfolded with the rising sun
Heard the swains shout and felt their freedom won.[52]

While the villages of Fenland were extending the farmland inland by drainage, coastal villages were also actively reclaiming land from the sea. On such a flat coastline, this was relatively easy to do, as Hills says:

> Along a coast of sedimentation reclamation is quite straightforward. Flocks of sheep and an adequate supply of labour to dig embankments and drains, and to keep the outfalls open, were sufficient to bring the sea- and river-borne silt into good pasture. By the early eighteenth century, the wash salt marshes were used not only to summer-feed livestock but also to produce large crops of grain and coleseed, and even of turnips … Ploughing in such superb pastureland was frowned upon by most landlords before 1730, and the object of reclamation round the coast was chiefly to supply 'hard' land farmers with summer grass for grazing or mowing.[53]

Windmills

Drainage mills, often known as 'engines', were first brought into the Fens in the later sixteenth century: like many forms of new technology, they met with a good deal of local opposition. In 1575 Peter Morrice petitioned Queen Elizabeth for the right to produce 'divers engins and instruments by motion wherof running stremes and springes may be drawn farr higher than their natu-

Fenland mills: Soham Mill.

rall levills or course and also dead waters very likely to be drayned from the depths into other passage whereby the ground under them will prove firm'. Several other designers followed Morrice, such as Sir Thomas Goldinge, who asked for a patent for his engines that could dry 'all places drowned or under water', and William Mostart in 1592.

As it turned out, Morrice was unable to build his engines and sold his rights to George Carleton and Humfrey Michell. They proposed setting up engines to drain grounds south of Ravens Dyke in Whaplode, Holbeach and Fleet, but opponents claimed the engines were 'of great charge and small performance' and permission was not granted: he was also unsuccessful in

Watlington. Mills.

Fenland mills: Watlington Mill. (Norfolk Record Office, C/WT 1/6/15)

his attempt to place an engine on the sea bank between Gedney and Sutton Gotes. He did build one engine at Holbeach, but it lasted just eight tides or four days before it was overthrown. It was destroyed not by wind or water but by a man, William Stowe. His story is told in full in the State papers.

Fenland mills: Moulton windmill.

One Sunday after attending church in Holbeach, Stowe called the town dike-reeves together, and, still in the church, told them that he marvelled that they would allow 'Toyes' to be set upon the sea bank. He led a crowd to the Town Bridge, where he spoke threatening words against Carleton, but the men would not follow him and the crowd dispersed. Two days later, the frame of the engine was cut through, all save one quarter of an inch. When the mill keeper went in the morning to set the sails going, he was just oiling the 'going gear' when the wind blew from the sea and threw down both man and mill. As

Fenland mills: Mill north of Holbeach: note the millstone.

late as 1702–03, a 'windmill or water engine' belonging to a Mrs Keate was destroyed by a mob of disorderly persons.

Despite this opposition, there were soon 'engines' at work in the Fens: a survey of 1604 mentions two engines at Over, and there was a mill or engine at Leverington by 1617. Casaubon saw one when he was travelling though the Fens in 1611 with the Bishop of Ely. Losing their way after leaving Wisbech, they came to a windmill: there they found a boy who showed them the right way

Fenland mills: a 'heined' (heightened) windmill.

to a ford (where the bishop's horse reared, causing him to fall off!). Dugdale's map of 1662 shows many mills in the Fens: not all these were for drainage, some being for grinding corn.

Drainage mills were usually of wood, with four sails, and did not have fantails: the mill was turned to face the wind by hand, by means of a winch. They were normally worked by two men, or by a family, who would be allowed to live in the mill rent-free. Mills had no windows: smoke from the fire went out through

Fenland mills: windmill, Tilney Fen End. (Norfolk Record Office, C/WT 1/6/1/4)

Fenland mills: the same windmill, after it had blown over, 1909.

cracks in the wood in the top of the mill, which itself helped preserve the wood. Mills worked for six or nine months, not usually in summer when there was not enough wind, which, of course, could not be depended upon. Mills need a wind speed of at least 6m per second to function: in the early nineteenth century, William Swanborough reckoned that mills worked on average just one day in five. Another difficulty was that the mill usually pumped into a tidal river: there would be times when the river level was too high for it to pump. It was possible to have a storage lake: mills could pump into the lake, from which water would run out through self-acting sluices at times when the tide was low enough. This was common in Holland, but there were only a few examples in England.

Records of the Bedford Level Corporation, which acted in its capacity as a Court of Sewers, show many examples of people being fined for having mills, or asking permission to erect them from the 1660s. In May 1663, John Trafford applied for permission to drain 500 acres at Tydd St Mary by an engine into Clough's Cross Drain. Permission was granted, provided it was not prejudicial to the venting of the waters from the Great Level.

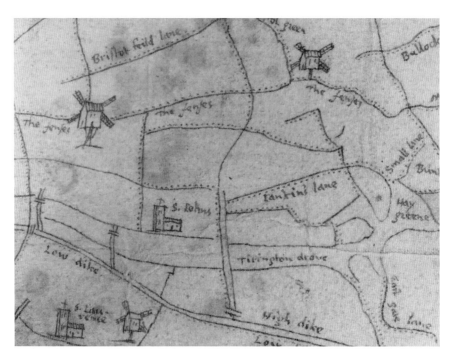

Windmills shown on Dugdale's map, mid-17th century (Norfolk Record Office, RYE 17/6).

Drainage mills along the river.

In 1680, the Corporation acted against some mills in Coldham and Waldersea, which had led to the Adventurers' grounds nearby being 'much dampnified'. They did not order the mills to be pulled down – this was beyond their powers, but they could levy fines. Instead they erected a bank to prevent the water thrown out by the mills running onto the Adventurers' grounds. However, this also caused problems as it meant the inhabitants had no way of getting rid of their water: they asked if they could cut a watercourse through the bank as a temporary expedient until a more satisfactory solution was found.

In three sessions between 1700 and 1708 the Corporation took action against the owners of no fewer than forty-four windmills and thirty-seven horse-mills. The owners were fined unless they ceased from working. However, the number of mills continued to increase: they were simply essential if the land was to be drained. By 1800, large mills were costing more than £1,000. Arthur Young mentions two at Wisbech costing £1,200 each, and one at Wilmington that cost £1,400. The Waterbeach Level paid £300 for a new mill in 1814.

As the land shrank, the height that the water had to be raised grew. This could lead to 'double mills', where one pumped the water into a storage basin, and a second mill pumped it from the basin into the river. The Littleport and Downham drainage area built a double mill in 1812, and the Waterbeach Level installed an 'inner mill' to lift water to their existing Dollard mill in 1814. In the Waldersea and Deeping Fen districts, each individual farmer had his own smaller mill to lift water from his fields into the main drain. The drainage authorities maintained larger mills to pump the water out of the main drains into the river: some of these small windmills were used even after the introduction of steam drainage. In the Netherlands, you can see three or even four windmills working in sequence.

Farming

Animal farming was flourishing in sixteenth-century Fenland. In 1560, the Lincolnshire Fens were required to produce thirty cart-horses for the royal use. The King's agent, Thomas Ogle, had the best horses and geldings brought before him. He chose fourteen at Spalding and another sixteen at Boston, paying between £2 and £3 6s 8d for each horse. Heckington Common was the subject of dispute in the reign of Charles I; the commons consisted of 2,330 acres, two-thirds being good quality grazing valued at 10s an acre: the remaining, wetter, third was valued at 5s an acre. The lord had the right to take in as many strangers' cattle as he liked from May Day to Martinmas. The commoners had unstinted rights. One woman, Mary Jenkinson, said that ever since the 1590s she had taken into the fen sixty cows, eight oxen, twenty young beasts, thirty horses and 1,000 sheep!

Water was still ever-present, and the Fenlander adapted to it. In 1724, according to Ogilby's *Britannia*, Crowland was 'so remote from pasture that the inhabitants are obliged to go a-milking by water in little boats called *skerrys*, which carry two or three persons at a time'. However, the success of drainage gradually led to a fundamental change in the landscape of Fenland, as Christopher Taylor recognised:

> From the 1650s onwards a rash of isolated farmsteads appeared everywhere but in the very deepest and wettest parts of the fens. The process continued throughout the eighteenth and nineteenth centuries but there are many farmsteads which can be definitely dated to the late seventeenth century. For example we know that a block of land to the north-west of the Old Bedford River was not drained until 1654. But in 1665, when describing the position of a break in the bank of the Bedford River, the Bedford Level Corporation recorded that it lay 'in Bedford North Bank neere Tubbes his house.' This exactly where the present Tubbs' farm stands today.[54]

Outsiders commented on the Fens after the 'great draining'. Near Ely, Dugdale noticed that: 'In the fen on both sides of this causey, were extraordinary numbers of cattel, feeding; the richness of the soile affording them sufficient pasturage'. Forty years later, Celia Fiennes was less complimentary: 'They are a slothful people and for little but the takeing care of their grounds and cattle which is of vast advantage; where the yeares prove drye they gaine so much that in case 6 or 7 wet yeares drown them all over the one good yeare sufficiently repaires their loss.'

More drained land also meant more arable. At first there was a rush to plough as many years as possible, with perhaps just a single year of fallow. Farmers soon learned it was best to grow a variety of crops with several years of grass – which, of course, was a valuable crop in itself. There was much diversification: new crops were introduced, most notably rapeseed (also known as cole-seed or colza), which had been imported from Europe through Lynn. It provided oil, which was needed in the finishing processes in the textile industry. Olive oil was normally used, imported from Spain, but after the Reformation Catholic Spain had become an enemy and alternative sources of oil were needed.

Rapeseed was grown in the Fens from the mid-sixteenth century, being noted by Turner in 1551 and by Langham in 1578: by the end of the decade, 2,000 quarters of rapeseed were being exported from Boston and Lynn to Flanders. Some 3,500 acres of rapeseed were being cultivated at Long Sutton in 1632. Wisbech was shipping 1,000 tons of oil a year in 1719, and the town also put the product to practical use, providing street lamps as early as 1700, unusually early for such a relatively small place.

Kerridge describes the process:

> The cole-seed, or giant rape, was brushed in at intervals from about May onwards, July being the peak month and the best for germination. Cole-seed produced about fifteen tons of green food an acre and no less than twenty hundredweights of starch equivalent, appreciably more than did common turnips. In summer it was reaped, spread on sail-cloth for about a month to dry and then threshed with ordinary flails. After winnowing, the seed was sold for farmers, or to oil-mills for crushing. The colza oil expressed gave illumination or lubrication or went to make soap. The stubble was useless for anything but burning where it stood.[55]

The crop was normally planted around midsummer, four to six weeks before the grain harvest: it thus provided employment during a slack period. Its green shoots made ideal winter fodder for cows and sheep.

Rapeseed was regarded with suspicion by some, because it was seen as a foreign import. In 1650, Sir William Maynard asked forcibly in the *Anti-Projector*, what 'is cole-seed and Rape, they are but Dutch commodities and but trash and trumpery'.

Another new crop was woad, an essential plant for dyeing textiles blue, it was mixed with madder for tawny colours and with weld for greens. Woad is an ancient crop, mentioned by Julius Caesar ('all the Britons dye themselves with woad, which makes them a sky blue colour and thereby more terrible to their enemies'). In the fourteenth century it was being imported into Boston from Amiens, Brabant and Picardy. It was exclusively imported from Europe until the mid-sixteenth century, when it began to be grown in Hampshire and surrounding counties. By the 1580s, Anthony Cope was growing woad at Wickham in Spalding. The actual process of fermenting woad produced a very unpleasant smell – for this reason, it was illegal to plant woad within 3 miles of a royal palace! The crop was grown on the estate of the Cotton family at Conington in Huntingdonshire – but Sir John Cotton was a non-resident landlord! It was gathered by hand, 'grasping the leaves of the plants, and taking them off with a twist': the plants were about 8in high. They went into baskets, made from locally grown osiers.

The woad harvest, early twentieth century.

In the early nineteenth century, Arthur Young drew attention to woad production at Brothertoft Farm, Boston: the farmer was J.C. Cartwright. Woad exhausts the soil, so it cannot be grown year after year on the same piece of land. Cartwright had 1,100 acres of land, which he exploited on a rotation system: the woad was followed by two years of rapeseed, another of oats, then seven or eight years under grass. This meant that at any given time he had 200 acres under woad. Cartwright set up a permanent woad mill, which employed thirty workmen and a foreman. They lived in a new settlement on the banks of the New Forty Foot Drain: it was called Isatica, after the Latin word for the woad plant. However, Young pointed out that demand for woad was limited, and advised farmers to be very cautious about growing the crop.

In 1837, when Joseph Fleckney died in Sibsey Fen aged 85, he was said in the newspaper notice of his death to have been engaged for fifty years in the woad trade. Fifty years later, in 1887, John Graves was said to be the largest woad grower in the Skirbeck area, and the mill was described in very dramatic terms: 'as the three enormous grinding wheels, fitted with almost countless steel teeth, speed on their roundabout course, devouring forkful upon forkful of unresisting woad leaves, the effect is as thrilling as an alligator feeding upon duskies'.[56]

Woad was not restricted to the Fens, but its production lasted longer there than anywhere else.

Madder enjoyed a brief boom in the Fens: it was being grown near Wisbech in the later seventeenth century. It took three years to yield its first crop, so was probably grown by a speculator: a good crop could make £32 an acre. It was being grown in Wisbech and Leverington in 1671. By the mid-1670s, however, the price had fallen to £16 an acre: the bubble had burst and madder ceased to be grown in the Fens.

Hemp and flax also provided oil. Hemp had many other uses: it was used in cloth making and for making rope. According to Ravensdale, hemp was grown at the boundary between the Fens proper and ploughland. The crop is mentioned at Cottenham in 1549, and at Waterbeach in the late seventeenth century. A sixteenth-century report said that rapeseed, flax and hemp 'will be more gainful to the owners of land than any corn'. At Ewell Fen near Willingham, Dugdale saw, 'a fair plantation of Onyons, Peas and Hempe' and noted approvingly that the onions had been sold in the previous year for £30 an acre. According to Hartlib, the same three crops were grown by Colonel Castle on newly drained land in Huntingdonshire.

There was even a small crop of mulberries, from which silk was made. Hartlib tells us that, on her wedding day, Colonel Castle's daughter gave pairs of silk stockings made from the product of silkworms, which she had bred herself. However, it did not develop beyond being a girl's hobby.

Draining was never entirely a benefit, even to farmers: an over-effective drainage system could be bad news as the land could become dusty while the water it needed was being carried away from it in rivers and drains. The way to remedy this was warping. Kerridge comments: 'The land might be dried not wisely but too well, so depriving it of essential sediments and solutions or laying it too dry for good grassland. Some soils were 'very dust' and had 'ther lieffe and succor from the waters overflowing'. When Cottenham common Fen was redrained, the commoners were driven to seek pastures elsewhere and to 'set barne dores overthwarte the river to stancke the water to help water into theire ditches for theire cattell'. Where basically poor or sandy soils were bereft of essential alluvial dressings, little ingenuity was required to pierce small slackers through the embankments to allow in as much silt as was needed … Although only brought to public notice by William Marshall, this practice was probably not much posterior to the drainage that necessitated it. With this remedy at hand, it is impossible to see anything but advantage in the draining of the peat fens.[57]

It was estimated that every tide left a 'leaf' of sediment ⅛ in thick: one disadvantage was that it left an absolutely level surface, which meant that standing water would not run off the land.

The old products of Fenland were still important in the undrained parts of the area, especially ducks and geese. In the Middle Ages, vast numbers of ducks were driven into V-shaped walls of netting, sometimes several thousand at one time: in 1607, one draught of the net in Lincolnshire took up 3,000 mallard. This was done in the summer months, when the ducks were moulting and unable to fly. An Act of 1534 attempted to preserve wildfowl during this vulnerable time in their lives by forbidding the taking of fowl between 31 May and 31 August: this Act was repealed in 1550. An Act of 1711 forbade taking of fowl between 1 July and 1 September, and in 1737, this was extended to the period 1 June to 1 October – the period when moult occurred.

A document held by the Spalding Gentleman's Society records between 300 and 400 birds *a day* being taken at Deeping Fen in 1728. It notes practices already centuries old and seen as the Fenman's inalienable rights:

The country People have Right of Common, Enclosing hundreds of acres with large Nets having pipes at their Ends and driving the moulted Mallards or Male Wildfowles into those Nets. N.B. There are very few female or Ducks when they being with their Young feeding out at Sea, but the Drakes being sick or unable to fly their Wing Feathers being gone with casting their Feathers amongst the Reeds and Rushes in the broad fresh Waters.

The fowl were not always killed at once, instead they might be captured and fattened up. This not only produced more meat but also a better taste: wild fowl tasted of what they had themselves eaten – 'some tasting of Fishe, some of mudde, and some of grasse'.

Special carts were employed to carry the fowl alive to London, as Defoe noticed in the 1720s:

They have of late invented a new method of carriage, being carts form'd on purpose, with four stories or stages, to put the creatures in, one above another, by which invention one cart will carry a very great number; and for the smoother going they drive with two horses abreast, like a coach, so quartering the road for the ease of the poultry, and changing horses, they travel night and day; so that they bring the fowls 70, 80, or 100 miles in two days and one night.

There was an innovation in the early seventeenth century, when the duck decoy was introduced in England. They were copied from the Dutch trap, the Dutch name being 'Eendecoy', and could take ducks in large numbers during the period allowed. Wheeler describes the new system:

A decoy consisted of pools surrounded by trees and plantations, and branching off from them were small channels or ditches called 'pipes'. At the time of catching the birds, these pipes were covered with nets, which rested on hoops, and were termi-nated by a drawing net. Into these the wild fowl were enticed by various devices: but the usual mode was by means of a decoy duck, trained for the purpose. This bird was taught to obey the whistle of the decoy man, who tempted it to swim up the trapping tunnel when he saw a number of wild fowl; these, following the tame one and being led into the channel, were then enclosed and ultimately taken by the net … Immense quantities of birds were caught in these decoys. In one season, a few winters previous to the inclosure of the East Fen, ten decoys, five of which were in

Friskney, furnished 31,2000 birds for the London market. It was not considered a good season unless the decoys yielded 5,000 birds. The birds usually taken in the decoy were the Mallard, the Teal and the Pochard.

There was big money involved. At Dowsby in 1765, 12,908 birds were taken in one the season – they were sold for almost £400. There were about 200 decoys in use in Fenland in the early 1800s, but that was their peak – they were in decline throughout the nineteenth century.

The goose also remained an essential part of the economy of many a Fen family, providing as they did eggs, flesh and fat, and requiring little more than some grass to feed upon. Some farmers produced them on a much larger scale with up to 2,000 birds, with coops made of wicker placed on top of each other: each bird soon identified its own pen to which it would return after being driven down to water. Geese were driven from the Fens to London: Defoe noted that there might be as many as 2,000 in a drove, and that this was done after the harvest in August so that the geese could feed on the stubble as they went. The droves continued into October 'when the roads begin to be too stiff and deep for their broad feet and short legs to march in'.

Other Fenmen left as work became scarce but are not well recorded, unless they came into conflict with authority. Such a man was John Smytheman of Ramsey. He journeyed to Norwich and got a job with a shoemaker, William Hellam, being paid piece work for making both plain shoes and for 'wooden heel work'. However, they had not gone through the necessary formalities: both men were punished, and Smytheman spent a week in Norwich Bridewell before being sent back to Ramsey. Others would go to sea. Lynn apprentice-ship records for the twenty years 1740–61 show young men from Fenland parishes signing on as apprentices to mariners, such as 14-year-old Roger Clarke of Wisbech in 1741, and George Draper, son of a Boston labourer, in the following year.[58]

People lived much closer to subsistence level than they do today: a bad har-vest or severe flooding could lead to people actually starving. Wheeler quotes a letter in the National Archives written in 1623 saying that people could not even find enough straw for their bedding, and that they were forced to eat dogs and horses. The writer knew of a case where someone was so desperate for food that they stole a sheep, tore off its leg and ate it raw: 'all this is most certain true'.

Dutch and French Incomers

Dutch and French immigrants, Protestant refugees fleeing persecution, brought their own skills into Fenland: even today a few places have names such as Frenchmans Farm or Dutch Farm. As early as 1584, a man named Latreille put forward proposals 'on the part of some Frenchmen' to drain the fens of England. In 1606, there was a proposal that French contractors should drain the Fens. Fenmen got up a petition saying that 'they need not the help of foreign undertakers'.

There was a large French refugee community at Thorney – the names French Drove and French Farm still survive in the parish. The refugees were first admitted on condition of being allowed to sell at any market, and of being exempt from taxes and from service overseas, the latter for forty years. They held their own services under their own pastors, and a register of baptisms survives, with 1,703 entries covering the period from 1654 to 1727. At its peak in the 1660s there were almost forty baptisms a year, so that the community was quite a large one. There was also a French church in Whittlesey. Not all the members of the refugee community came directly from France, quite a large number having been first at a French community at Sandtoft on Hatfield Chase in Yorkshire, but they were not welcomed by the local peasants there, so they asked the Earl of Bedford for land on his Thorney estate, which they would drain and cultivate. Others came from communities of refugees at Canterbury and Norwich. Some of the community were in fact Dutch rather than French speakers. Other people did come directly from Europe to Thorney. Some of the incomers were trained drainers, who received wages for their work, while others were farmers and a small number were capitalists who sometimes joined the body of the Adventurers.

In 1600, a licence was granted for Stephen de Carsol, a Frenchman, to preach at Thorney in either French or Latin. A stone in Thorney Church south wall is to Ezekiel Daniels, who died in 1674: he is called the first minister of the French colony that began to assemble in 1652. The pastor of the Whittlesey congregation in 1646 was a man named du Perrier: when Whittlesey was united with Thorney some time between 1646 and 1656, he became pastor at Southampton. The Church of England did its best to help distressed French ministers, one being appointed to Parson Drove, for example: a Henry Pujolas was pastor there in the 1690s, where he received only a small stipend as the chapel wardens, according to an enquiry held in Wisbech in 1696, held on to most of the money due to him from rents on church land in Leverington and Parson Drove.

The community declined in the early eighteenth century, as its members merged with local families: there was an average of only four baptisms a year in the 1720s. However, a writer in 1744 says that French was still spoken in private conversation by the descendants of the refugees, and some of the French surnames survived in anglicised form well into the nineteenth century if not later. They include Wanty (from Wantier) and Bayley (from Bailleul).

The contribution of incomers to drainage was reinforced in the 1650s. Because of shortage of labour for Vermuyden's second efforts at draining the Fens, Scottish prisoners of war were brought in after the Battle of Dunbar in 1650, and Dutch prisoners after Blake's victory over van Tromp in 1652. The Dutch prisoners were not always very satisfactory workers: the Earl of Bedford complained that they went on strike claiming that, as prisoners of war, they should not be forced to work. They often ran away, and were frequently sheltered by sympathetic Fenmen.

The contribution of the incomers was recognised by many observers. When Dugdale was at Sandtoft in 1657, he noted 'there is a Chapell (very ruinous) built about 20 years since by those French and Dutch, who adventured in the improving of this Isle, by draining'. The nearby drain was named Dutchman's drain. In 1683, Gregorio Leti described French refugees settling on newly reclaimed land at Thorney: they 'began to sow a kind of wild cabbage called colza, from which they extracted an oil, which is not only useful for lamps, but also is used in the preparation of wool; and of this they succeeded in making, during the first few years, a very advantageous harvest.'[59]

Arthur Young thought that the custom of paring and burning in the Cambridgeshire Fens originated with the French. When he visited Thorney and Whittlesey, he was told by a Mr Grounds, of the latter place, that the paring plough was known as the French plough. Young points out that burning had long been common agricultural practice in France.

The Ports of Boston and Lynn

Boston was at its height in the Middle Ages: in just one decade, from 1280 to 1290, the wool of 3 million sheep was exported from the town. The wealth and population of Boston was declining by the sixteenth century due to the

River traffic at Lynn …

… and at Boston.

collapse of the export trade in wool, especially to the Baltic. Leland attributed this to a specific event, the murder of one of the 'Esterling' traders in Boston by Boston merchant Humfrey Litilbyri – as a consequence, the Esterlings stopped coming and the town was soon 'sore decayed'. However, from about 1615 this was more than compensated for by a great growth in trade with the newly independent Dutch Republic, which brought in French wine, Norwegian deals and rye from the Baltic, now coming via Amsterdam rather than directly. As R.W.K. Hilton noted:

> The Dutch invasion must have been as obvious to anyone watching the port as it is to anyone looking at the port books today. At first arrives a single ship of Amsterdam. It returns, makes repeated visits, plies as fast as it can sail to and fro across the North Sea. One sees the shipmaster building up his business. He becomes a familiar figure in the port books, as he must have been at the quayside among the merchants of Boston.[60]

In the early seventeenth century, Lynn was a much more important port than Boston: Alan Metters estimates that it had four times as much overseas trade, much from the Low Countries, but also a good deal of continuing trade from the countries around the Baltic. Several ships carried what sounds like rubbish to Dieppe: bones, broken glass, enormous quantities of old shoes – perhaps an early example of disposing of waste by exporting it.[61]

THE LANGUAGE OF THE FENS

The landscape of the Fens has produced its own language, almost always relating to drainage. Some of these are:

DELF or DELPH: a ditch, usually a drain running parallel with and at the foot of a bank.

GOTE: a Saxon term for a sluice, usually between fresh and salt water.

GULL: a hole made by water breaching a bank.

HURNE or HYRNE: a corner or a sharp angle.

SASSE: a sluice with doors for keeping out the tides.

WASHLAND: land beside a river reserved for storage of flood water.

Six

EIGHTEENTH-CENTURY FENLAND

Then bankes came downe with ruin and rout –
Then beaten foam flew round about –
Then all the mighty floods were out.

The feet had hardly time to flee
Before it brake against the knee,
And all the world was in the sea.[62]

In 1726, 'Proposals and inducements' were issued 'for a considerable number of people to join in the purchase of several thousand acres of drowned and derelict lands in several counties of England'. The writer refuted a complaint made in 1653 'alledging that it was worth as much before the draining in reed and sedge as since', and dismissed the objectors as 'some few people that had formerly nothing to live on, but what they got by Fishing and Fowling, and some discontented Persons, that would neither do themselves good, or suffer others, are apt to clamour against this noble work of Draining, and the Undertakers thereof'. The future was with the drainers. Pishey Thompson, Boston's first historian, even says that people who perfected drainage works in Lincolnshire, thereby removing the cause of sickness and disease, were known as dragon-slayers: 'John Rennie was the great dragon-slayer in the Fens of Lincolnshire.' There had been earlier schemes, on a smaller scale: Earl Fitzwilliam drained the 10,000 acres of the Holland Fen in 1720. In 1756, a small 'Cradge Bank' was built on the north side of New Bedford River. A dam was built at Welmore Lake to allow the water to flow out of the Washes – a hole was just made through the dam, which was then blocked up when not required! A proper sluice, the Welmore Lake Sluice, was built in 1825.

'Cradge' is a word for a bank placed on top of an old one. Joseph Scott, in his plans for improving Fenland drainage, thought that there should be stocks of material kept ready for emergency cradging:

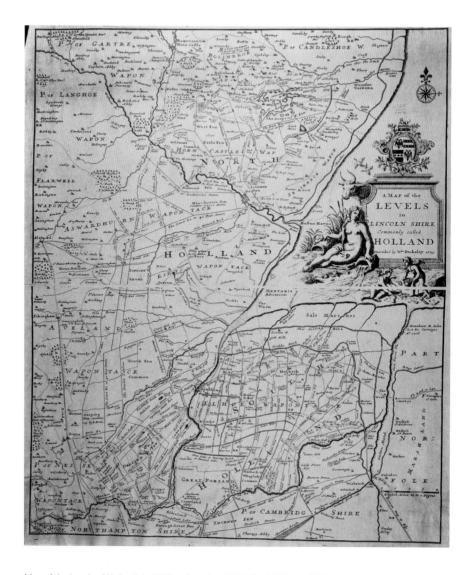

Map of the Levels of Holland, by William Stukeley, 1723. (Norfolk Record Office, BL 7a/10)

Instead of the slow process of going to adjoining estates and cutting down young plantations, and cropping trees, sticking boughs in the banks, and making hedges in the water etc, there should always be hundreds of hurdles kept in readiness, and in dangerous floods many of these should be put into lighters, and instantly conveyed to such parts of the bank where they are wanted. And most of the hurdles should be made small and light, to be handy, but a few of them should be made large and strong, for parts that require such.[63]

The origins of the Boston Grand Sluice go back as far as 1142 when a 'great sluice' was erected across the River Witham at Boston, though by 1316 this wooden structure was 'ruinous and in great decay'. The river became tidal again, until in 1500 a Dutchman, May Hake, built a masonry and timber structure across the narrowest part of the river, just upstream of the present Town Bridge. Although the sluice itself functioned barely 100 years, the bridge above the sluice lasted until 1807, although it was decrepit in its later years. Hake's sluice consisted of a pair of waterways, closed against the tide by horizontally hinged flap doors suspended from iron hooks.

Flooding was still a problem. During the winter of 1762 and the spring of 1763, 22,000 acres of Holland Fen were flooded. Subsequently the Black Sluice was built to connect the South Forty Foot Drain with the River Witham near Boston. The River Witham itself was still proving a problem. Individual proprietors had made piecemeal attempts to improve their section of the river by cutting drains, erecting mills and embanking, but the need for effective strategic action had become apparent. The fall from High Bridge at Lincoln to Boston was only 16ft; the river was 'crooked', and as little as 18ft wide in places. Winter usually brought flooding. The preamble to the 1762 Witham Act made clear the situation: 'by the sand and silt brought in by the tide, the outfalls thereof into the sea hath, for many years long past, been greatly hindered and obstructed, and is now, in a great measure, stopped up, lost and destroyed and thereby great part of the low lands and fens lying on both sides of the said river (together about one hundred thousand acres) are frequently overflowed, and rendered useless and unprofitable, to the great loss of the respective owners thereof'.

The River Witham was straightened under the 1762 Act and construction of the Grand Sluice at Boston began in 1766, designed by Langley Edwards of King's Lynn: it is possibly the earliest tidal outfall sluice still extant in a substantially original state. Much of the Black Sluice Lock survives on the Haven side of London Road – three piers and three original iron winches. Most of the western side was destroyed when the pumping station was extended in the 1960s.[64]

In 1774, Vernatt's Drain was extended to join the Welland near the sea at Surfleet. This was the work of yet another Dutch engineer, Sir Philiberti Vernatti. The success of the improvements was reflected in rising land values:

by the end of the eighteenth century, land rentals along the Witham had risen from 1s 6d per acre to between 11 and 17s.

There was one enormous tract still undrained: the 40,000 acres of the inter-commons of West, East Fen and Wildmore Fen. The commoners gave a lively description of East and West Fen before it was drained:

The fen called the West Fen is the place where the ruffs and reeves resort in the greatest numbers, and many other sorts of water fowl which do not require the shelter of reeds and rushes migrate hither to breed, for this fen is bare, having been imperfectly drained by narrow canals which intersect it for many miles. Twenty parishes in the Soke of Bolingbroke have a right of common on it, but an enclosure is now in agitation. The East Fen is quite in a state of nature, and exhibits a specimen of what the country was before the introduction of draining.

It is a vast tract of morass, intermixed with numbers of lakes, from half a mile to two or three miles in circuit, communicating with each other by narrow, reedy straits. They are very shallow, none above four or five feet deep, but abound with pike, perch, ruffs, bream, tench, dace, eels etc. The reeds which cover the fens are cut annually for thatching not only cottages, but many very good houses. The multitudes of stares that roost in these reeds in winter break down many by perching on them. A stock of reeds well harvested and stacked is worth two or three hundred pounds.

The birds which inhabit the different fens are very numerous. Besides the common wild duck, wild geese, garganies, pochards, shovellers, and teal breed here, peewit, gulls and black terns abound; a few of the great terns or tickets are seen among them. The great crested grebes, called gaunts, are found in the East Fen. The lesser crested, the black and dusty, and the little grebe, cootes, water-hens and spotted water-hens, water-rails, ruffs, red-shanks, lapwings or wypes, red-breasted godwits, and whimbrels are inhabitants of these fens.

'Improvers' took a contrary view. In 1794, Stone wrote of East, West and Wildmore Fens:

They are extremely wet and unprofitable in their present state, standing much in need of drainage, are generally overstocked, and dug up for turf and fuel. The cattle and sheep depastured upon them are often very unhealthy, and of an inferior sort, occasioned by the scantiness, as well as the bad quality, of their food, and the wetness of their lair ... It is not a constant practice with the commoners, to take all their

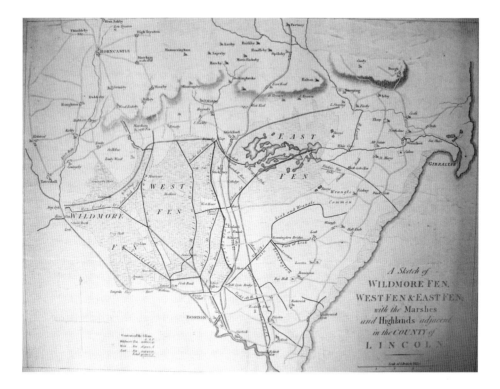

Westmore, West and East Fens.

cattle off the fens upon the approach of winter; but some of the worst of the neat cattle, with the horses; and particularly those upon Wildmore Fen, are left to abide the event of the winter season; and it seldom happens that of the neat cattle many escape the effects of a severe winter. The horses are driven to such distress for food, that they eat up every remaining dead thistle, and are said to devour the hair of the manes and tails of each other, and also the dung of geese.

Theft of animals was a continual problem as well: Stone thought that these commons were 'the frequent resort of thieves, who convey the cattle into distant Counties for sale'. Sheep fared even worse than larger beasts: in 1793 it was estimated that 40,000 sheep rotted on the three fens, and they were even more likely to be stolen: 'the number stole is incredible: they are taken off by whole flocks. So wild a country nurses up a people as wild as the fen.'

In 1799 John Rennie was asked by Sir Joseph Banks of Revesby Abbey, which overlooked West Fen where he leased a large area of land from the

Duchy of Lancaster, to undertake surveys of Wildmore and East and West Fens. Banks had succeeded to the estates in 1761 while still a minor, becoming a Drainage Commissioner when he came of age in 1764. He recognised that the main problem was the overflow of upland waters in the Fens and the poor outfalls. The work that followed was substantial. A catch-water drain was constructed from Coningsby in the west to join the Gote Syke Drain, and the Maud Foster Sluice was moved and enlarged. The East Fen was serviced by a catchwater drain from Little Steeping to join the West Fen Catchwater south of Stickford. In addition, a new sluice called Hobhole Sluice was constructed down river from the Maud Foster Drain, which was fed from the Hobhole Drain extending up to Stickney, eventually allowing water to bypass Maud Foster. These advantages, with the construction of numerous minor dykes and of a new River Witham channel at its outfall, had a major effect on the entire river north of Boston.

> The great bull at Revesby [Young's description of Banks] had brought about a scheme for the united drainage of all three fens under the most capable civil engineer of the day, a scheme which would work as planned until fifty years of drainage caused the peat of the East Fen to shrink so much that drainage by gravity was no longer possible, but which, with assistance from pumping, continues to operate to the present day.[65]

It should not be forgotten that these enormous drainage enterprises were largely undertaken by bands of itinerant workers using manpower and the simplest of tools. Many of these 'navvies' had been the bands of canal builders during the eighteenth century and were to become the railway builders of the nineteenth century. For the first time the power of the shovel was assisted by the use of steam engines, placed on barges. It was these straight rivers that were noticed by Philip Larkin travelling by train: 'The river's level drifting breath began/Where sky and Lincolnshire and water meet.'[66]

The great marshes of the Fens were now conquered. The former quagmire now began to be used for crops. The changes were obvious to any observer. As John Clarke wrote in 1852:

> The fields are now divided by neat whitethorn hedges, and the surface, both of clay, silty loam, and peat earth, is under a high state of cultivation. The farms are nearly all in tillage instead of pasture, wheat, oat, beans, and barley, seeds, turnips,

and coleseed yielding bulky and wealthy crops, for market, for grazing long-wooled sheep, and feeding large cattle.[67]

As Pevsner noted, the area maintains its own unique landscape: 'the roads are grid-like and run in straight lines for miles.' In addition, the new townships of Eastville, Midville, Frithville, Carrington, Westville and Thornton-le-Fen were established after 1812, and these soon developed into new communities. Each of the new communities needed a parish church, and six churches for the area were sanctioned by an Act of Parliament of 1812. Five were designed by Jeptha Pacey, although the last, Eastville, was not built until 1840, by C.J. Carter, probably a pupil of Pacey.

Deeping Fen, extending for 11 miles between Deeping and Spalding, was also crying out for 'improvement'. Stone commented in 1794:

Every kind of depredation is made upon this land, in cutting up the best of the turf for fuel; and the farmers in the neighbourhood having common rights, availing themselves of a fine season turn on 7 or 800 sheep each, to ease their inclosed land, while the mere cottager cannot get a bite for a cow; but yet the cottager, in his turn, in a colourable way, takes the stock of a foreigner as his own, who occasionally turns on immense quantities of stock in good seasons. The cattle and sheep which are constantly depastured on this common, are of very unthrifty ill-shapen kind, from being frequently starved, and no attention paid to their breed.

The land was sold for about £3 an acre, and rented out at 7 or 8s an acre 'and a great deal was in such a state that nobody would rent it'. Twenty years later, the Fen had been drained and everything was very different: land was now changing hands at £20 an acre, and rents had rocketed to 20s an acre. The very richness of the soil brought in a new pest – mice, 'which have multiplied to such a degree in the pastures as almost to starve the sheep. The land is alive with them. Mr Greaves has, in a field of a few acres, killed eight or ten by his horse treading on them.'

There was still much work to be done, but on a smaller scale. At least one venture utilised the unemployed of the area. Woodhouse Marsh Cut, straightening the River Nene north of Wisbech, was begun in 1827 and completed in 1832. It was known as Paupers' Cut because it was built by labourers thrown on the poor rate. Tycho Wing summed up the success of the Second North Level major improvement scheme by observing that 'in the winter 1836, we

Wisbech in 1756.

actually saw the water moving in the Wryde Drain at Thorney which no man had seen before'.[68]

The other major campaigns of the eighteenth century involved attempts to improve the outfalls of the rivers. The importance of a clear and adequate outfall where the River Nene flows into the Wash had long been known to play a vital part in the drainage of the northern Fens. The River Nene ran through salt marshes and frequently changed course. In about 1720, Charles Kinderley put forward a scheme to confine the stream to a narrow channel. His scheme was adopted by the Bedford Level Corporation, but the Wisbech authorities filed a petition in Chancery to stop the work – it was suspended for fifty years. In 1751, Nathaniel Kinderley revived his father's scheme. He was initially unsuccessful, but years of inundations followed, and in 1773 an Act was passed reviving the scheme: the finished channel was called Kinderley's Cut in honour of its proposer. The cut ran from Wisbech to Gunthorpe Sluice and immediately improved the outfall. Nathaniel Kinderley was also the first to propose in 1751 what – seven decades later – became the Eau Brink Cut. The two Kinderleys, father and son, are both buried in Moulton churchyard.

The value of Kinderley's Cut was progressively negated by the silting of the rivers at Cross Keys Wash. At the beginning of the nineteenth century, the consulting engineer, John Rennie, drew up plans to cut a new channel 200ft wide and 5 miles long, close to the former bank of Cross Keys Wash. The work was carried out between 1827 and 1830 under the direction of Thomas Telford, who had been appointed as Rennie's successor. The contractors, Joliffe & Banks,

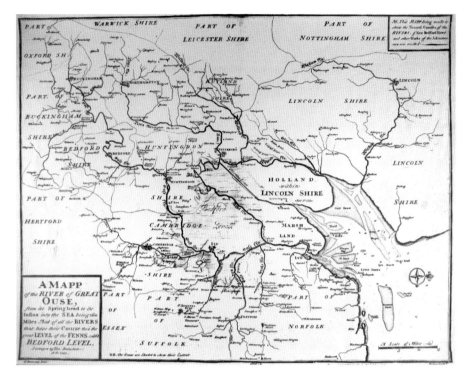

Thomas Badeslade's map of the Great Ouse, 1723 (Norfolk Record Office, BL 7a/12)

employed up to 1,500 men to make the cut. On completion, the old river was closed off and the full discharge from the Nene was then sufficient to scour out the new channel to the required depth for navigation within a few months. The banks of the new cut were protected with 10,000 tons of stone pitching.

Telford described the work on the Nene Outfall Cut:

On the 4th of June 1830, the dam at the lower end being removed, and the upper dam on the 7th, the tide was permitted to flow up the new cut, and this continued until the 14th, but while the river was permitted to pass partly down the old channel, there was not a rush of sufficient down the new cut to scour out the silt brought by the flowing tide; so that it became absolutely necessary to close the old channel by making an embankment across it, so as to turn the whole of the river down the new cut. Three hundred workmen with one hundred carts worked day and night for six days to close up the old river: barges or lighters were sunk to help form a barrier.

Fenland drowned.

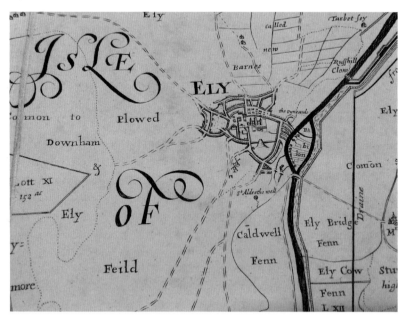

Eighteenth-century Ely: from Jonas Moore's map of 1706. (Norfolk Record Office, BR 318/1)

He continued proudly:

> There is now a safe and daily communication between Wisbech and the sea at all periods of the tides, and in all weather, for vessels of the above [60 tons] burden, and on spring tides for ships of much larger capacity, and drawing not less than fourteen feet of water. Vessels carrying 400 tons reach Sutton Wash on spring tides ... The trade of the port, which before the Nene Outfall was made was not more than 50,000 tons a year, has since progressively increased and reached in the last year [1836] to 108,000 tons.

The Nene Outfall Amendment Act of 1829 authorised the River Commissioners to erect two lighthouses at the mouth of the river, without the sanction of Trinity House. They still exist: the brick towers are 40ft high with small cottages attached and are now privately owned. The towers have never displayed lights but served as landmarks for shipping entering the outfall channel.[69]

The River Nene meets the sea.

Although the major impact of drainage was on the Fens, continual marshland reclamation of the coastal strip should not be forgotten. Attempts were made during the medieval period to safeguard the coastline from inundation from the sea with the construction of clay banks; and also in the seventeenth century when more than 17,000 acres was saved from the sea along the coast principally south of the River Welland. The main impetus to recover the marshes came at times of high prosperity: during the French wars of 1793–1815, more than 5,000 acres of marshlands were embanked in Spalding, Moulton, Whaplode, Holbeach and Gedney and a further 700 acres between Frieston and Friskney. Throughout the nineteenth century, nearly all Fen coastal parishes were enlarged by new land reclaimed from the marsh, even to the extent that a completely new 3,193-acre parish of Wingland was created. Saltmarsh was reclaimed at Wainfleet/Croft, 1789, and the South Holland Embankment built from Fosdyke to Gedney (1793–1811) to reclaim 4,695 acres.

Floods

In 1713, the Denver Sluice was destroyed by a combination of violent floods and an exceptionally high tide. Although this removed the obstacle to navigation, it was disastrous for the South Fens. Badeslade wrote that the land was drowned:

> to such a Depth, that the Sun cannot exhale the Waters, nor dry them up: and from *Haddenham* Hills in our View of the Fen, we observed they were all to the *South* and *East* bright, excepting here and there a Reed or sallow Bush, and some small Tract of Grounds which appeared above the waters; and those heretofore rich Meadows from *Audrey* Bridge to *Stretham* Ferry, we found drowned on both sides of the River.

The Denver Sluice was rebuilt by a Swiss engineer named Labelye between 1748 and 1750. The sluice that he constructed lasted until the present sluice, the third on this site, was designed and built by Rennie: in December 1831, he issued a 'Specification of three new sluice openings and a lock for the proposed enlargement of Denver Sluice'. The new sluice was completed in 1834.

Eyewitnesses record many floods in the eighteenth century. A sea flood in 1736 was described at the time as the worst for 135 years: seventeen breaches

The river bank, Spalding.

were made in the bank between Spalding and Wisbech and hundreds of acres were under water. Several houses were washed away, including that of Thomas Hayes, a Gedney fisherman. According to a newspaper report, he lost everything except his wife and a barrel of ale, 'to both of which he had been wedded for above 50 years'. As the waters rose, he had to save one or the other and eventually let the cask go: he and his wife were both saved.

When Charles Labeleye passed through fen country in 1743, 'the fens were then in a most beautiful condition, and so dry that from Cambridge to Denver's Ferry our horses had but one occasion to wet their hooves in wading through waters': by 1745, however, the Fens were again in a very poor state. There was a great flood in winter of 1763 – of the whole 22,000 acres of Holland Fen, not a single acre remained dry. In 1769, the left bank of the River Welland gave way, flooding Deeping Fen to a depth of 6 or 7ft. On the following day, the north bank of the Nene also gave way, near Guyhirne, and the water flooded the whole of the North Level, reaching Long Sutton churchyard and the turnpike road between Sutton and Gedney.

There was another 'Great Drowning' in 1770, when the north bank of Morton's Leam burst at Abel's Gull in November. S. Egar of Thorney wrote: 'the whole country for miles around was flooded to a depth of six feet or more

… The breach in the bank was 130 yards long and 36 feet deep. So sudden was the irruption that many were ruined. Some, barely escaping with their lives, found a temporary asylum in the Abbey Church of Thorney, and in buildings on the higher lands. Tenants gave up their lands in despair. It was not until the spring of 1773 that the land was brought again under cultivation.' In January 1771 John Fearnside wrote from Wisbech that: 'it was a very poor time for customs house officers, with nothing in prospect for a drowned country until the waters are drawn off by engines or evaporated chiefly into the clouds.'[70]

John Golborne wrote a report on the Middle and South Levels in 1777:

> Look which way you will, you will see nothing but misery and desolation: go but half a mile from Ely, and you come to Middle-fen, a tract of sixteen thousand acres, given up an abandoned; there you see the ruins of Windmills, the last efforts of an industrious people. If to Ramsey, there you will find more than ten thousand Acres occupied by the waters, and see houses without Inhabitants, and lands incapable of either Pasturage or Tillage.

A New Year's gale on 1 January 1779 coincided with an unusually high tide: a ship laden with iron and coal was wrecked on Walpole Marsh and became so embedded in the sand that it could not be recovered: the mast remained, surrounded by grass marsh, until the enclosure of Wingland in 1831.

Arthur Young noted the bad floods of 1799: more than 25,000 acres were under water until May 1800 to the south of the hundred-foot drain, and 'all much annoyed by the flood … it was a melancholy examination I took of the country between Whittlesea and March, the middle of July, in all which tract of ten miles, usually under great crops of cole, oats, and wheat, there was nothing to be seen but desolation, with here and there a crop of oats or barley, sown so late that they can come to nothing.' He focused on the problems of one Fenland resident:

> In Draper's delph there lives, or rather swims, Wm Fletcher, a labourer, with a wife and three children, During the summer of 1799, they could live below stairs but one month, the sea was so deep upon the ground floor; all last winter it was two feet deep, and they have not been downstairs yet, but to get their boat, which brings them to and fro; the water is now (July) in the house after this dry season. For this habitation they pay two guineas a year. His family lives within one hundred yards of half a last of coleseed per acre. Such contrasts are incredible to a person who was never in the Fens.

In the same year, according to William Chapman, 'most of the new enclosed fens bordering the Witham' were flooded so that 'many hundred acres of the harvest of 1799 were reaped by men in boats'.

There was a great storm in the Fens on Sunday, 4 May 1800, especially at Bourne, where £700 worth of damage was done in the parish. A Mr Hopkinson was in the church with many women and children and noted that the hailstones sounded like a volley of musket balls for half an hour. The windows that were not properly secured were shattered and there was a sudden explosion within the church, 'not unlike a gun discharged in a cavern or with its muzzle close to a wall': a bolt of lightning had struck a young man in the church, burning his leg. As Hopkinson recorded, 'The cottage of the poor man, as well as the mansions of the rich, suffered in the general wreck. Five neighbouring villages suffered resembling houses in the metropolis after they have recently been rescued from the ravages of fire, by dashing out the windows, and by seasonable exertions of the engines.'

A flood in December 1821 was recorded in the *Gentleman's Magazine*:

The River Glen bank broke at a short distance from the Guthram Gote, and, in consequence, the fen was inundated from Tongue End (near Bourn) to Pinchbeck Six Houses (some distance east of Spalding). The turn-pike road near Spalding toll-bar was overflowed by the river Welland, a tunnel having blown up. The whole of the country was in great alarm, and numbers of men were employed in what is provincially called *cradging* (strengthening banks with hurdles, stakes etc.) and endeavouring to stop the progress of the waters.

'Blown up' does not imply the use of gun powder, it is the term used when a bank or tunnel gives way entirely.

According to Peter Charnley, there were major breaches in the North Barrier Bank in 1763, 1764, 1767, 1770 and 1773; 'all these breaches can be seen on the ground today between Peterborough and Guyhirn; they are shown on the Ordnance Survey maps and all are named.' How were they repaired? Charnley tells us:

The task of closing a breach meant all materials had to be transported by boat, including clay, which came from Whittlesey. The ends of the breach had to be secured by wooden piles driven by hand, sealed with faggots and puddled clay. The counter bank, curved toward the river, had then to be constructed from both ends, driving piles by hand in flowing water, cutting down the flow through the piles with straw and faggots, weighted with clay; the ends of each day's work sealed off and secured to prevent them washing away until the work approached the centre of the breach. As the hole became smaller the velocity of the water increased and the scour hole at the back became deeper. Time was of the essence. Men worked at night, with inefficient lighting, in dangerous and wet condition, usually in winter. Not a job for the faint-hearted. The closing of the breached counter bank was crucial. All materials required for the repair had to be at hand, laid along the existing bank. When the gap was reduced enough to span timbers, the piles were driven and immediately straw and faggots were dropped from boats on the river side and sucked into the gap. As the water slowed, clay was dropped over the front to be puddled in by poles. When water was reduced to a trickle, the size and depth of the scour-hole at the back could be assessed. This was a crucial stage for the restoration, for unless the temporary piled bank was backed by clay in time for the next rise of water, associated with the high tide, the water would blow out the piled works leading to a new scour-hole and ultimate collapse.[71]

Mills

In 1726, the first sub-district of the levels was established at Haddenham in the South Level, and over the next 150 years all the levels were divided in this way. Each district was concerned only with its own drainage, small cuts leading to a central drain that got rid of its water by pumping it up into one of the large arterial drains. People had to pay rates to local districts and also to the larger authority controlling the level. Local solutions would cause problems in the next village. In the middle of the eighteenth century, Thomas Neale blamed the 'ruinous state of the parish of Manea' on the number of mills in the Middle Level: 'a great number of these mills throw their water directly upon Manea'. He also blamed a tunnel built in 1712, because of which water from a tract of nearly 10,00 acres now came into the village's 20ft drain, and the decay in the Ouse outfall since the collapse of Denver Sluice. 'I have heard ancient people say, that if Manea heretofore were drowned two feet deep in February by a breach of banks, for it was never drowned otherwise, they could plow and sow those lands with oats that same year; but now it is too well known, if it be drowned but one foot deep at that time, it can scarce be got dry all summer.'

A Fenland scoop wheel.

The remedy, Neale thought, was to obtain a Drainage Act and erect mills, and this was duly done.

One problem was universal: as soon as the land dried out, it began to sink and the surface of the land began to drop. Water could no longer naturally flow away on the main drains and rivers – it had to be pumped up into them. Early engines were powered by horses, but the windmill transformed drainage – and the landscape. By 1763, there were fifty windmills at work in Deeping Fen, and by the end of the century there were sixty-three along the banks of the South

Forty Foot drain. The overall effect of these improvements can be judged by the increase in land values. In 1799 Arthur Young reported 'twenty years ago the land sold for about £3 an acre; some was then let at 7s or 8s an acre; and a good deal was in such a state that nobody would rent it; now it is in general worth 20s an acre, and sells at £20 an acre.' However, the situation deteriorated because the effectiveness of drainage caused the level of the Fens to continue to drop: windmills became unable to cope. John Rennie stated in 1810: '… especially when the wet weather is succeeded by calm weather, the mill cannot work, and therefore water lies on the surface of the Fens, and does incalculable injury'.

Joseph Scott thought that the banks along the rivers could be strengthened by tree planting:

> When I saw the awful effects of the former breeches of banks, an idea occurred to me that the light-soiled fen-banks might be greatly strengthened by planting them with oziers etc … Ozier-cuttings should be pricked into the lower parts of all fen-banks, and cuttings of elder on the higher parts; and stock might browse the tops and keep them short, and then they would not interrupt navigation. There are elders now growing on Wisbech Bank, near the Toll-gate; and if many were planted along the brink, it would strengthen the bank, and soon make the road several feet wider, by causing the bank to stand more perpendicular.[72]

Transport and Communication

The droving roads from Scotland into Norfolk went by Spalding and Wisbech: in 1750, 20,000 Scots cattle passed along the Wisbech road. Spalding was the lowest bridging point on the Welland, but it was not essential to go so far inland:

> For cattle, sheep and travellers wishing to get from the north of England into Norfolk it was not necessary to pass through Spalding or Wisbech. There was a shorter but more dangerous route which forded the Welland and Nene well below the lowest bridging points. This was the Washway Road, so called because it involved crossing the wide and dangerous Fosdyke and Cross Keys washes. Through these washes the rivers were constantly changing their courses, and the main danger came from the tides and quicksands. Anyone wishing to cross needed a guide and even then accidents were not unknown.[73]

Meadows Taylor of Diss travelled to Harrogate and Manchester in the summer of 1786. Travelling by horseback, he and his party left Norwich on 5 July, spending the night at Grimston. The next day they went to Lynn, where they 'crossed the River in the ferry boat with our horses', on to Cross Keys and 'across the

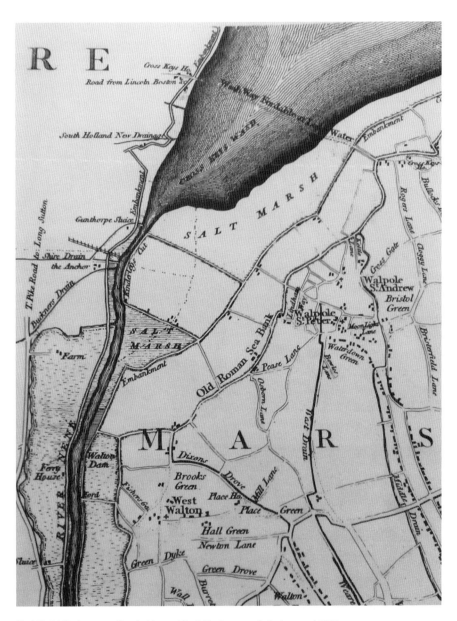

The Wash Way between Lincolnshire and Norfolk, shown on Faden's map of 1797.

Wash with a Guide to Long Sutton – din'd at the Bull'. Then 'to Fosdyke Wash … & drank Tea there. Across the Wash – a very good Inn and Bathing house on the Fosdike side.' He then went onto 'Kirktown' [Kirton-in-Holland] and to Boston for the night. Boston was, of course, at the heart of northern Fenland: here goods were transferred between sea-going vessels and river boats, the Corporation benefitting from the dues charged for cranage.

Boston warehouses, with satellite dishes.

Boston warehouses.

The 'bathing house' at Fosdyke reflects how Fenland participated in the late eighteenth-century craze for sea-bathing, albeit to a limited extent. There were hotels for bathers at Skirbeck and Freiston Shore as well, the latter once memorably described as 'the Brighton of the middle classes of Lincolnshire'. Occasional visitors came from the Midlands, but land enclosures pushed the sea shore further and further out, and the resorts declined and disappeared in the later nineteenth century.

This route north became safer after the construction of the Fosdyke Bridge and embankment in 1812–15, and the Cross Keys Bridge and Embankment in 1827–31: the first stagecoach to use the route was the Union, travelling from Norwich to Newark, which crossed to a large welcoming crowd on 4 July 1831. The last of the Fenland guides was Charles Wrigglesworth of Sutton Bridge, who died in 1840 aged 52; his grave can be seen in Long Sutton churchyard. Perhaps significantly, guiding was no longer his full-time occupation – he was also a coal merchant.

Wild and lonely roads encouraged highwaymen. Two who held up a coach near Wisbech in 1727 were caught and sent to Norwich Castle. In 1742 a man named Wrigglesworth, alias Smith, was confined to Newgate Prison in London for robbing the Wisbech mail, taking bills of exchange and bank notes: one of the latter was found on him when he was arrested. Dick Turpin, perhaps the most well-known highwayman of the age, arrived in Long Sutton in July 1737, calling himself John Palmer, a horse dealer. After living in the town for about nine months, he was suspected of sheep stealing but when the constable went to his house to arrest him, Turpin knocked him down and escaped. Two years later he was hanged at York. Dr John Bailey of Long Sutton was robbed and murdered by a gang in April 1795; 'the instrument with which it was perpetrated was a plank hook, which entered the left eye, dividing the nose, and came out of the lower jaw'. More than 1,000 people attended his funeral and his memorial, reading 'Alas, Poor Bailey', can still be seen in the church. His watch was pawned by the murderers at Great Addington, but they were never caught.

Taylor recorded the state of Fenland roads as they were in 1786. He was on his return journey on 29 July, travelling to Thrapston: 'country all open field. Road hard but good, composed of a soft stone, which dissolves into a sort of clay, and grows firm as a barn floor … Huntingdon – dined at the Fountain, this is the largest Inn, but not so comfortable as the Crown. This Town is new paved with Freiston Causeway. The country from Thrapston mostly open fields tho' some Inclosures have taken place. The Road good.'

Taylor left Huntingdon on the Cambridge road, for Earith, 'where I was com-pelled to stop all night on acct of the Rain at the sign of the George, a neat public house in this village. The road thus far very fine Turnpike … mostly open field here.' He left Earith the next day (30 July) and was now in the real Fens: 'leaving Earith, at the end of the street passed over an old bridge thrown across the old Bedford Drain now grown up and disused, a little fur[the]r cross over

a wooden bridge which is navigable, at the foot of the bridge on the other side stands a house called the Hermitage.'

He then turned and followed the bank for several miles, before turning away and heading for Sutton: 'a remarkable thick steeple to the church. The road along the bank is a good Horse way but not a way for carriages, they go about a mile around by a bridge called Gotts & the Black barr, but these are roads fit only for a dry summer. As soon as you pass Sutton church, turn on the left into a narrow lane or bridleway & in a few rods you enter the Turnpike Road leading from Ely to Chatteris,' which he calls 'a fine road'. He breakfasted at the Lamb in Ely. 'Leaving Ely by the Turnpike Road to Newmarket passing thro a level enclosed country chiefly pasture. At 6 m[iles] measured is Soham. The town neat. On the other side [of] the town enter the Open Field land country which gently rises before you.' He had left the Fens.[74]

Much transportation naturally exploited the rivers. When the poet John Clare was a young man living at Helpston, he was offered a job in Wisbech, 'a

The White Horse Inn, Spalding.

Chequers Inn, Holbeach. (Norfolk Record Office, WLS lxi/29)

Long Sutton inn preserving the memory of highwayman and local resident Dick Turpin.

The New Saracen's Head, on the drovers' route north of Holbeach.

foreign land to me' (it was 40 miles away!). He walked to Peterborough, and boarded a horse-drawn barge: the journey cost him 18*d*. After an unsuccessful interview on Friday, he had to wait until Sunday to make the return journey.[75]

A Parliamentary report noted that between 4 May 1776 and 3 February 1777, 2,692 boats and lighters had passed along the Hundred Foot River, pulled by 1,265 'pretty large horses'. In the same period, no fewer than 7,070 boats and lighters, pulled by 3,694 horses, had passed through Denver Sluice. This was known locally as 'haling' – haling paths still exist along the Little Ouse – and had a detrimental effect where the horses travelled on the tops of banks that protected the land from flooding. As the report noted, 'the banks were very greatly damaged ... the horses do not travel in a right line one behind the other, but obliquely, and so cover a larger space'.

A flood in January 1763 was directly blamed on haling. Horses were pulling lighters along the river: when they were suddenly whipped by their drivers, the lighters behind them were pulled into the bank. The resultant breach was

60 yards long and 33ft deep: many families were drowned and many stacks of corn lost.

Thomas Hawkes described Spalding in 1792:

> All the corn grown in the interior parts of this country is brought up for the use of the inhabitants and the surplus is sent to London in boats belonging to Boston etc. The chief of the trade is in Oats and some little coalseed, very little other grains being produced in this neighbourhood ... From Stamford and Deeping they send down Gangs of Lighters to be loaded with Coals for the supply of those parts of the country and a large district in the neighbourhood of Stamford.

All channels had to be continuously maintained. Springall Brown, a Peterborough merchant who ran gangs of lighters between there and Wisbech, told Parliament that due to the low level of water and the many obstructions it could take ten days to navigate between the two towns in summer, a distance of

Boston: church and bridge.

Boston: bridge and river.

PER·MARE·ET·PER·TERRAM

The arms of Boston Corporation.

just 21 miles! Had the river been kept in a proper state, he though the journey would take just six to eight hours. Horse traffic was partly responsible: 'the haling upon the banks causes them to *moulder* into the rivers, which contributes to the increase of weeds'.

In 1802, barges carrying up to 60 tons could reach Spalding, but two decades later this had fallen to 40 tons. The channel was improved in the 1830s: barges carrying up to 120 tons could now reach the town. Eighteen vessels carrying coal arrived in Spalding in just one week in January 1839. Like all water-borne traffic, competition from the railway led to a rapid decline in the second half of the nineteenth century. A small amount of water-borne trade continued down to the 1930s, with two barges carrying loads from Spalding to Fossdyke, where they were transferred to sea-going vessels bound for Hull.

In 1796, the town of Wisbech opened a 5¼-mile canal to Outwell, with a lock at each end: the canal was on the line of the old Wellstream and restored the link between the Ouse and the Nene river systems. However, tides brought silt into the channel, and the situation was made worse because local people were continually throwing their rubbish into it! Its peak time was in the 1840s, when it was chiefly used for carrying coal: however, with the coming of the railway it ceased to be much used. It finally closed in the 1920s. Much of it has now disappeared beneath gardens and, ironically, a road has been built on the section of canal in the centre of Wisbech.

Horse-drawn barge passing under Welney suspension bridge.

River transport, Albert Bridge, Spalding. (Ayscoughfee Hall, Spalding)

River transport in the Fens. (Ayscoughfee Hall, Spalding)

The wildness of the coast made it a haunt of smugglers – John Ransford of Wisbech was master of a smuggling boat seized at Fosdyke by a customs vessel in 1737: he was found to have 1,400 hundredweight of tea on board, with brandy and other contraband items. Ransom and his crew were imprisoned in Norwich Castle gaol. Tales current in the boyhood of a Fenland writer in the 1890s included the story of a Wisbech man who had a cutter in which he brought spirits from Holland into the Wash, until he was caught in the Lynn Deeps by the revenue cutter.

The most ambitious scheme of all was a proposed canal from London to Cambridge:

This canal will connect the entire eastern-side of England (South of Peterborough) with London, forming the great trunk, or confluence of navigable branches, cuts, and streams, now in existence, whose aggregate length amounts to one thousand miles, and of other navigable cuts, hereafter to be made necessary to it. It will be the conduit to London of the whole surplus produce of the fen Countries, the richest portion of five of the finest counties in the island, which have long been the granary of the capital, at one third of the present price by land carriage.

Proposed canal between the Fens and London. (Norfolk Record Office)

Fenland Heroes

Matthew Flinders (1774–1814)

Flinders was born at Donington, where his father and grandfather had practised as surgeons, on 16 March 1774. He went to Donington Free School and
to grammar school at Horbling, and was inspired to go to sea by his reading of
Robinson Crusoe. He first went to sea in 1790 and in the following year joined
the *Bellerophon* under Captain William Bligh, sailing to the South Seas to trans-
plant the breadfruit tree from Tahiti to the West Indies.

Flinders returned to Britain in 1793, and then voyaged to New South Wales
on board the *Reliance,* arriving at Port Jackson in September 1795. For the
next five years he, often with the assistance of the ship's surgeon George Bass,
explored and surveyed in Australia. In 1801 he was appointed to survey New
Holland on board the *Investigator*. Flinders circumnavigated Australia 1803–
05: with him was an aborigine who had become his friend, Bongaree. Many
of the geographical features he surveyed were given names based on places in
his native Lincolnshire, such as Cape Donington, Boston Island and Spalding
Cove. Flinders invented the technique of using iron bars to compensate for
the magnetic deviations caused by the iron on a ship, now called 'Flinders
bars' in his honour.

He returned to England in 1810, after being kept in confinement for several
months at Mauritius, where he had landed on his return journey. He wrote up
an account of his voyage, and returned to Donington, but died in his London
home on 19 July 1814. He was buried in London, but there is a memorial tablet
to him in Donington Church. He became a hero in Australia: there are statues
to him in Sydney, Melbourne and Adelaide; Flinders River, Flinders Island and
Flinders University are all named after him. This fame is deserved as Flinders,
if he did not actually invent the name 'Australia', brought it into popular usage
in his writings.

Flinders' grave illustrates well the vicissitudes of history. He was buried in
St James's Gardens but when Euston station was built the grave and its
headstone disappeared. However, his coffin, and the skeleton, within, were
recovered in January 2019 during archaeological work in the area prior to the
building of the HS2 railway line from London to Birmingham and the north.
The coffin could be identified because it still bore its lead identification plate.

The body, along with 61,000 other skeletons in the cemetery, is to be removed before construction of the new railway begins.

Flinders' cat, Trim, also circumnavigated Australia and Tasmania with Flinders, but disappeared in Mauritius. A statue of Flinders – and Trim – was erected in Donington Market Place in 2006, and a new Flinders Park has been created in the town.

Bass, from a Boston family, was an explorer in his own right: going with Flinders to Australia, he discovered the straits now called Bass Straits in 1796. In 1803, he set sail with twenty-five men on the *Venus* but the ship and crew were all lost: what happened to them is not known.

Thomas Clarkson (1760–1846) and John Clarkson (1764–1828)

Conybeare, in 1910, wrote: 'Wisbech plays but little part in history.' He had forgotten Thomas Clarkson, one of the greatest men in world history. Clarkson's brother, John, played his part, too. Thomas Clarkson was born at Wisbech Grammar School on 28 March 1760: he was the eldest of three children. His father was the headmaster, and his mother Anne was of Huguenot descent. Clarkson went to his father's school, then to St Paul's School in London and then to university at St John's Cambridge. While there he wrote an essay to a topic set by the vice-chancellor titled 'Is it lawful to enslave the unconsenting?' He won the prize but his life was changed: he now dedicated himself to the abolition of slavery. Clarkson's essay was published by a Quaker bookseller in 1786, and he wrote many other anti-slavery pamphlets. He was one of twelve members of a committee for the abolition of slavery set up in 1787. Clarkson visited London, the two main slaving ports of Bristol and Liverpool, and many other towns in the cause. The conditions on board ships were appalling; slaves were manacled and crowded together in the holds of ships owned by men of Bristol and Liverpool – almost half of them died on the long voyage from Africa to the West Indies, where the surviving slaves were put to work on sugar and tobacco plantations. In his *History of the Slave Trade*, Clarkson published a diagram showing the interior of a slave ship, which became one of the most striking images of the campaign, appearing on the walls of many schools run by Quakers and other sympathisers. Clarkson was a great believer in trade with Africa, arguing that there were many possibilities rather than slaves. He had a whole chest of African products, which he would show to people to encourage them to enter into trade with the conti-

nent: this chest and its contents can be seen in Wisbech and Fenland Museum, one of the most significant exhibits in Fenland.

Thomas Clarkson became ill from all his work, which included the risk of physical attack from slave-ship owners, and he bought an estate in the Lake District to recuperate: there he came into contact with the Lake Poets. William Wordsworth admired him so much that he addressed a sonnet to him after the abolition of the slave trade in 1807. The poem begins 'Clarkson! It was an obstinate hill to climb' and concludes:

And thou henceforth wilt have a good man's calm
A great man's happiness; thy zeal shall find
Repose at length, firm friend of human kind.

However, the 1807 Act only outlawed the slave trade, it did not abolish slavery itself. Clarkson had more work to do: in the 1820s he campaigned as a leading member of the Anti-Slavery Society. The Act abolishing slavery in the British Empire was passed in 1834: some 800,000 slaves, mainly in the West Indies were freed.

Clarkson had married Catherine Buck in 1796 and they lived at Bury St Edmunds between 1806 and 1816 and then at Playford Hall, also in Suffolk. Clarkson died there on 26 September 1846 and was buried in the local church. A large monument to his memory designed by Gilbert Scott was erected at Wisbech in 1880, and in 1996 a tablet to him was placed in Westminster Abbey close to the other leading abolitionist, William Wilberforce.

His brother, John, also played an important part in the struggle. Another abolitionist, Granville Sharp, had established a 'province of freedom' in Sierra Leone, and in 1792, John Clarkson led a fleet of fifteen vessels carrying 1,196 black settlers from Nova Scotia: they were former American slaves who had fought for the British in the war of independence, for which they had been promised land and freedom. He acted as first governor of the colony of Sierra Leone, but was dismissed because he was more concerned with the Nova Scotians' welfare than making the profits required by the directors of the company. John Clarkson died on 2 April 1828: he is buried in Woodbridge, Suffolk.

Monument to Thomas Clarkson at Wisbech.

Susannah Centlivre (1669–1723)

Susannah Centlivre was born Susannah Freeman. It is always said that she was born in Holbeach: she could well be the Susanna Freeman baptised in nearby Whaplode on 20 November 1669. She married for the first time at the age of 16 and was widowed twice before her marriage to Joseph Centlivre in 1706: he was cook to Queen Anne at Windsor. She began her career as an actress, but her fame rests on the plays that she began writing under her second married name of Susannah Carroll: eighteen of her plays were produced in her lifetime, the first being *The Perjured Husband*, produced in London in 1700. Others included *The Gamester* (1705), *The Wonder; A Woman Keeps a Secret'* (1714) and *A Bold Stroke For a Wife* (1718), the last two starring David Garrick and Anne Oldfield when first produced in London. The plays were very popular in their time. *A Bold Stroke* concerns Colonel Fainall, who impersonates a Quaker preacher, Simon Pure, to win his lady love: he is unmasked when Pure arrives: and proves himself 'the real Simon Pure', a phrase that was long in common use. Susannah Centlivre's last play appeared in 1722: she died in the following year.

Interest in Centlivre has revived because of her perceived feminism: As her character Violante in *The Wonder* says:

> The Custom of our Country inslaves us from our very Cradles,
> first to our Parents, next to our Husbands;
> and when Heaven is so kind to rid us of both these,
> our Brothers still usurp Authority, and expect a blind Obedience from us;
> so that Maids, Wives or Widows, we are little better than Slaves to the Tyrant Man.

Fenland has another link to the stage: Oliver Goldsmith is said to have written *She Stoops to Conquer* (1773) while staying in Leverington with the Lumpkin family.

Seven

VICTORIAN FENLAND

The old sea wall, he cried, is downe,
The rising tide comes on apace,
And boats adrift in yonder towne
Go sailing uppe the marketplace.[76]

Victorian Fenland saw the development of the technology of steam drainage: as the levels of the peat shrank, more and more power was needed to lift excess water from the fields into the rivers and drainage channels. The steam engine was first patented by Thomas Savery in 1698, but the first really practical one was that developed by Thomas Newcomen by 1712: a Newcomen engine in the Netherlands in 1776 was probably the first steam engine used solely for land drainage. Steam engines began to be used to pump out water when drains were being built, for example by Rennie from 1804 when he was draining the East, West and Wildmore Fens. Two engines in boats helped scour out the Eau Brink. In 1805, Arthur Young noted: 'The application of steam engines to the drainage of the fens, instead of windmills, is a desideratum that has been often mentioned, but none yet executed: when it is considered that the windmills have been known to remain idle for two months together, and at seasons when their work is most wanted, it must be evident that the power of steam could nowhere be employed with greater efficacy of profit.' He was soon proved right.

The first ever steam engine used solely for drainage in the Fens was at Sutton St Edmund in about 1816: it is not clear just when it was built, but it is first recorded in a report by Tycho Wing in August 1820: 'Sutton St Edmund has one Steam Engine, the yearly expense of working and repairing which is laid at two hundred pound per annum.' It had a 12hp engine and drained more than 4,000 acres. It was probably this machine that men from the Littleport and Downham District saw in 1818, when they went to view a steam engine near Wisbech: they reported that a steam engine would be most beneficial for their own district. The second one was at Ten Mile Bank: ordered in 1818, it had 30hp and had two scoop wheels, the only Fen engine to do so. Rennie visited it on its third day of operation, commenting: 'the quantity of land to be drained is 20,000 acres – but she was only considered as equal to the draining of half that quantity and another of equal power is proposed to be erected'.

Others soon followed, including a pair at Pode Hole by 1825, and another at Spalding Marsh by 1833. By 1830, Joseph Glynn could write: 'Before steam power was used, there were seventy-five windmills in this district; and often has the Fen farmer, in despair, watched their motionless arms [motionless because there was no wind] whilst his fair fields gradually disappeared below the rising waters, and the district assumed the appearance of an immense lake.' The days of wind power for drainage appeared to be over. John Clarke noted in 1852:

> The number of wind-mills formerly at work on the whole of the fens between Lincoln and Cambridge probably exceeded 700; at present they may be about 50 mills in the Lincolnshire part of the level, and perhaps 170 in the Bedford Level and adjacent fens; or a total of 220. The number of steam-engines may be estimated at 17 in the Lincolnshire part, varying from 10 to 80 horsepower each, and upwards of 43 in the remainder of the level. They lift water from 6 to 16 or even 20 feet; and the area of land which they drain may be computed at not less than 222,000 acres.

The new machines brought their own problems. The pumps used scoop wheels, and, as the peat continued shrinking, the wheel often had to be lowered, which was both difficult and expensive: often the opportunity was taken to enlarge the scoop wheel, which added to the cost. New technology came along in the mid-nineteenth century: the Appold pump, exhibited at the Great Exhibition of 1851. This was a centrifugal pump, moving the water radially outward. It was eventually to lead to the turbine pump of the twentieth century, but many Fenland drainers preferred to stick with what they knew, scoop wheels being easier and cheaper to maintain. They also had one very real advantage: when the drains were full, a scoop wheel initially pumped the water out more quickly than the centrifugal pump and this could make the difference between saving a crop and losing it.

The centrifugal pump came into its own when the technology was used in 1867 to drain the West, East and Wildmore Fens. These had been shrinking ever since Rennie had first drained them, and by 1866–67 the East Fen was under water for weeks: in January, the rainfall was 3.32in and 10,000 to 12,000 acres were flooded. A new pumping station was installed, with two sets of machinery each consisting of a steam engine driving an Appold pump: their success was proved almost at once as no less than 5.28in of rain fell in December 1870, yet the Fens remained dry.

Red-brick buildings and tall chimneys became a new feature of the flat landscape as windmills had been. The builders took pride in the power of their new engines, several recording their new technology on their buildings. Several pump houses survive, such that at Pymore by district engineer William Harrison, with a telling verse on a plaque.

These fens have oft times been by Water drown'd.
Science a remedy in Water found.
The powers of Steam she said shall be employ'd
And the Destroyer by Itself destroy'd.

Steam came to Fenland in other ways beside drainage pumps. Steam mills were introduced in the early nineteenth century for production of flour, like the South Holland Mills at Spalding, in about 1807. The technology of the steam engine could be used in the field too, but was not without danger. In March 1867, the boiler of a steam engine being worked in a field near Watlington exploded with such force that it was thrown a distance of 40 yards. Five people were killed instantly and seven more severely injured, two of them dying the next day. The operator was to blame: he had tied down the safety valve to increase the pressure in the boiler.

Although mills powered by wind might be unable to lift water, they still played an important role in farming, grinding corn as they had done for centuries past. It has been said that it was in Lincolnshire and adjacent counties during the nineteenth century that windmill technology reached its peak. Surviving corn windmills include: Maud Foster Mill, Boston, a five-sailer mill with an ogee cap, built in 1819 at a cost of £1,826, and Sibsey Trader Mill, built as late as 1877. Most dramatic of all is Moulton, 'looking like a giraffe', according to Pevsner: it was the tallest mill in the country. The mill was built in 1822, and is 24m high with nine internal floors. It was used until 1994, has been lovingly restored and is now a visitor attraction, as is the Maud Foster Mill.

In 1860, Joseph Webb, an Emneth miller, brought an action against the local vicar, J.W. Berryman, and his churchwardens for 'stealing his wind': the case was heard at Norwich Assizes on 31 March. Webb had bought Gaultree Mill

A lovingly cared for traction engine from Wisbech.

in 1856, paying about £225 and spending about £100 on repairs. In August 1859, the vicar and churchwardens had built a school for elementary children. It was only about 25 yards west of the mill, and, Webb claimed, when the wind was from that direction the building 'interfered with the currents of air which should have set the sail of the windmill in motion'. He had sent to the builders, saying 'my children will want bread – is there no redress for me?', but was told that there was none, hence the legal case. The judge said that he did not know of any case in which a man who built a windmill was entitled to all the air that came near it: if that were the case, then anyone could put up a mill and so prevent his neighbours from erecting buildings on their land! He urged the two sides to settle the matter by arbitration, to which they agreed. Both the mill and the school stayed, and in 1895, under a later miller, the mill was 'heined' to use a Norfolk word, that is, it was heightened so that its sails were well above the school buildings.

Farming

In early Victorian Fenland, corn production was at its height and the area became known as the 'breadbasket of England'. Armstrong in 1854 noted that a Fenland farm might produce nine quarters per acre, compared to the national average of four quarters an acre. The methods used were largely traditional ones. After harvest, the corn had to be carried from the field to the stack-yard. This was done by a team of seven men and some boys, known as a 'running set'. Each man had his own task, though these would be swapped. Two men were in the field, one pitching the sheaves onto the wagon, the other stacking them. The other five were in the stack-yard, one unloading the cart, one passing the sheaves onto the stack, and two on the stack itself, building it up. The seventh man tidied up loose straw into sheaves. The wagons, pulled by horses of course, were actually driven by the boys, and the skill was to organise them so that gave a constant flow of corn to the men in the stack-yard: as they were on piece-work they could not afford to be kept waiting. If it was too wet for work, there would be no pay, except for the foreman who was on a fixed wage. The work was unending, from early childhood to extreme old age. Two men killed by lightning while working on the harvest at Holbeach in 1894 – John Barsby and Richard Barney – were both over 70 years old. In such a flat landscape, the stacks stood out as prominent features in the landscape: Frances Cornford recalled 'the stacks, like blunt impressive temples, rise/Across flat fields against the autumnal skies': I noticed just the same on my last visit to the Fens in 2018.[77]

In the middle of the nineteenth century, John Clarke described the winners and the losers in Fenland agriculture. The 'winners' were the farmers:

The fenland farmer has made a great progress within the present century, which may well vie with the improvements upon the bleak stony wastes of Norfolk and Lincolnshire. And his advance is at a quicker rate now than formerly; inasmuch as his method of wading upon high stilts through water-flags and cotton-grass has been abandoned for speedy driving upon turnpike roads and railways over sheep-fed and corn-clad fields. If you doubt the fact of his rapid and wonderful improvements, you need simply turn to one branch of husbandry, contrast in your own mind the antique *animals* of the past with the *neat* cattle and sheep of the present age. Contrast the hair and teeth of those thistle-fed horses with the strong teams of our day; the rough-boned ox with hide distended over sharp hip and wiry rib, with the gentler beast of modern breed, the large-headed, thick-legged shaggy remnant of a half rotted flock, with the comely well-conditioned sheep now grazing on our dry meads, rich clovers, and luxuriant cole.

The 'losers' were the farm labourers:

> When their common-rights, for the defence of which they so manfully struggled, were absorbed into the hands of large occupiers, was not their independence lost, and their private property diminished and taken away? Are they much advantaged by having to pay exorbitant rents for houses, and being driven by proprietors unwilling to augment the poor's-rate, to crowded freehold villages many miles from their place of labour, instead of inhabiting even mud cottages close by their own plot of ground, and the farm where they worked, and feeding not merely a pig or two at a time, but also having a cow pastured upon the common? Does the present price of coals recompense them for the lost privilege of digging turf-fuel? Is the labourer's present life, with the fear of the Union-house as the final reward of his toil, and without the hope of leaving to his children any better lot, so vastly preferable to what the fishing, bird-catching, free but often hard living of the poorer fenman once was?

Farmland pests included rats and rabbits. Wheeler noted that: 'by so precarious a tenure is the fen land held and so great is the necessity for constant and unremitting vigilance and care, that with the least neglect, only, perhaps, an unseen rat hole, the waving corn fields may be turned into a sea of water'. An Act

The potato harvest. (Ayscoughfee Hall, Spalding)

Fenland harvest, with horses carts and traction engine. (Ayscoughfee Hall, Spalding)

of 1765 for preserving rabbits in warrens specifically exempted Lincolnshire: anyone could 'kill and destroy' any rabbits found on any sea or river bank in the county. It was forbidden under the laws of the Court of Sewers to keep rabbits on the banks: in about 1750 two Freiston men were charged with keeping rabbits so near the sea bank as to damage it – they were ordered to destroy their rabbits and repair the damage to the bank, under a penalty of £10. The Deeping Fen Act of 1856 imposed a fine of 40s on anyone keeping rabbits or geese on any of the banks or forelands.

The price of wheat fell dramatically from the 1870s because of cheap American imports. Farmers needed to diversify: fortunately, there were other crops to be grown on such fertile soil:

> Falling profits and rents from the traditional corn-growing enabled enterprising men to acquire land for fruit, bulbs, vegetables and flowers, using as the basis of fertility the town manure which could be obtained virtually for the cost of carriage; the railways that took away the produce to the towns brought back the manure. Soils around Wisbech were already proved to be suitable for plums and other tree fruit.

Fruit had been grown in the Isle of Ely for centuries. When Alice Mash of Wisbech was about to give birth on Shrove Tuesday 1657, her midwife refused to lay hands on her unless she named the father: she named Luke Chapman of Walsoken Marsh, recalling wistfully that the child was conceived 'in cherry

time'. In fact, the couple traded in fruit: it was on the occasion when they went together to see 'a bargain of fruit' that the incident (in which Luke strenuously denied any involvement) had supposedly occurred.[78]

It was a time when fruit was increasingly cultivated. Cherries had been regarded as medicinal since the sixteenth century: Sir William Temple thought them an 'unfailing cure' for indigestion. Gooseberries (grown primarily for jam) were planted between Bramley apple trees in the Wisbech area and many small allotments turned out strawberries. Apple orchards also developed, if only slowly: there were no orchards in the 1880s, a few in 1906 – but many more were planted over the twentieth century.

One of the staple crops of the Fens was hay, cut in the spring and stacked, so as to be ready for use as fodder for the animals on the farm in the following winter. The surplus would be sent to market. In the later nineteenth century the hay press was introduced, which compressed the hay, making it easier and cheaper to transport. Mustard was another important crop – the supply in England was almost all from the Fens. A mustard market was held at Wisbech in October and November. Flax was much grown, especially round Swineshead. There were flax mills at Surfleet and in the East Fen, and a fair for flax and hemp used to be held every 27 April at Spalding. Peppermint was grown and distilled in the Holbeach area, its memory preserved in the name Distillery Farm, and also in the name of the latest project intended to develop technology in the agri-food sector – Peppermint Park.

Potato growing expanded greatly at the very end of the nineteenth century: they were grown in the Isle of Ely, the fenlands of Norfolk and the Holland division of Lincolnshire: 'It was the large commercial growers in these regions who were the best customers for the Scottish seed potatoes: they supplied London and the midland towns with potatoes after Christmas, first clamping them in straw-lined pits and dressing them out in the biting winds of January and February.'[79]

Poultry, pigs, fruit, vegetables, early potatoes: these could provide a decent income for a small farm in the East Anglian Fens.

Reclaiming the Wash

There was major progress in another area, the reclaiming of more land from the sea. Extensive new areas around the Wash became farmland. Small areas of

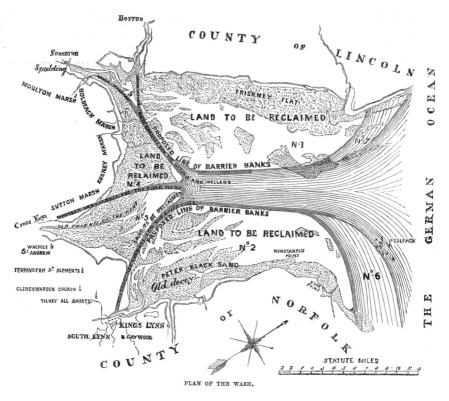

Mid-nineteenth century plan to reclaim the Wash (Norfolk Record Office, HMN 3/86/3)

about 200 to 400 acres were enclosed by high banks, and thus protected from inundation by spring tides. The banks were around 24ft high and had sluices through which surplus water drained away at low tide. Following enclosure, the marsh was grazed by sheep for two or three years, by the end of which time the marine grasses had been displaced by land grasses and clover. Reclamation of saltmarsh had continued on and off in west Norfolk since the Middle Ages, but a new spurt of activity, directed more towards the mudflats and the salt-ings, commenced with the establishment in 1839 of the Norfolk Estuary Company, a body with ambitious aims: the creation of an entire new county called Victoria, which would extend over an area of more than 200,000 acres, by channelling all the main rivers flowing into the Wash into a single river. The actual achievements of the Company were rather less than this, but remain impressive nevertheless.

In 1846 an Act of Parliament authorised the reclamation of 32,000 acres of saltmarsh on the margins of the Wash, in two sections: a northern section running from near Snettisham to as far north as Wootton; and a southern, in the vicinity of King's Lynn. The latter involved the construction of a new channel to carry the River Great Ouse out to the sea, the former changes to the much smaller Babingley River. Further acts were passed in 1849, 1853 and 1857 that, among other things, laid out the compensation due to the Crown in lieu of its loss of foreshore rights, and to the 'front-agers', those whose land had recently formed part of the coast. The works were directed by Rennie, and by 1851 it was reported that 600 men and about 200 horses were employed on the scheme, and were moving round 5,000 cubic metres of earth daily, figures shortly rising to 800 men, 300 horses and 7,000 cubic yards. The northern reclamations were in four blocks, two of which were completed in 1858 and others in in 1861 and 1866; the southern, in the vicinity of Lynn, were in two blocks, completed in 1865 and 1881. Most of the reclaimed land was leased, rather than sold, to local farmers and estates.

Irish Itinerant Workers

Just as in the twenty-first century, farm work brought in workers from afar. There were Irish workers in the Fens at harvest time from at least the early eighteenth century. There were inevitable tensions between the incomers and local men, who resented the Irish willingness to work for lower wages. In 1737 a mob of Irish labourers plundered the village of Benwick and went on to attack March: they were met by a force of local men and eventually fled, leaving five of their number wounded on the ground.

Four Irish itinerant workers were involved in a murder case in 1795. James Culley, Michael Quin, Thomas Quin and Thomas Markin were lodgers with William Marriott, a shepherd of Wisbech High Fen. One July night, they waited for him to come back to the house with a bucket of water: on his return they beat him to death and then did the same (so they thought) to his wife and another lodger, ransacked the house and fled with a watch, spoons and cash. Unfortunately for them wife and lodger survived and were able to identify the criminals. They were caught at Uttoxeter, brought back to Wisbech and hanged. The bodies of two of them were handed over for dissection, the other two hung upon a gibbet at Gedney, which survived long enough to be marked on the 1834 Ordnance Survey map.

In 1832, there was trouble at Holbeach where a local farmer named Richardson was employing a large number of Irish. The local farm workers gathered at the farm armed with pitchforks, spades and bludgeons. Richardson called in neighbouring farmers and they – and the Irish workers – beat back the mob, capturing sixteen of them, whom they loaded onto a wagon and drove to the Chequers Inn, where they were held in custody. Supporters gathered around the inn throwing stones, and eventually forced their way in and released the prisoners. They then threw the cart in which the prisoners had travelled into the ditch and set fire to it.

The presence of families of Irish labourers can also be inferred from a tragedy in Wisbech Fen in August 1850. Four people died within a day: Patrick Hunt (18), Winifred Garvey (28), her 2-year-old daughter, and another child, Thomas Howd: all four were Irish. Hunt had seen what he thought were mushrooms by the side of the road and gathered them and taken them back to his lodgings, where he and the Garveys had eaten them. All three were ill the following day, Hunt dying at eight in the evening. Mr Garvey returned home at about this time and summoned medical assistance for his wife but she died in the morning, followed on the next day by their daughter. It was never made clear how Thomas had obtained some of the mushrooms but they proved fatal to him as well.

Another murder case, in 1866, shows up some details of how the Irish itinerants lived. Hugh Kelley left Ireland on 2 August and began to work for an Algarkirk Fen farmer two days later: he slept in the barn, as he had done before in previous years, and there were other Irish workers sleeping there, too. On the night of 12 August, Kelley was very badly beaten up and taken to Boston workhouse. He identified his assailants as Irishmen working on a nearby farm – Lawrence Garland (still working at the age of 78!), his sons Patrick and James, another family member called Barney Garland, and a fifth man, Thomas McGuinness. All lived within 5 miles of each other in Armagh. Other people involved in the case were also in family groups – 'two brothers named Kirk' and three men named Thomas, Peter and 'Laddie' Crekin. One witness had seen the accused in a local public house, but could not understand what they were saying as they were talking in Irish. The case became one of murder after Kelley died from his injuries and came before the Assizes in December. The four Garlands were sentenced to terms of imprisonment, but

McGuinness had fled and could not be found by the authorities: he had probably returned to Ireland.

The population of the countryside increased in the first half of the nineteenth century, but then fell: 'The average population increase in the Fen parishes in the period 1800–50, excluding Boston and Spalding, was 101%. This was encouraged by enclosure and the need for labour, as well as the impact of speculative builders and the lack of control by an individual dominant landowner.'[80] However, in the second half of the century the population declined by 11 per cent, as farmers began to adopt new labour-saving machinery: this was made worse by the agricultural depression in the last quarter of the century.

In the days before any social assistance, rural poverty was a great problem, and Union Workhouses were established in the area under the Poor Law Act of 1834: Lincolnshire, for example, had Union Workhouses at Boston, Holbeach and Bourne. There were others at Ely, Wisbech and Whittlesey, that at Wisbech serving the surrounding parishes in both Cambridgeshire and Norfolk. Workhouses were hated because paupers forced into them felt humiliated – families were split up, with separate wards for men, women and children. They were paid for out of the Poor Rate, with ratepayers querying any

Wisbech, the North Bank.

extravagance: the Bourne guardians were severely reprimanded for providing a Christmas dinner for the inmates of the Workhouse there! There was a scandal at Holbeach Workhouse in 1882 involving a 22-year-old man called Bingham or Ringham. There was an outbreak of disease called 'itch' in the Workhouse and an apparatus was procured to disinfect the inmates. This involved standing in a large box with just one's head sticking out at the top: sulphur was burned in the box as a fumigant. Bingham was placed in the box, the sulphur added – and he was then apparently forgotten. His screams were heard eventually but it was too late – when pulled out, he was 'very much charred and burnt, and skin and flesh fell from different parts of his body'. He died a few hours later.

The violence endemic in the countryside in the first years of the nineteenth century had largely passed. Nine fires did occur in a short time in Mildenhall in 1861, mostly in sheds or out-houses: seven were blamed on a local 'half-witted youth', and one had been started out of spite by a bricklayer. Only one had a direct link with agricultural discontent. According to *The Times* of 24 June 1844, the commissioners for fen drainage were now letting out 'droves', broad paths – about 80 yards wide – with ditches on each side, which had been driven through the Fens to help in 'claying'. Herbage grew along the droves, upon which the poor would feed their pigs and donkeys. The drainage commissioners were now letting the droves out, which caused resentment. The final fire in Mildenhall might have had this cause: 'the farmer on whose farm this occurred is a commissioner of fen drainage, and attempted as such, to let part of the "droves" … and, as nobody would bid for them, he himself hired a part of them for some other person. The very next day his barn was set fire to.' The reporter heard that many persons locally suspected the labourers deprived of the droves on which they fed their donkeys.

The 'claying' mentioned in this report was an important innovation – it was described as a 'very modern practice' in 1830. The peat surface lay over a substratum of clay, which might lie between 2 and 20ft below the peat. It could not be exploited before the drainage had been improved as the water would otherwise flood the diggings. Once dug up, the clay was spread over the peat: it neutralised acidity and also helped prevent the peat blowing away. It was a key factor in the changeover from growing oats to growing wheat, increasing the fertility of the latter crop from about 20 to about 30 bushels per acre. The land gained when Whittlesea Mere was drained in 1850 was then clayed, an important factor in the subsequent fertility of the soil.

Arthur Randell, writing in the 1960s, recalled:

In my father's time, though not in mine, Fenmen still used to work at claying in winter. They would dig trenches four feet wide, at regularly spaced intervals across a field, lift out the clay and spread it between the trenches where it mixed with the lighter topsoil. The men worked in gangs of two and I have often heard my parents say that my grandfather and my Aunt Polly would work together and could beat any other gang in the field, for my aunt was a big strong woman and as hard as nails. Even now, long after claying has become a forgotten craft, it is possible to see the courses of the old clay dykes, as the trenches were called, for in spring the young corn which now grows there is a darker green than elsewhere.[81]

Claying continued even later than this suggests. Norman Wymer, writing in the present tense, describes the practice in 1948, calling it 'gaulting'; 'trenches are dug from end to end on either side of a field and clay thrown over the intermediate section to prevent its blowing away during ploughing'.[82]

There was a case of incendiarism at Holbeach in 1884 when 16-year-old William Gove set fire to a stack of wheat at the farm of William Rowell. Gove had previously worked for Rowell and had a grudge against him: he was sentenced to eighteen months' hard labour. Random acts of violence, often fuelled by alcohol, occurred as in any other age. In 1863, Thomas Bloom, a local shoemaker, was killed by a farmer's son named Franks during a fight in a Holbeach pub. The coroner thought that strong drink was the cause, and that the case might be considered as manslaughter rather than murder. However, he objected to the weapon that Franks used: 'The use of the knife was a dastardly and un-English thing and strongly to be condemned.' Crimes of passion occurred as always in human existence, such as that of Henry and Maria Scott. They had recently separated after twenty-five years of marriage and Maria was staying with relatives at the Saracen's Head in Holbeach. On 17 June 1901, Scott, a farmer, butcher and former policeman, bought a pistol from a Holbeach salesman, walked to the pub and shot Maria, then cutting his own throat. Both survived for some days: Maria eventually died and Scott lived to be tried for his wife's murder.

The case shows that there was no difficulty in obtaining a gun in Victorian Holbeach, which offered a wide range of facilities including watch-making. One such watch-maker a generation earlier was William Rippin. He became blind at the age of 28, but was able to continue his trade, learning to take apart and put together a watch despite his disability: he needed the help of his wife only in pinning and unpinning the hair-spring. The 'blind watchmaker of Holbeach', as he was known, continued his trade until he died in 1857, the business continuing in the hands of his wife and daughter.

A more idealised approach to living led to the establishment of a utopian settlement at Manea in 1838. It was funded by William Hodson, a farmer, Methodist lay preacher and follower of the socialist Robert Owen. Cottages, a school and a windmill were built on a 200-acre site. The community adopted the moto 'Each for All' and published a weekly newspaper called *The Working Bee*. Male members of the community wore suits of Lincoln green. The colony was short-lived, Hodson withdrawing his support in 1841. Some of the houses were later occupied by local brick-workers.

Floods

In spite of the new steam pumps, there were many years when there was severe flooding: much land was still 'drowned' every winter. Charles Lucas, writing in 1930, recalled:

> In October 1856 my father bought a seven-acre dolver (small holding) in High Town Drove, next to Toft Farm, as it is called now. In November, he went to the vendor and asked him to show him the land. The man had to take my father in a boat from the Anchor Bridge, rowing across the Fen for about one mile. Everything was then under water. When he came to the place, the man put a pole down into the water and said, 'This, Doctor, is your land.'

In 1862, the sluice at Wiggenhall St Germans blew up through pressure of water upon it, causing severe flooding in Marshland. As far away as East Dereham in central Norfolk, the vicar, Benjamin Armstrong, noted in his diary on 30 May 1862: 'On account of the breaking of a sluice-gate in the Fens near Lynn, the sea has reasserted its sway over 50,000 acres, and steamers are plying over farms, roads, and luxuriant crops. This is a sad disaster.' The flood was known as 'the Great Drown', an eyewitness recalling; 'a vast extent of water covered the whole surface of the district before us. Nothing was to be seen but water, except that an occasional farmhouse, and willows, a few posts, and the tops of hedges just appeared above what was now a lake. Here and there was a boat going to or returning from an inundated residence to save the wreck of furniture'. In fact, not all those in the boats were well-intentioned: they included

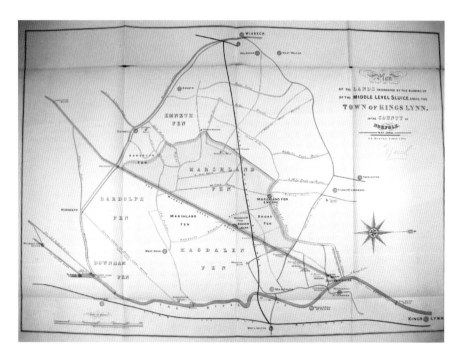

'The Great Drowning' of 1862: the area flooded (Norfolk Record Office)

FALL OF THE MIDDLE LEVEL SLUICE ON THE WEST BANK OF THE OUSE, ABOUT FOUR MILES FROM LYNN, NORFOLK.—

'The Great Drowning': fall of the Middle Level Sluice. (Norfolk Record Office)

'The Great Drowning'; scene near Washbank Bridge. (Norfolk Record Office)

'The Great Drowning': the Fens flooded. (Norfolk Record Office)

'The Great Drowning': damming the Middle Level Drain. (Norfolk Record Office, BL/BG 3/9/41,42)

'The Great Drowning': the dam in course of construction. (Norfolk Record Office, BL/BG 3/9/41,42)

people from London, who had come out by train, and were busy trying to loot houses that had been left by their owners.

George Walter Scott, whose widowed mother ran a pub at Saddlebow, recalled this flood almost eight decades later:

> In May the sluice at St Germans blew up, it was on a Sunday night, and thousands of areas of land was covered with water. Cattle, sheep and pigs were drowned. I can remember how the Buses ran from King's Lynn and passed through our village to see the great sight at St Germans. Mother did a good trade as all kinds of carriages drew up to our house with men and women to have a drink. It was many months before the land was drained of all the water, some land was made better by the floods, and other land was made much worse as the water carried the soil from one district to another and so made some of the land very low, and of clay and very hard to cultivate, while other land was made very fertile and the best in Marshland.[83]

Railways

The railway brought great changes to Fenland. Their development enabled rapid transportation of farm produce, which could be delivered fresh to London and the cities of the Midlands and the north for the first time. D.I. Gordon noted the significance of these long-disappeared railways to farms in the Wisbech area:

> Above all these lines are to be remembered for the aid they gave to agriculture, and particularly in enabling farmers to specialise in perishable produce; by 1900, for example, there were 5,000 acres of fruit, flowers and general horticultural crops within 7 miles of Wisbech alone. In 1896 the M&GN carried 4,400 tons of fruit (soft varieties followed by plums and apples) out of Wisbech between June and September, and in 1898 3,980 tons by goods train, 230 by passenger services; similar totals were achieved by the GER, averaging 60 tons a day over the season.[84]

One especially loved line was the Wisbech and Upwell Tramway, a standard gauge line running alongside the Wisbech–Upwell canal of 1794. The line opened first in 1883 and by 1888 was carrying up to 500 tons of agricultural produce a week. The engines had cow-catchers attached.

Spalding railway station in its prime.

Holbeach railway station after its closure.

Railways in Lincolnshire were associated with the port at Boston. They began with a loop line from Peterborough through Spalding and Boston to Lincoln, and the railway from Boston to Louth and Grimsby in 1848. The line from Spalding to Holbeach was built in 1858: the first train, a goods, arrived at Holbeach on 9 August, carrying coal and flour, followed by the first passenger train on 15 November. The age of the railway lasted just one century: passenger trains ceased at Holbeach in 1959, goods services stopped in 1965. Holbeach was a typical Fenland railway station, important for locally grown potatoes, flowers and fruit – flowers (daffodils, narcissi, hyacinths, tulips) in the early part of the year, fruit from May onwards (gooseberries, strawberries, raspberries and red and blackcurrants), vegetables (lettuces, cabbages, broccoli, green peas, potatoes) – fruit used to go in carriages attached to passenger trains, while vegetables made up a goods train. The line continued on to Sutton Bridge in 1862 and to King's Lynn in 1864.[85]

Getting to Lynn involved crossing the River Nene, a major engineering challenge. The first bridge was a road bridge, built by Sir John Rennie in 1825. It was 650ft long, consisting of fourteen timber spans and a cast-iron opening span of 52ft. The bridge opened up like Tower Bridge: the bascule mechanism being operated by hand, an arduous task because of the frequent passage of ships to and from Wisbech.

Twenty-five years later it became necessary to reconstruct the bridge because of changes in the river channel. The replacement bridge was built by Robert Stephenson in 1850 to a more elaborate design than the earlier structure. This was a swing bridge: a span of 193ft pivoted at the centre on a pier in the river. The bridge was designed to be converted to dual road and rail use. The third bridge, the present one, was designed by J. Allen McDonald of the Midland Railway. It was completed in 1897. The bridge swung by hydraulic power and, for the first time at this site, the control cabin was built on top of the swing span. Tolls were levied – a halfpenny for a person, a farthing per goose and ten pennies for a score of sheep. The toll was abolished in 1903.[86]

Railways led to the development of ports and harbours. An attempt was made to create a harbour at Long Sutton, but this soon collapsed into the mud: however, there are still cranes operating on the river bank. The railway company ran the docks at Grimsby, but those at Boston were owned by the Corporation and were improved by them in the early 1880s, taking advantage of the railway links. The channel to the Wash was improved at the same time, to allow the passage of sea-going vessels. Boston had even briefly been the main operating

Long Sutton Bridge.

base for the Great Northern Railway, but this moved to Doncaster in 1853. The company tried to buy up the competition: the GNR took over the leases of the Witham Navigation and the Fosse Dyke Canal, but because prices of steam packets between Boston and Lincoln were so low the railway had to introduce a rare fourth class ticket of just a halfpenny a mile to compete. However, the train won out because it was so much quicker: by 1863 the steam packets were out of business.

In 1845, the people of Ely were said to be 'almost in ecstasy at the idea of having a first class station in the city': it was built at the bottom of the steep hill in a marshy swamp and cost £81,500. In the cloister at Ely Cathedral there is a monument to William Pickering (30) and Richard Edger (24), killed on Christmas Eve 1845 in building the railway line into Ely. It begins:

The line to Heaven by Christ was made
With heavenly truth the Rails are laid
From Earth to Heaven the Line extends,
To Life Eternal where it ends.

Cranes at Long Sutton.

Long Sutton Harbour.

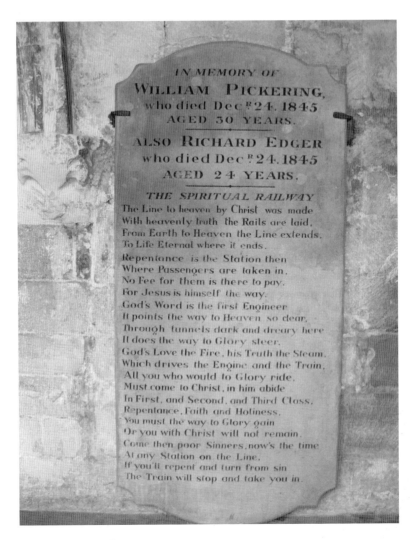

IN MEMORY OF
WILLIAM PICKERING,
who died Decr 24. 1845
AGED 30 YEARS.

ALSO RICHARD EDGER
who died Decr 24. 1845
AGED 24 YEARS,

THE SPIRITUAL RAILWAY
The Line to heaven by Christ was made
With heavenly truth the Rails are laid,
From Earth to Heaven the Line extends,
To Life Eternal where it ends.
Repentance is the Station then
Where Passengers are taken in,
No Fee for them is there to pay,
For Jesus is himself the way.
God's Word is the first Engineer
It points the way to Heaven so dear,
Through tunnels dark and dreary here
It does the way to Glory steer.
God's Love the Fire, his Truth the Steam,
Which drives the Engine and the Train,
All you who would to Glory ride,
Must come to Christ, in him abide
In First, and Second, and Third Class,
Repentance, Faith and Holiness,
You must the way to Glory gain
Or you with Christ will not remain,
Come then poor Sinners, now's the time
At any Station on the Line.
If you'll repent and turn from sin
The Train will stop and take you in

The Spiritual Railway, Ely.

The line between Ely and Peterborough was built by Samuel Morton Peto, noted for his concern for the moral and spiritual welfare of his navvies; 'tommy-shops' were banned and the sale of beer prohibited on his workings. On this line he employed ten scripture readers to read to the men and keep them morally as well as literally 'in line': the Dean of Ely confirmed that, during their two years in the Fens, Peto's navvies had been 'an example to the district'. Bear this high moral tone in mind as you travel today between Peterborough and

Ely, one of the few lines in Britain to have a cathedral prominent in the vista at each end.

Victorian Ely was both a port and a railway hub, and improvements in links to London opened up the markets of the metropolis to local farmers: the 1869 Trade Directory noted that Ely was famous for its asparagus, grown there and sent to the capital.

Railway engineering in the Fens did not require the major tunnels and viaducts of elsewhere, but did require a stable base. In the 1890s a man at Holme recalled:

> I mind the time well when they made this line across the fen. The mere did not come within a quarter-of-a-mile of it, but the fen here was like a sponge. They raised this railway bank with great difficulty, long planks of wood were laid on the fen, and if one of the workmen stepped off the plank he used to slip up to his middle in the bog and had to be helped out.

Because of this, railway lines are usually elevated a few feet above the surrounding fields. This could be an advantage: when Armstrong travelled by train from Dereham in Norfolk to London in November 1852, he noted that the entire countryside between Ely and Cambridge had become one vast sea through which the train could run, although road traffic was useless: the locals, used to the situation, reached their houses by boat.

The isolation of Fenland cottages is shown in several nineteenth-century incidents. At the beginning of the nineteenth century a Gedney farmer became ill in the depth of winter. The nearest doctor was in Wisbech, 10 miles away: his servant set off at about four in the morning and was at the doctor's house by nine: the doctor was ready in an hour and they began the return journey; 'wading through the mud and mire until they passed Parson Drove [and] came by a very fine expanse of water, when the man said, "This is the nearest way, Sir, if you have no objection to go, only you must be prepared to jump on your horse, for he will have to swim sometimes." The doctor objected to this and they made their way around the standing water: when they finally reached the farm, the man had been dead some hours. It was far too late for the doctor to return to Wisbech, so he had to stay the night, not returning home until the middle of the next day.

In 1883, the coroner of Marshland was accused of neglecting his duties in a letter in the *Telegraph*, a free newspaper published in Wisbech on Saturdays and patronised by the 'lower class' attending the town's market. A labourer called James Hunt lived at West Walton. He went bathing in the River Nene on Sunday, 24 June but got into difficulties and was washed away by the current: his body was recovered on the following Thursday and taken to his cottage. He left a widow and a child. The coroner was informed but failed to turn up for four days, by which time 'decomposition rapidly set in, and the corpse became shriekingly offensive, so much so that the family could not remain in or near the house'. This was not the only difficulty: the local men eventually summoned to be the jury at the inquest were told it would be at the public house by Ferry station on Monday, 2 July, and gathered there. The coroner did not turn up for some hours and, when he did, it was at the Dunn Inn on the other side of the river! The jurymen had to find boats and get themselves across the river to attend. The letter went on to allege that: 'This is not the first nor the second case in which the same Coroner has delayed holding inquests, to the great inconvenience of the sorrowing relatives.' The charges may have been exaggerated – the coroner, Mr Wilkin, sued and obtained £150 damages – but it makes a good point: and West Walton is only 12 miles from Lynn!

In such an isolated country, river transport and the horse-drawn barge remained key elements in local transport, as Tennyson appreciated:

By the margin, willow-veiled,
Slide the heavy barges trailed
By slow horses; and unhailed
The shallop flitteth silken sailed.

Coprolites

There was a brief flurry of industrial activity in Victorian Fenland, based on the exploitation of coprolites, nodules of phosphorised clay, often said (wrongly) to be dinosaur droppings. They were apparently first exploited by John Ball, a Burwell miller in 1851: he found them beneath his allotment, and ground them in his mill to produce powder, which could be used as a fertilizer. There was a rush to exploit the new discovery, which was done by digging trenches through the peat soil: one coprolite miner was killed at Bottisham Lode in 1876. By 1890 the industry was in decline as it was proving cheaper to import phosphate from America for fertiliser.

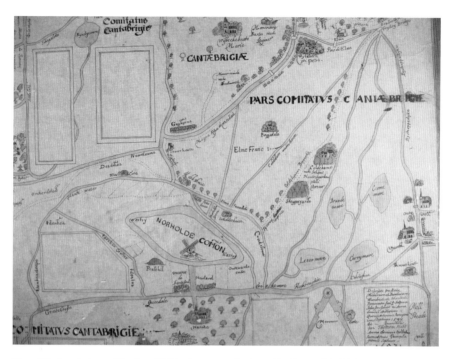

Map of the Fens between March and Wisbech; a water-dominated landscape. (Norfolk Record Office)

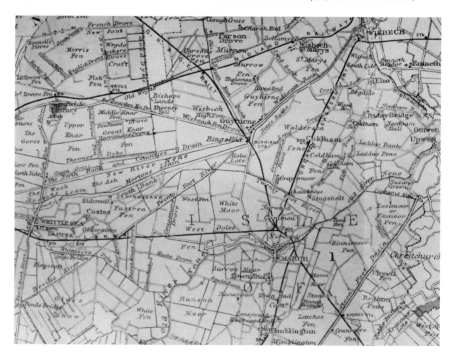

The same area after the coming of the railway.

Marsh Ague and the Use of Opium

Ague, or malaria, now known to be transmitted to people by the mosquito, was endemic in Fenland: a visitation by ague was the origin of the saying that a man was 'arrested by the Bailiff of Marshland'. Wheeler says: 'The persons suffering from ague were attacked intermittently with severe shiverings, which shook the whole body and even the chair or bed on which the sufferer was resting, accompanied by intense pains in the limbs. At one time, they were burning hot, and at another equally cold, and fever and thirst ensued.'

W. Watson wrote in 1827 that people were 'fearful of entering the fens of Cambridgeshire, lest the Marsh Miasma should shorten their lives'. One cure was to eat a spider or a spider's web, said in the *Lancet* to have been used by poor in Lincolnshire. However, most common ague was alleviated by taking opium: 'There was not a labourer's house ... without its penny stick or pill of opium, and not a child that did not have it in some form.' In public houses, it was often added to beer, whether by the customer himself or by the landlord. Very many Fen gardens had a patch of white poppies, and poppyhead tea was not only drunk by adults, many taking it to work, but also fed to babies as a sedative, especially during teething troubles. It was commonly dispensed by doctors. Thomas Stiles, writing as a very old man in 1894, recalled that in Wisbech where he practised from 1813: 'daily I supplied a vast number with either opium or laudanum'. By the mid-nineteenth century, opium was being imported: a study made in 1867 by the British Medical Association found that half the opium imported into Britain went to Lincolnshire and Norfolk. In the following year, the Pharmacy Act made opium preparations harder to obtain and there was a decline in its use in the later years of the century: by its end opium was classified as a dangerous drug and its use severely restricted.

According to Wheeler, a typical opium user might take as much as a dram a day, spending 1s or 18d a week on his habit. A dram was a piece about the size of a small walnut, the amount taken at one time being about the size of a pea. Wheeler thought it was less harmful than excessive alcohol: 'The man or woman who takes opium is never riotous or disorderly, and gives no trouble to the police as an effect of its use. It tends however to make the taker silent and morose.'

Constant use of opium – known locally as 'stuff' – affected the physical appearance, Charles Lucas noting: 'A graphic description of the complaint which I have heard from Fen people was "He is as yellow as a pagel and shakes like a puppy". He thought use of it from childhood affected the brain as well:

To children during the teething period the poppyhead tea was often given, and I do think this was the cause of the feeble-minded and idiotic people frequently met with in the Fens. I have known people of this calibre, when they wanted to go to the shop, put one or two children into an empty brewing copper, give them a piece of bread, then put on the lid, and there the children would remain until their considerate parents returned perhaps late in the afternoon.

In 1850, the *Christian Socialist* picked up a report in the *Morning Chronicle*, which said that the taking of opium was almost entirely confined to the Fenland district, citing the towns of Ely, St Ives, Chatteris, Wisbech and Whittlesea as places where a great deal of opium was sold. The price for laudanum was just a few pence per ounce, and for opium less than 2s an ounce:

One great cause of the extent to which the drug is used is its comparative cheapness as compared with ardent spirits: the same effects may be obtained, I was informed, from a penny worth of opium as from a shilling's worth of spirituous liquors. Indeed, there is very little spirits drunk in these parts, for the opium appears to have almost entirely superseded it, and so deeply has the practice taken root among the people that the drug has come to be considered by them as almost an article of necessity. One old woman in Wisbech was habitually taking 96 grains a day.

It was the practice of giving opium to children that most shocked the reporter. It was usually given in the form of Godfrey's Cordial: one ounce of Godfrey generally contained about a grain of opium. The habit was especially common during gleaning, when as many people as possible would be out at work, leaving a large number of babies in the care of one person. 'I always take care,' said a young girl of about 14, who had been employed on several occasions to take charge of a number of children in the absence of their parents, 'that they leave me plenty of "stuff", 'cause then, when they begins to cry, or gets troublesome, I shoves some of it in their mouths and that stops em.'

Opium use declined in the latter half of the nineteenth century. Lucas thought that the use of opium and the drinking of poppyhead tea was seldom met with after the year 1860, when drainage was well established. However, as late as 1920, when a man died in London after taking laudanum, the chemist who had supplied it said at the inquest that in the Fen country people took laudanum in half-pints. Christopher Morris, writing in 1947, comments: 'There are people still living who have seen opium pills on sale in Cambridge market place to comfort the victims of the Fenland agues.'

Another disease common in Fenland, as elsewhere, was smallpox. This left scars and could cause blindness: one victim was Nicholas Saunderson, born in 1682 and blinded as a child. He overcame this to become a teacher of mathematics at Cambridge and a doctor of law. He died in 1739 and is buried at Bottisham. Some of the most detailed descriptions of Fenland men are those who ran away leaving wives and children dependent upon the Poor Law. These often mention smallpox scars, as in the case of Edward Johnson, a labourer, aged 36, about 5ft 6in tall, dark complexion, black hair, whiskers meeting under the chin, much marked with the smallpox, with a scar on his nose and bald on the crown of his head. The reputation of milkmaids for beauty is connected with the prevalence of smallpox. They frequently caught cowpox from close contact with their animals, but this was less potent than smallpox: it immunised the girls against smallpox and left no scars, hence they were always fresh-faced, unlike other village girls.

The most important factor that brought the old ways to an end was the establishment of universal education. The reign of Queen Victoria saw the setting up of many local schools, most of those in the Fens being established by the National Society, such as those at Pinchbeck and Moulton Seas End. From the 1870s schools were set up in every town and village and, for the first time in history, almost everyone learned to read and write. An inspirational teacher could change a child's life. Elizabeth Jennings recalled how in a classroom where 'the day was wide and that whole room was wide/the sun slanting across the desks, the dust/of chalk rising', a teacher reading *Lepanto* made her a poet for life.[87]

Laws were passed to prevent very young children being made to go out to work: under an Act of 1867, no one under the age of 8 was to be employed and an Act of 1873 forbade the use of children under 10 in agricultural gangs. All this took some time to gain acceptance. When Sybil Marshall's father was walking to school one morning, he passed a farm worker, who was heard to say: 'Look at that bloody greet ol' boor still a gooing to school. Oughter bin getting his own living.' Her father was then aged 9! He had started school shortly before his fifth birthday, walking 3 miles there and 3 miles back every day: he recalled that every Monday he would be given a clean white bag, containing his 'dockey', that is, his lunch: 'sometimes there 'ud be bread and cheese, some-times sandwiches, and usually a bit o' cake o' some sort'. The boys used to hit each other on the head with their dockey bags: 'when we come to eat our grub, it 'ud all be mammygagged together into a solid lump'. He left school when he was 12 years old.

There had, of course, been a number of schools in Fenland in earlier years, such as the Grammar School at Wisbech, founded in 1549, and that at Bourne, founded in 1636 under the will of William Trollope: both were successors to guild or religious schools that had closed at the time of the Reformation. Spalding Grammar School was established in 1588, and survived hard times in the later eighteenth century, at one point having two masters and just one pupil! Holbeach Free School was founded in 1669 by George Farmer.

The school at Stickney had perhaps the most famous teacher – the French 'decadent' poet Paul Verlaine taught there in 1876 and 1877 after his release from a gaol in Brussels: he taught French and the classics but was best remem-bered by pupils for his skill at drawing. Verlaine then moved briefly to Boston, where he stayed for a while at the Whale Inn: he can hardly have missed its main attraction, a 53ft long skeleton of a whale that had been caught in Boston Deeps in 1847. His time in the Fens is commemorated in his poem 'Paysage en Lincolnshire'.

Health was also being brought under control in Victorian Fenland. The large towns, Boston and Lynn, had hospitals by the 1870s, followed by smaller towns including Spalding (1881) and Bourne (1900).

Whittlesea Mere

There were many large bodies of shallow water in Fenland, known as 'meres' – locals often spelled the word 'meers' in Dutch style. They included Yaxley Mere – reeds cut from it were sent by horse-wagon to Oxford and Nottingham. Ramsey Mere covered 1,500 acres, but the largest of all was Whittlesea Mere, which covered 1,870 acres in summer and 3,000 acres at times of winter flooding.

William Dutt describes the scene:

Until the middle of the nineteenth century there were tracts of unreclaimed fen, and though by that time nearly all the meres had been drained, Whittlesea remained,

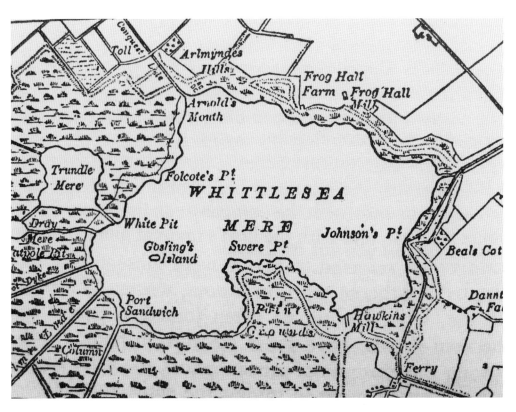

Whittlesea Mere.

and on its waters and around its reedy shores a few fenmen were able to live much after the fashion of their forefathers. In spring and autumn they devoted themselves to eel-catching; at midwinter they gathered in their annual reed harvest; all through the winter they kept a watch for the wildfowl which flocked to the mere, and the rare birds which often alighted on its reeds and on its quiet waters.[88]

The mere was between 2ftt and 7ft deep. It was used for boating, bathing, fishing and fowling in summer, and for skating when it froze over in winter. A new outfall through the Middle Level drain to the Ouse estuary was created in 1848 to take away excess water: this made drainage possible in 1851. Astbury tells us that hundreds of local people arrived 'provided with sacks and baskets to catch the fish floundering in the ever decreasing waters of the mere. Some even came with carts and gathered fish by the ton to send it to markets in Birmingham and Manchester.'[89]

In the following year, ditches were cut and roads and boundaries of farms laid out, but on 12 November 1852, the new banks bust and 1,000 acres of land were covered with 2½ft of water: the mere could not be conquered so easily. It had to be pumped continuously for three weeks to clear the water away. Within a couple of years, the landscape completely altered: 'the wind, which, in the autumn of 1851, was curling the blue water of the lake, in the autumn of 1853 was blowing in the same place over fields of yellow corn'.[90]

By 1860, crops were being grown on 2,100 acres with a value estimated at £12,350 a year. The crops were wheat (800 acres), oats (700 acres), coleseed (300 acres), mangolds (100 acres), grass (100 acres) and green crops (100 acres). The wheat alone could feed 3,000 people for a year, while the beef and mutton raised on the grassland could feed more than 300 people for a year. One unforeseen result was almost instant shrinkage of nearby areas of peat – the railway embankment across the Holme Fen had to be strengthened.

Ice Skating: A Fenland Sport

The lakes and many of the drainage channels in Fenland often froze in winter, and the area was the home of skating. Skates were originally made out of animal bone; the Dutch are said to have brought over skates with metal blades in the seventeenth century. The Spalding Gentleman's Society minutes of 1728 record: 'Mr Harrison Baker of this town goes on ice skates with a velocity and grace equal to a Dutch Hollander and can do a mile in three minutes.' The first recorded speed-skating event was held in 1763. The great age of Fenland skating was in the Victorian period: the National Skating Association was set up in 1879.

William Dutt was an enthusiast:

Where else can skaters go for an out-and-home run of seventy miles in a day, as has been done between Earith and Wisbech; or enjoy such an outing as did two sons of a Huntingdon farmer, 'We skated from Holme station, by way of Benwick, March and Upwell, to Wisbech, and after witnessing four races, skated home on the same day, covering a distance of sixty-six miles?' When the floods are 'out', as they sometimes are even now, in spite of an excellent drainage system, portions of the Great level are, in frosty weather, transformed in to immense icy playgrounds, where not only casual pleasure-seekers and professional skaters disport them-

Fenland skaters. (Ayscoughfee Hall, Spalding)

Skating racers. (Ayscoughfee Hall, Spalding)

selves, but even companies of volunteers have been known to drill and manoeuvre on 'patterns'.[91]

Alan Bloom recorded that in the 1870s, a skater raced a train for a wager from Sandhill Bridge in Littleport to Ely railway bridge. His opponents tried to slow him down by placing clinkers and ash on the course – but he still beat the train by half a minute! A review of Bloom's book in *The Times* in 1958 talked of 'the

Fenmen, tough, laconic of speech, still a race apart, living in Chatteris and Crowland, Upwell and Over, to whom skating is a natural form of self-expression, the very breath of life'.[92]

The ecologist Roger Deakin was also an enthusiast: 'The great fenland sport is as evanescent as the ice itself. As soon as there's ice thick enough, the normally deserted Ouse washes from Welney to Earith can still wake up to a sudden throng of skaters and spectators, and word goes round somehow that the Fenland Championships are on; held whenever, and wherever, the weather permits'. Arthur Randell's father was keen, too:

> My father used to talk of the sharp winter of 1875 when, for several weeks, the Great Ouse was frozen over for about half a mile each side of Magdalen Bridge. Skating matches were held with prizes of flour, bacon and other foodstuffs to help the poor who were out of work on account of the weather. It was not real skating, though, he said, but more like 'running on pattens' because the surface of the ice was so rough and there were huge ice floes, several feet thick, which had come up with the tide and piled against the bridge.[93]

J.M. Heathcote, of Conington, described a typical skating scene. The course was laid out with barrels and ropes. At one end:

> there is an old woman sitting 'with chestnuts in her lap' and roasting others in an old grate. A Dutch oven is by her side and a crowd of buyers round her close by. On one side a rude, oblong box on bones and drawn by two dogs, imported a little gin for those who were thirsty. Many thousands are collected together and groups are skating in various directions. But the larger number are occupied in superintending that portion of the ice which was marked out for the course.[94]

Skating had its dangers of course, especially for foolhardy children, three of whom died in just one week in January 1817. A 13-year-old boy was drowned after the ice gave way when he was skating on a large mill-drain in Thorney, while two brothers aged just 6 and 7 were drowned at Walsoken when venturing out onto the ice before it was strong enough.

An early form of ice hockey was also played on the frozen lakes of Fenland. This was known as 'bandy', which was also the name of the bat, made from willow: the ball was known as the 'cat'. Villages would compete against each other, the traditional prize being a leg of mutton.

Fenland Heroes

Jean Ingelow (1820–97)

Tell the green rushes, O, so glossy green –
The rushes they would whisper, rustle, shake;
And forth on floating gauze, no jewelled queen
So rich, the green-eyed dragonflies would break,
And hover on the flowers – aerial things,
With little rainbows flickering on their wings.
'The Four Bridges'

Jean Ingelow was born in Boston in 1820: her father was a banker. Her early verse was admired by Alfred, Lord Tennyson, and she came to prominence when her book simply called *Poems* was published in 1863: it is said to have sold 200,000 copies in America, where the sentimentality of her verses had an enormous appeal. Her most well-known poem was 'High Tide on the coast of Lincolnshire, 1571', which is cited approvingly by writers as diverse as Rudyard Kipling, D.H. Lawrence and Anthony Powell. She also wrote novels and children's stories, the most famous of which was *Mopsa the Fairy*, published in 1869. She moved away from Fenland and was largely forgotten by the time of her death in London in 1897.

Octavia Hill (1838–1912)

Octavia was born at 8, South Brink in Wisbech, on 3 December 1838. Her father was James Hill, a corn merchant, but he went bankrupt when she was just 2, had a nervous breakdown and largely disappeared from the family. Octavia was bought up by her mother, Caroline, and her grandfather, Dr Southwood Smith, a health reformer who worked at the London Hospital in the East End: he was an inspiration in her life as was her mother, who had an interest in progressive education. The family lived in Finchley and when Octavia was 14 moved to Russell Place in central London. Octavia devoted her life to improving housing conditions of the London poor, and she put so much of herself into the cause that in 1877 she collapsed under the strain. From 1884 she worked with the ecclesiastical commissioners in improving the housing on church property in Deptford, Southwark and above all in

Wisbech: the birthplace of Octavia Hill.

Walworth where she was consulted on the rebuilding of the estate. She was also a founder of the National Trust, which arose from her interest in providing open spaces for the poor in London. Octavia died at her London home on 13 August 1912.

Sir Harry Smith (1787–1860)

Sir 'Harry' Smith, Britain's most decorated soldier, was born in Whittlesey in 1787: his father was a surgeon. He fought throughout the world – in South America, Spain, the United States, and was at the Battle of Waterloo in 1815. He was in South Africa in the 1820s and '30s, on one occasion riding 700 miles over rough country in six days. He became adjutant-general of the

Queen's troops in India in 1840, fighting in several battles: he is known as 'the Hero of Aliwal' as he led the final charge that won that battle. He returned to South Africa as governor of the Cape in 1847, a position he held until 1852. He returned to England, dying in 1860: he is buried in St Mary's Church in Whittlesey. His name is indirectly still known throughout the world: the city of Ladysmith in South Africa is named in honour of his wife.

MURDERERS FROM BOSTON: CATHERINE WILSON AND GEORGE HENRY METCALF

Less benign emigrants from the Fens were Catherine Wilson and George Henry Metcalf, both brought up in Boston – and both murderers, acquiring notoriety in a world at least as fond of melodrama as our own.

Catherine Wilson as a young girl had several jobs in Boston and Spalding as housekeeper or nurse: she later became the object of one of London's most sensational murder trials. It was alleged that she was in the habit of persuading her grateful employers to make out a will in her favour – and then poisoning them! She was actually convicted of the murder of Maria Soames in London in 1856, but the suspicion was that at least six others had suffered death at her hands. One was Peter Mawer, a retired sea captain in Boston, who left everything he had to her. It was thanks to the income that she obtained from the rents of his Boston property that she was able to set up in London as a respectable lodger with a servant, also from Boston, Elizabeth Hill. Her misdeeds were only uncovered as a result of a failed poisoning attempt by her in 1862. She was hanged at Newgate on 20 October 1862 in front of a crowd of 20,000 – the last woman to be publicly hanged in London.

George Henry Metcalf was the son (by her first husband) of the woman who ran the Boston Corporation swimming baths, and was apprenticed to a Boston hatter. He received his moment of fame in 1886 when he murdered his wife in Brighton, subsequently committing suicide. After his death, his body was brought back to Boston and he was buried in Boston Cemetery.

Eight

THE TWENTIETH CENTURY
AND BEYOND

The austere sun descends above the fen,
An orange cyclops-eye, scorning to look
Longer on this landscape of chagrin.[95]

The turn of the century saw the start of attempts to preserve the landscape of 'Old Fenland' for future generations. In 1899, the National Trust purchased 2 acres of land at Wicken Fen for £10: this was the very first National Trust property. In 1911, a further 97 acres at Wicken Fen were bequeathed. The first keeper appointed by the Trust was local man, George 'Bill' Barnes. In those days, the old habits of 'preserving' rare specimens by shooting birds or collecting eggs were still common. Barnes later recalled the time when a rare Montagu's Harrier nested on the Fen: egg-collectors gathered and were only deterred by a white lie, when he informed them that the nest was in marsh too dangerous to visit!

Drainage

The twentieth century saw a new technological development in the continual struggle to control flooding: as their boilers became unsafe, steam pumping engines were replaced with the more compact diesel or petrol engine. These could be started up at once – unlike the steam engines that took hours to get going – which meant that they were much more suitable for intermittent running. Small oil-driven pumps were in use by 1900: the first large oil engine was introduced in the Methwold and Feltwell District. Some new steam pumps were still erected, however, such as at Rummers in the North Level, which was built in 1927 and drove an Appold centrifugal pump. Another new introduction, to become common a few decades later, was the use of concrete for bridge building. Horseshoe Bridge at Spalding Common was one of a pair built in 1910 for the Deeping Fen Trustees by the Liverpool Ferro-Concrete Company: the entire structure was built in reinforced concrete. Its twin, Money Bridge over the River Glen near Pinchbeck, was demolished in the 1980s.

It might be thought that with the onset of the agricultural depression the work of reclaiming the Wash would have come to an abrupt end. Instead, at a meeting held in 1900, it was declared that the reclamations were still in their infancy, and the potential for further reclamations was discussed. A new embankment was to be constructed, parallel to the existing line of reclamations, which was to be called the Century Bank: seven new blocks of enclosed marsh would be made in its lee. The required money was raised from mortgages secured on the value of the two blocks of land already reclaimed. By 1904 the first of the new enclosures, covering 571 acres, had been completed at a cost of £6,799. When, in 1906, most of the existing enclosures were sold off – mainly to large landowners, some of whom were members of the Board – the sales raised sufficient cash to clear the mortgages and to leave £4,697 to invest in further reclamation work.

In 1908 it was estimated that the rest of the proposed new enclosures in the lee of the Century Bank could be completed at a cost of £1,045. The bank itself had now been standing so long that it was partly derelict, and a replacement was needed to complete the scheme. Further large blocks of land, to the north of the 1904 reclamations, were completed in 1910 and 1911, and another small area just to the north of Lynn was reclaimed in 1914. During the First World War some maintenance work was carried out on the banks, using German prisoners of war. The Company continued to operate, selling land and putting forward new plans, but only in 1923 did work on embanking recommence, now in the area between the 1904 enclosures and the land reclaimed in 1882, to the north of Lynn. In August 1927 the main sea wall around this second batch of enclosures was completed and the water excluded from 300 acres. In 1928, the work was completed and two new enclosures made.

At this time the government proposed taking over the assets and liabilities of the company through the Ouse Drainage Bill, but the plan came to nothing and embanking continued. A further 175 acres at the northern end of the reclamations, and abutting on the block enclosed in 1911, was completed in 1933; the new land was valued at £5,250. However, no further intakes from the marshes were made, in part because of fears that the Great Ouse Catchment Board would make a claim on the Company under the terms of the Drainage

Act on the grounds that the land reclaimed had largely been created as a result of the work that the Board itself had carried out in changing the character of the river outfalls. The Second World War ended further work, and only after the war had ended were further reclamations begun, with three further blocks being enclosed from the saltings in 1949. The Company was taken over by the Crown Estate under the Norfolk Estuary Act of 1964, and some further reclamations were made into the late 1960s.[96]

Reclamations at Wingland between 1910 and 1974 totalled more than 2,000 acres. Borstal boys at North Sea Camp started reclamation work in 1936, later enclosures down to 1979 completing a 970-acre project that became the Camp Farm.

Of course, nature could not be completely tamed. There were floods, the most notable being those of 1912, fully reported in the press:

> In the Isle of Ely and in many parts of Norfolk large areas of cultivated land are under water and the loss inflicted upon farmers is enormous. In the majority of cases the ground is only under a few inches of water, but in low-lying parts the hedge tops are barely visible above the floods. Cut wheat and barley can be seen in places

A common Fenland scene; flooded fields in 1912. (Norfolk Record Office)

The great flood of August 1912, Hilgay. (Norfolk Record Office)

half submerged by the flood water, and the rain is widespread. In one apple orchard adjoining the Ely–Norwich line the water reached to the fruit on the trees. Many fields had become lakes ... All the streets at Bourne were flooded yesterday, and furniture was floating about in inundated houses. The Fens around Bourne are under water to the depth of more than two feet and cut corn is floating on the surface. Potatoes and mangolds have been washed away.[97]

Farming

The Small Holdings Act of 1892 allowed – but did not compel – county councils to buy land for smallholdings, which were to be sold to the occupants over several years. Lincolnshire county councillor Richard Winfrey set up the Lincolnshire Small Holdings Association in 1894, the first of its kind in the country. The Association rented 650 acres around Spalding and sub-let them to 202 separate tenants: tenancy rather than ownership proved to be the way forward. The movement spread to Norfolk, again under Winfrey's leadership. Tom Williamson takes up the story:

In 1902, 130 labourers in Nordelph asked Winfrey to help them obtain smallholdings. They petitioned Norfolk County Council for 500 acres and Winfrey bought 50 acres in the parish, but this was only a start and in 1904 the county council purchased a further ninety-one acres at Chapel Farm. Thirty-five holdings of between one and twelve acres were laid out. The tenants included twenty-eight agricultural labourers, a carpenter, a baker, a grocer, and a man who worked as a travelling show-man in the summer and in the winter hired his horses to their neighbours to work in their fields. The success of the scheme was attributed to the local availability of part-time work and the fertility of the soil.[98]

A child bought up at Southery recalled life there in about 1915, writing about Southery Common:

It was mostly black earth bordered with grass and weeds, just a wide drove that continued onto the fen from Common Lane … For many months of the year the footpath beside the dyke was very slippery. Only farm workers with waggons, tum-brils and animals used the drove, where there were many deep holes filled with thick, black mud – known locally as 'slub' – into which the horses sank to their bellies. During the dry period of summer, clouds of soot-like dust arose from the animals' feet, dulling the weeds and grass; and to ride in a cart was reminiscent of a monster switchback where one wheel went down into a hole while the other went up over a mound and people and packages were tipped from side to side.[99]

Fens prosperity was built on diversification – market gardening, pea production for canning, bulbs, sugar beet factories at Spalding, Ely and Lynn, HL Foods based at Little Sutton, pre-packed foods; and distribution companies such as Leverton's of Spalding.

Woad

Woad production continued in a few places in the Fens through the nineteenth century and into the twentieth. In Young's time, it was grown at Brothertoft, as we have seen, on Moulton Common before its enclosure, and at three other places, which he does not name. There was still a woad mill at Tattershall Road in Boston in the 1840s: seven families are listed in the 1841 census as working there, an unpleasant task and not just because of the smell: the dye stained one's skin. The site was cleared for railway development in the mid-1840s.

Woad was still being grown in the Fens, however: Benjamin Armstrong noted it in 1854. In Wheeler's time, in the 1880s, woad was being grown at Algarkirk, Skirbeck, Wyberton and Parson Drove. Wheeler reiterates that woad gives the

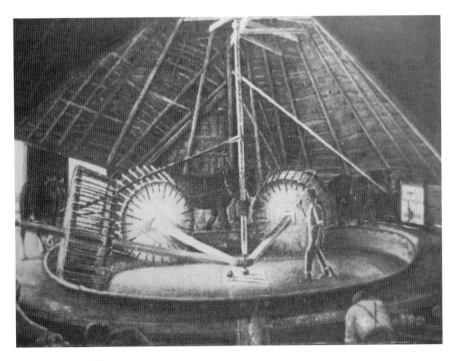

Interior of a woad mill.

land a thorough cleaning, often being followed by very good crops of oats and then wheat on the land. A 1907 newspaper article notes that woad at that date was grown only in the Boston and Wisbech areas.

The woad mill at Parson Drove is often said to be the last place in England where woad was grown and milled:

The plant grows about six feet high, and has a blue-green leaf and bright yellow flower ... It is weeded by men and women clad in hardened skirts and leathern knee-caps, who creep along the ground and take out the weeds with a curious little handspade which fits into the palm. The plant is picked by hand. The leaves are crushed to a pulp in the mill by rude conical crushing wheels dragged round by horses, and are then worked by hand into large balls and laid on 'fleaks' of twined hazel, or on planks, in special sheds, for three months to dry. After this the balls are thrown together, mixed with water and allowed to ferment in a dark house for five or six weeks. The woad is then rammed into casks and is ready to be sold to cloth manufacturers.

John Dawbarn, writing in 1952, recalled:

> The old woad mill stood on the right hand nearly opposite the church as one takes
> the Wisbech road from the village. Old residents can remember the horse-pro-
> pelled crushing wheel in action, pulping the leaves of the woad plant, after which
> process the pulp would be worked by hand into balls as big as Dutch cheeses then
> left to shrink by exposure to sun and air. The writer remembers as a boy being
> taken to see the huge wooden drying sheds, then tumbling rapidly into decay.
> Here men used to work in the dark, for light would spoil the dye. A few specimens
> of isatis tinctoria, last relics of a dead industry may still be seen growing in cot-
> tage gardens.

The last woad mill at Parson Drove was demolished in 1914: built of blocks of
turf with timber and reed-thatched roof, it was a temporary structure which
could be moved every few years. Woad continued to be grown as a commercial
crop at Skirbeck until 1932, when the mill there was demolished.[100]

The name now survives only in the occasional Woad Lane or Woad Cottage.

Flower-Growing

The tulip is not native to the British Isles, the first known mention of it being
in 1578, having been spreading across Europe from Turkey where it originated:
the name may derive from the Turkish word 'tulband', meaning turban. 'It is
from the Dutch fields that our English garden varieties have come, from there
that the stocks planted in the English fields originated, and from there that
many Dutchmen have come to England, at first to sell and soon to begin growing bulbs here.'[101]

The selling and growing of bulbs began around Spalding; late nineteenth-
century trade directories list bulb growers there and at Whaplode and Bourne.
The introduction of Darwin tulips in 1905 helped the expansion: they were long
stemmed and gave both a crop of bulbs and a good cut flower. By 1933, there
were about 150 bulb growers cultivating 2,500 acres of bulbs in the Spalding
and Wisbech districts. Dominicus van Konynenburg came over from Noordwyk
in Holland in 1922 and became the leading daffodil producer in Britain and
a major producer of tulips, building up the Spalding Bulb Company. Other
Dutch families included Moerman, Nell, Lindhout, Buschman – and van

Springfields, Spalding.

Geest. The latter are more generally known for importing bananas but are also major bulb producers: they have taken over the Spalding Bulb Company. At peak periods Spalding railway station was handling many thousands of boxes of fresh flowers every night, but by the 1950s road transport was beginning to take over. Bulb auctions were first held at Spalding in 1948. A Tulip Week was first held in the same year, developing into 'Tulip Time' in 1950, and the first Spalding Flower Parade in May 1958: up to 400,000 people came to see the increasingly sophisticated floats, climaxing with the arrivals of Miss Tulipland on a magnificent floral throne. The popularity of the parade declined somewhat in the early years of the twenty-first century, but the Flower Festival remains a major tourist attraction.

The growing of flowers is an iconic symbol of modern Fenland, typified in Springfields Garden outside Spalding, which opened in 1966, Len van Geest playing a major role in its development. Whole fields of daffodils are grown in the Spalding area, while at Wisbech, East Anglia's leading church flower festival is held each July.

Fruit

Fruit picking was another speciality and people would travel from London for the seasonal work it offered. Many of these were very young and so vulnerable. One such was a London girl called Minnie Morris, found strangled in Burrett Road in Walsoken on 16 July 1912. A young local man, Robert Galloway, walked into Wisbech police station the same day to confess to the crime. He cited jealousy as the cause: Minnie had been friendly to him, but also to another local lad, with whom Galloway had earlier had a fight: all were regular drinkers in the Black Bear in Walsoken. Galloway was tried in Norwich in October and hanged in Norwich Prison on 5 November. Some doubted if he was really of sufficient intelligence to be responsible for his actions, the local newspaper querying if it was not society as a whole that was to be blamed for young men 'of his way of life, ill trained and at a loose end'. One correspondent to the paper urged that the case showed that capital punishment should be abolished in Britain: he was half a century ahead of his time.

Migrant workers included many from Ireland who continued to come over in the summer to work on the fields, especially in Deeping Fen where they helped harvest crops of corn and potatoes. This caused resentment in 1916, because many of those coming over were young men who were excluded from being called up for war service. Fen folk felt that whereas their young men were earning just 1s a day in the forces, and in some cases even serving in Ireland, the

young Irishmen could come to the Fens and earn up to 6s a day in the fields. English people refused to work on farms employing Irishmen, some of whom were therefore dismissed – and publicans and shopkeepers refused to provide them with their usual accommodation.

Daily Life

Many inhabitants of Fenland have recorded their memories of daily life in the early twentieth-century Fens. Two of the most important are Sybil Marshall and Arthur Randell. Sybil Marshall, born in 1914, was a primary school teacher in the 1930s, teaching at a typical small Fenland school where twenty-six children, whose ages ranged from 4 to 11, were taught in a single class. She published *Fenland Chronicle*, recollections of her parents, in 1963. In later life, she taught at Sheffield and Sussex Universities. Marshall died in 2005. Arthur Randell was born at Wiggenhall St Mary Magdalen in 1901, and worked on the railways and as a mole catcher. In the 1960s he published several books of reminiscences, edited by Enid Porter, curator of the Cambridge and County Folk Museum. Randell died in 1988. These writers, and others, enable us to enter into a Fenland world that has been completely lost.

Ted Brand was another man who published his reminiscences. He was born in Warboys in 1903: his father was a farm labourer and his grandfather a smallholder and miller. He is very good on the details of daily life in a Fenland home in the early years of the twentieth century:

How hard Mother worked. She was always busy cooking, baking bread, jam making, pickling, wine making and ham curing. A washerwoman came in on Mondays from 7 am until 4 and earned two shillings (10p). We gave her breakfast and dinner as well, otherwise Mother did all the work. She baked our bread in one of those big brick ovens and used a long stick with a flat steel bottom to reach it. She also baked wonderful Yorkshire pudding and ham done in a crust. My word, we may have been poor, but like most country folk we knew how to live … There was no indoor sanitation. Outside we had a double seater, a commodious privy. As children we used a chamber pot that was kept at the back of the house. My earliest memory concerns that chamber pot. I was sitting on it when it broke in half. I remember hopping into the house on one leg crying with pain.[102]

It is impossible now to imagine how hard life was just a century ago. Even that most basic necessity, fresh water, was often not available. Sybil Marshall's mother told her daughter:

> I know most folks think there's too much water in the fen, but they ought to be there in summer time. Then the rivers and drains and dykes all dry up till there ain't a spoonful of water nowhere, and it used to be all anybody could do to get enough to drink. Most houses 'ould have a rainwater tub, but that 'ould be green and shiny and full o' striddlebags, little wriggling creatures that 'ould turn into gnats afore long. That warn't very good tack to drink, but it were better than the muck from the dykes. Many's the time I've seen a man or woman in the bottom o' the dyke, waiting for the water to seep into a tablespoon to be put into a kettle for the one cup o' tea o' the day.

Winifred E. Long recalled: 'The fen people all drank the river water. On our summer walks we would see the women going down to the bank and dipping their buckets into the river. We used to talk to one old woman who was well over 70 and she said she had always drunk river water and loved the taste of it.'[103]

Arthur Randell's descriptions of his work on Fenland railways bring back the flavour of working life a century ago. For example, he worked at Wisbech Harbour:

> Every morning an engine would come down from Wisbech Goods drawing fifty to seventy trucks laden with coal, timber, potatoes, oranges and other goods. These were sorted out and placed either in English's Sidings (Messrs English Brothers, timber importers), the Gas Works Sidings, or in Wilson's Manure Siding, while the remainder were pulled by horses into sidings, where engines were not allowed to go. Wisbech Harbour at that time was a very busy place and often the engine would have to make two trips, especially when boats had come in with Scotch seed potatoes or with timber from the Baltic … I enjoyed working down at the harbour. The men of the London Scottish were friendly chaps who used to give us pint mugs of tea and big slices of oat cake, and it was interesting to meet the foreign seamen off the timber ships. But all this is now in the past.[104]

Brian Short looked at two villages in the Cambridgeshire Fens, Isleham and Willingham. The most prominent family in the former was the Robins family of Isleham Hall, with about 20 per cent of the land in Short's sample, but the most

significant fact in both villages was the number of smallholdings – just under half the holdings in both village were of less than an acre. The small size of holdings was especially notable at Willingham, where 'it is clear that some two centuries after the close of Spufforth's study, landholding in Willingham was still unusually fragmented, with no hereditaments in the sample being as large as 75 acres. This was virtually identical with the position in 1720. The large Fenland-edge farm had no place here, in either the seventeenth or the twentieth centuries.' Of 141 houses in Isleham and Willingham in 1910, fifty-two had four rooms, eleven had three rooms and eight had just two rooms. A few of these cottages were built of clunch and most had earth closets often shared with other cottages: Short cites the example of a Mr Ball, who rented a cottage owned by an Ely man, made of clunch with a tile roof and a three-up, one-down structure with an earth closet.[105]

The rivers were key elements in the transport of the area, with steam slowly replacing the horse, as Randell recalled:

> Up and down the great Ouse used to go the strings of horse-drawn barges or lighters as we used to call them, bringing goods of all kinds from King's Lynn as far as Cambridge. There was also in my young days a steam tug called the *Nancy* which hauled about ten big barges. She could get along much more quickly than the lighters which had to stop at each bridge they came to so that the towing horses could be untied before they galloped along the towpath while the barges drifted under the bridge.

Where there were rivers, there had to be bridges, not always well maintained: 'In 1913 a new bridge was built over the Ouse at Magdalen to replace the old oak one. The wooden one had been dangerous for a long time because tugs had knocked out eight of the twenty-four piles, few railings were left and for most of the way across there were only a couple of planks to walk on; yet people continued to go over it as though it were as safe as London Bridge. During my time several people fell through and were drowned, the body of one of them being recovered right out at Skegness which, to Magdalen folk, seemed as far away as China'.[106]

Although the rivers were generally calm enough, boating, of course, had its dangers. Four people were sailing near Denver Sluice on 28 September 1912 when the boat overturned and two were drowned: a 9-year-old boy named Eric Hyner, and an adult, Leonard Gainsbury. Gainsbury was an expert yachtsman and the cause of the tragedy was never discovered: the fact that the sluices were open at the time, with the consequent rush of water, was thought to have been a factor.

Sir Norman Angell (1872–1967), Nobel Peace Prize winner

Angell was born Ralph Norman Angell Lane in the Manor House, Holbeach, on 26 December 1872: his father owned a small chain of shops. He was educated at a preparatory school, then at a local school kept by an Anglican clergyman, and later in France. He then worked as a journalist in England and in Switzerland. In 1891 he emigrated to America, where he worked as a rancher and then in journalism: he returned to England probably in 1897, and moved to Paris the following year. Between 1905 and 1912 he was managing editor of a new continental edition of the *Daily Mail*. He married Beatrice Cuvellier,

Birthplace of Norman Angell, Holbeach.

the daughter of an American lawyer: they parted in 1912, but were not legally separated until 1932.

In 1909 he issued a pamphlet called *Europe's Optical Illusion*, which was published as a book, *The Great Illusion,* in 1910: it is on this book that his fame rests. He argued that even a successful war of conquest would be counterproductive because of the high costs of the economic dislocation that would be associated with such a war. The book became a best-seller, being translated into twenty-five languages and selling more than a million copies. Many people interpreted his message to be that war was no longer possible: sadly, events a few years later proved how wrong this was.

Angell was one of the international leaders of anti-war movements and peace campaigns during the First World War, much of which he spent in America. He joined the Labour Party and served as MP for Bradford North for two years from 1929. He was a strong supporter of the League of Nations, and in 1933 he defended the legitimacy of international force against aggression, while insisting that in his personal views he remained a pacifist. For this work, he was awarded the Nobel Peace Prize in 1934. Angell spent the Second World War, like the First, in America, returning in 1951 to live in Surrey. He died in a nursing home in Croydon on 7 October 1967.

Fenland in the First World War

The First World War was the first total war, involving every family in Fenland as elsewhere. Many men volunteered for service and after 1916, when conscription was introduced, all men had to serve. For the first time, war involved women as well, whether as nurses, on the land, or in engineering and munition making. The war also saw the first air raids, and the introduction of rationing.

Fear of invasion was felt by Arthur Randell, as he later recalled:

One day, just after the 1914 War broke out, my father and I were out mole-catching and met a foreman we knew on one of the farms; we stopped to have a word with him and naturally our talk was all of the war. This chap was a big man who always quoted texts from the Bible whenever he could and had a habit of grinding his teeth together.

'Teddy, bor,' he said to my father that day, 'when the Germans come marching along the road I'll say to them; 'March on, my bors, and blow the Big House up'.

We asked if he really expected to see any Germans round Magdalen. 'Oh yes,' he assured us, 'I'm expecting them to come along any time now,' and he seemed so sure of it that my father, being no scholar, thought he must be right and it so put the wind up us that I am quite sure that if we had met a gang of men on the road home we'd have done something silly. It wasn't until we had a chat with Charlie Self who told us that the Germans had no more chance of landing in England, let alone coming to Magdalen, than an ice-cream had in Hell, that we felt really at ease.[107]

Lynn saw one of the earliest Zeppelin raids in Britain in January 1915: two people were killed. On 29 July 1916 one bomb fell at Fiskerton and on 2 September four bombs were dropped at Boston, one falling 250 yards from the church: one boy of 16 was killed in the raid. A blackout was introduced. Bishop Hicks noted that the mission preacher at Boston filled the Scala Theatre on Sunday evenings during the war: the authorities had forbidden the lighting up of the parish church: 'now they have got back into church, these informal services are much missed'.[108]

Scott recalled the raids: 'We had several big Zeps over us, I saw one quite plain over our house, it looked just like a big cigar. Lynn had been bombed and some lives were lost. I remember we were up all night as they were going over to the Midlands, we heard several bombs dropped. I watched them coming back and saw the flashes as they dropped their bombs. A nurseryman had nearly all his glass blowed out near Lynn.'

It was not only through the Zeppelins that the outer world reached Fenland, as Scott recollected: 'One night I heard a big explosion but did not know what it was, I thought it was quite near. I rang up the telephone office to see if they knew where it was but they did not seem to know, but in the morning the papers told of a big explosion at Silvertown near London, a hundred miles away and yet I heard it quite plain.'[109]

The war saw many Fen men leave their home villages and town for the first time. Scott recalled:

We were told to plough up all the strawberry beds and plant potatoes. One of my men was in the Reserves and he went out at the start, was taken prisoner of war at Mons and sent to work at the coal mines in Germany. As the Germans kept gaining ground all my young men were taken from me, so I had only the old men left to carry on, three of my young men were with the Norfolks and was sent to Gallipoli,

and never heard of more. Then I had to apply to the Army to send me men to work on the Farm, and the Army sent me all sorts of young men, some had been clerks, one had been working in an Engineers' shop, but not one had been used to the land, so you can guess what a lot of trouble this caused me.

It also saw many incomers. Ayscoughfee Hall housed six families of Belgian refugees. In 1917, German and British prisoners of war were exchanged through Boston Dock.

After the war, many striking war memorials were erected. They include the memorial at Wainfleet Cemetery in shape of a triumphal arch and Lutyens' war memorial in Ayscoughfee Hall grounds. The memorial at Walpole St Andrew is a big bronze cross in churchyard, with animals on the shaft, in memory of twenty-one men who did not come back. March has a soldier in First World War battledress, head bowed, rifle pointed to the ground, and there is another soldier at Soham, more prominent as he stands on top of the monument rather than in front of it, as he does at March. 1923. The 'Thinking Soldier' war memorial at Huntingdon was designed by Kathleen Scott (widow of Scott of the Antarctic): it was unveiled in 1923. There is another statue at Whittlesey, this time not a soldier but an allegorical figure – a knight in armour holding a sword. Elm, like many villages, has a cross of sacrifice: the names here include Charles Barker, reported killed in action in France on 21 August 1915: he was just 15 years old.

Between the Wars

Drainage
Drainage work was still a vital part of Fenland life. In 1919, there was another great flood in the Fens and the Stretham drainage engine pumped day and night for forty-seven days. In the 1920s, the unemployed were used on drainage work in the North Level. A new 'eye' or sluiceway was added to Denver Sluice in 1923 to improve the discharge of the sluice under flood conditions.

The year 1934 saw a major step forward in Fen drainage:

A significant event in the long history, covering a period of 300 years, of the struggle to master the problem of the drainage of the fens took place on September 28 [1934], when Mr Walter Elliot, Minister of Agriculture, inaugurated the new sluice and pumping station at St Germans Norfolk, which by its ability to discharge up to 3,000 tons of water per minute will materially relieve the difficulties which have hitherto attended the drainage of the Middle Level, an area of 173,000 acres lying between the Rivers Nene and Ouse. The greater part of the Fen district consists of peat, and, by reason of its reclamation an adaptation to agriculture, the soil has dried and shrunk, causing settlement averaging half an inch per annum, but attaining as much as 6 ft in some places during the last fifty years. Simultaneously the River Ouse has been gradually silting up, making it impossible in times of flood for inland water to gravitate to the sea, and necessitating the employment of pumps to raise the water to enable it to escape. The new sluice is the third of its kind which has been installed, its predecessors, the first of which dates back to 1848, having proved insufficient to cope with the quantity of tidal water to be excluded. Advocated after the disastrous flood of 1912, the present scheme, which has cost about £224,000, did not take place until 1929, when, on the advice of their chief engineer, Major R G Clark, the Middle Level Commissioners decided to proceed with the work to his design which incorporated a pumping system of three units. Mr Elliot described the pumping system as 'the biggest in the world – more powerful than anything in Holland, the great land of drains, engineers, and water pumps'. The four sluice gates provided are designed to withstand and operate against a maximum difference of 30 ft from the Ouse side and of 17 ft from the drain side. The weight of each gate is approximately 28 tons.[110]

The *Victoria County History of Huntingdonshire*, published in 1936 identified two problems. The first was technical – the continued lowering of the Fens:

The result, after a time, becomes, critical. The banks, straining unevenly towards the fen, are weakened; and the difficulty of pumping water up into the high drains is increased. Thus it is that the works of one generation have become inadequate for the needs of the next. And, all the time, attention has been directed not so much to this fundamental phenomenon as to the rival merits of different schemes. Some of these schemes may have brought relief for a time, but, ultimately, like a powerful machine in a threatening disease, they have left the Fens weaker against the changes of subsequent years. Because the more satisfactory the drainage has become, the more rapid has been the shrinkage and wastage of the peat. To combat this seemingly inevitable evil, we can only look with hope towards the increasing triumphs of engineering skill.

The other problem was administrative:

> A cursory glance at a map of the Bedford Level shows a tangled network of drains, leams, eaus, and rivers – all running apparently at random. The confusion of the streams on the map has been, alas, paralleled by a confusion in their administration. Everywhere there has been a multiplicity of authorities without any real authority; everywhere mutual dependence without a complete co-operation. Both nature and man, by many intersecting channels, have made interdependent all portions of the Level; indeed, all portions of the whole Fenland. Yet even before the initial Bedford Level schemes had been completed, the beginnings of separate interests were already apparent. This fact has been of no little importance in the failure of successive generations to arrive at, and, to carry out, a satisfactory programme of draining. And it may well be doubted whether any system of drainage in the Fens can be permanently successful unless it is based on some enlarged and comprehensive scheme.

A Royal Commission had been set up in 1927 to look at the working of Drainage Boards. This led to the Land Drainage Act of 1930. Four Catchment Boards were established for Fenland: Witham and Steeping; Welland; Nene; Great Ouse. These became River Boards in 1948 and River Authorities in 1964, at which time the ones for the Welland and the Nene were combined. In 1974, ten all-purpose Regional Water Authorities were created in England and Wales, to govern all aspects of water management, including amenities such as angling and boating, navigation issues, land drainage and flood protection. The whole of the Fens came within the Anglian Water Authority, three of its river divisions covering the area: Great Ouse; Welland and Nene; Lincolnshire.

In 1937 it was feared that one of the barrier banks along the Bedford rivers might give way, causing flooding all over Fenland. The Great Ouse Catchment Board called in consulting engineers Sir Murdoch Macdonald and Partners, whose report came out in 1940: it proposed a relief channel from Denver to St Germans, running parallel to the Ouse, and a cut-off channel round the eastern edge of the Fenland from the River Cam at Grantchester to Denver. If this was too expensive, the cut-off channel could be omitted and the board decided to adopt this course, but even this work was interrupted by the war.

Suggestions were revived of a dam from Friskney to Hunstanton so that all the land behind it could be reclaimed: comparisons were made with the Zuiderzee in the Netherlands. However, there are differences, as H.C. Darby pointed out: the tidal range in the Wash is over 25ft, whereas that of the Zuiderzee is less than 5ft: in any case, whereas the bed of the Zuiderzee is good soil, that of the Wash is merely sand! Charles Lucas, writing in 1930, was an enthusiast: 'If this outrush of upland water were properly bridled it might produce enough electricity to light Lynn, Yarmouth and Norwich, and at the same time provide sufficient funds to pay all the working expenses of the barrage.'[111]

Farming

In 1926, *The Times* summed up the Fenland scene: 'To a person unfamiliar with the district the landscape, though flat, is much less 'Fenny' than the name Fenland would suggest, for it is now well cultivated and yields heavy crops of corn and potatoes – 13 tons to the acre was one wayside report – besides roots, including sugar beet, and such frivolities as mustard.'

The railways were a key factor in the prosperity of Fenland farming. As D.I. Gordon wrote:

[By the] 1930s further growth had occurred and at the peak of the season small stations like Sutton Bridge, Murrow (East), Long Sutton, Gedney and Holbeach were each despatching trains of up to sixty vans daily for centres such as London, Manchester, Liverpool, Birmingham, Cardiff, Leeds, Sheffield and Edinburgh. And this was not all. Pea traffic coincided with the soft fruit, potatoes were carried the whole year, shortly after Christmas the movement of flowers began and continued for four months, steam-heated vacuum stock for their carriage being provided between Lynn and Bourne by the 1930s, in the early spring large quantities of cabbage and broccoli were conveyed, and later in the year came plums, apples and pears, and sugar-beet. Only after World War II did these heavy traffics begin to flag.[112]

Cyril Marsters recalled this from his own experience:

In June and July loads of gooseberries and strawberries would be delivered to the station yard. The gooseberries were contained in circular wooden skeps; the strawberries in oblong 'chip' baskets … Fruit crops would be loaded into closed container wagons – 'box vans' we called them – which dad would previously have inspected for cleanliness … Fruit such as gooseberries, plums or apples would be delivered in the wicker skeps. These were circular baskets, the larger 'bushel' size being about 24 inches in diameter and fourteen inches in height; the smaller sized ones, known as 'strikes', were approximately fifteen inches in diameter and ten or twelve inches high … Following on after the strawberries and gooseberries would be the plums, and these again were transported in the sturdy wicker skeps.[113]

Fruit growing involved the development of new strains, for example, specialist apples, such as the Magdalen Wonder. There may have been an earlier apple of this name, but the one now known was developed by Harry Bridges of Wiggenhall St Mary Magdalen in the 1920s, probably from the cox and one of the laxtons, and using grafting techniques to improve its colour. It was much grown in the area in the Second World War. One of the most progressive farmers was Herbert Carter (1862–1944), who farmed at Holbeach Hurn, with George Hovenden Worth: his enlightened methods added a new dimension to the agriculture of the area. His name lives on in Holbeach: he gave the recreation ground now known as Carter's Park to the town: it was the early training ground of Geoff Capes, Olympic shot putter, and, on three occasions, Britain's strongest man.

Celebrating the coronation of 1953, the gates of Carter Park, Holbeach.

One result of the drying out of the peat was that the fields were liable to catch fire. A stray bonfire could spread to the underlying peat and, once started, it was almost impossible to put out, burning until it reached the barrier of a stream or dyke: one fire near Littleport burned for nearly two years before extinguishing itself. Such fires made a spectacular sight at night time. One fire in Conington Fen in 1871 burned for weeks: according to Astbury, 'at night the little hillocks of flame which burst from the surface of the burning soil gave a brilliant display which could be seen clearly by those travelling on the nearby main line of the Great Northern Railway'. Astbury points out that these fires are far from uncommon: in the dry summer of 1949, Ely fire brigade was called to nearly forty peat fires.[114]

Sugar Beet

Sugar beet became a boom crop in the 1920s, after sugar had been rationed during the war as so much of it was imported. It is sown in March, and is labour intensive as it is densely planted to prevent the growth of weeds: the plants then have to be 'singled', in which multiple seedlings are removed, and 'chopped out', removing more of the plants so that the remainder are evenly spaced. These jobs were done by men or often by women, using a hoe. They are harvested between September and Christmas, while the sugar content is at its highest and before winter frosts damage the crop. This was also labour intensive – the beets could be lifted by a horse team but had to be shaken to loosen the attached soil, and crown and leaves were cut off: they were then forked into a cart and taken to the roadside waiting to be transported to the factory: the leaves could be ploughed back into the ground or used as animal fodder. The sight of beet piled high beside a Fenland roadside is a common one: children are said to take a few and carve them into lanterns for Hallowe'en.

On reaching the factory the beets are cut into thin slices, known as cossettes, which are placed in water and the liquid produced boiled to produce a thick liquid in which form the crystals that are the sugar. The used cossettes are pulped and used as animal feed.

In 1925, a big new sugar beet factory was built at Queen Adelaide near Ely. Others followed. *The Times* of 7 October 1930 reported on the new crop and its effect upon the landscape:

Upon either side of the seaward-flowing Ouse thousands of acres, once bearing cereals, are now covered with the broad, pale-coloured leaves of the sugar-beet …

At constant intervals along both banks of the 16-mile stretch from Ely to Denver Sluice ... are wooden platforms and 'chutes', whither the surrounding farmers bring their loads of beets. These have been pulled and topped in the fields. They are rather like rotund and orange-tinted parsnips. And the procession from the fields has already begun. Frequently, from the river, no more is seen of this than the golden crowns of the cart-loads, jogging along some road parallel to the water, but for the most part hidden by the intervening banks. Here and there, however, at the stout wooden stages, piles of beets have been unloaded or are being rolled down in their scores of hundreds into strings of waiting barges. Some, indeed, are full and under way, teams of half-a-dozen or more behind their steam tugs. And it is these lighters plying upstream to Ely or down-stream to King's Lynn that have displaced the wagons creaking across the stubble, laden with sheaves for the farmyard stacks ... The factories need coal as well as beets, so that the lighters and tugs fulfil a double function.

E.P. Brand recalled working with sugar beet:

Handling the beet was neither quick nor particularly easy. Cutting out – making a gap of six to twelve inches, depending on the type of land – and singling usually

Sugar beet factory being built: this factory was at Saddlebow, south of King's Lynn.

The Saddlebow sugar beet factory, 1927.

done by a woman, for example, were very delicate jobs. We lifted our own crops with an old style lifter, cut the tops off by hand, put the beet in heaps, and later cleaned the dirt off with a piece of sharp wood or a piece of steel. But then mechanisation arrived.[115]

As we have seen, it was not just sugar beet that depended upon the railway, but also fruit and potatoes. It was a boom time for the train. The railway sidings at March were redesigned on a massive scale between 1925 and 1933. The Whitemoor marshalling yard served the whole of the eastern counties. By 1953 it had a capacity of 7,000 wagons a day, but traffic reduced by the 1970s. Passenger services on the Wisbech and Upwell Tramway were withdrawn in 1928. By 1962, there was just one freight train a day except in the fruit season. The line finally closed in 1966. It is immortalised in *Toby the Tram Engine* (1952) by Rev Wilbert Awdry, part of the *Thomas the Tank Engine* series of books: Awdry was vicar of Emneth for twelve years, so counts as one of Fenland's literary residents.

Because the country was so flat, roads usually crossed the railway by level crossing rather than by bridge. This involved risk: as early as August 1860, the crossing keeper at Spalding had been killed trying to open the gates before the arrival of a train shunting coal trucks. On 1 June 1939, four people were killed at Hilgay when an express hit a lorry at the Cross Drove level crossing. The train was running from Hunstanton to Ely, while the lorry was loaded with straw. The leading carriages came off the line and collided with wagons in a neighbouring siding: three people died at the scene and a fourth the following day, with a further five being seriously injured. The lorry driver escaped with cuts and bruises.

Oil

The 1920s saw a brief boom in one industry in Fenland: oil. The shortage of oil during the First World War had led to the search for English oil, with the hope that oil reserves could be extracted from naturally occurring oil shales – shades of the fracking schemes of almost a century later! Doctor William Forbes-Leslie built treatment works at Setchey and began drilling. It was claimed that hundreds of millions of tons of oil could be recovered by the company English Oilfields Limited.

Arthur Randell recalled:

> In 1919 and 1920 the main topic of conversation round Magdalen Road and in the neighbouring villages was the oil which had been discovered at Setch, three miles from the station. A tall chimney was erected, with buildings alongside it, retorts were built and big offices, and a railway line was laid down with sidings and a signal-box … Hundreds of navvies came down and a host of clerks and chemists, while many farm workers left the land in order to earn big money in the English Oilfields as they were called. All this made Magdalen Road an even busier station because most of the machinery and building material was unloaded there by crane to go on to Setch by road. There was even talk of a pipe-line being laid from the oilfields to King's Lynn.[116]

However, in 1921, oil samples from the Setchey field proved to be of no commercial value at all because of their high sulphur content, which could not (then) be taken out. The scheme collapsed: even the tower fell victim to the Fenland wind, blowing down some years later.

Daily Life

Some villages in the Fens were still very isolated. A report of 1938 about Feltwell Anchor Fen says:

> The school and hamlet were virtually removed from contact with the outside world and although the provision of a road which now links with the nearest village has made transport easier, many of the pupils have little or no knowledge of the world beyond their own homes. Dependence upon broadcasting is increased by the fact that the hamlet receives daily newspapers only three times a week and then twenty-four hours after publication.

Cyril Marsters had personal experience of the primitive conditions. He was about 12 when the family moved out of Lynn to Wilburton when his father became station master there in 1940:

> Just outside the kitchen door was a small, enclosed yard. This gave access to a flush toilet on the left-hand side and, on the far side, a wash-house. There was no bathroom in the house so we would have to revert to the use of a tin bath, in the wash-house, which Mum regarded as a very backward step, having become used to the convenient bathroom in the house we had just left.

Cyril went to the village school:

> The school was run by the Headmaster (nicknamed Nonny) and one other woman teacher and, as far as I can remember, there were only two classrooms. The larger of these was a long rectangular room with numerous rows of desks arranged behind one another across the shorter width of the room and facing one of the long walls. On this wall was a series of blackboards and between the wall and the front desks a wide gangway. The groups of desks accommodated two or three different classes, all in the same room and Nonny would move along the front gangway to deal with them in turn. While he was dealing with one class the other would be kept busy with work he had given them to do.[117]

The 1930s saw a new development in Cambridgeshire: the village college. These provide secondary education for 11- to 16-year-olds, and also educational and

leisure facilities for adults. They were the brainchild of Henry Morris, the Chief Education Officer for the county, who had a vision of a school that would cater for all ages under one roof. The first to be opened in Fenland was at Bottisham in 1937, with others following at Swavesey, Soham and Burwell (the last actually a primary school).

Each village had its own character, and even its own ways of speech, as Arthur Randell found out: 'Although Coldham is only fourteen miles from Magdalen as the crow flies, and though both are in the Fens, I found that the dialect spoken by my new mates was quite different from mine. I used to wonder at first what they were laughing at when I shouted out to one of them; my Norfolk brogue seemed to amuse them.'[118]

One great advance was related to the removal of much marshland: the malarial mosquito was finally eliminated from Fenland, along with the disease, around 1920. Other diseases still prevailed. In 1928, there was an outbreak of diphtheria in Whittlesea, with twenty-five cases in the first two months, including three deaths. According to *The Times*, 'the surface water wells of the town are thought

Spalding Water Tower, a prominent feature in the town.

to be contaminated with sewage and many of the inhabitants are drinking rain water'. Day and Sunday schools in the Isle of Ely were closed – all the books in one school being burnt – and children's matinees in cinemas banned.

Dorothy Leigh Sayers (1893–1950)

Most people today think of Agatha Christie as the doyenne of detective stories, but in the 1930s Dorothy Sayers was an equally popular author. Dorothy was born in Oxford, where her father was choirmaster at Christ Church, but moved to the Fens at the age of 4 when he took over the living of Bluntisham-cum-Earith. As her biographer, Sir William Hutchison, wrote: 'Each year of her childhood from that time on, she saw the bleak fenland washes flooded to protect the pastures enclosed by the Fens' extensive system of dykes … Able to read by the age of four, she began devouring books from the rectory's library. The young Dorothy Sayers also wrote sketches and plays, which she performed to the delight of an indulgent household.' In her teens the family moved to another Fenland parish, Christchurch in Cambridgeshire.

Dorothy was educated at home until she was 16, when she went to the Godolphin school in Salisbury. She went to Somerville College in 1912, graduating in 1915 with a first-class degree in French. After trying teaching, she became a copywriter in an advertising agency: she created the Mustard Club scheme for Colman's Mustard and invented the slogan 'My Goodness, my Guinness!'

In the 1920s and '30s she rivalled Agatha Christie in writing best-selling thrillers, with two popular detectives Lord Peter Wimsey and Harriet Vane. One of the best, *The Nine Tailors*, published in 1934, has a Fenland setting:

> Mile after mile the flat road reeled behind them. Here a windmill, there a solitary farmhouse, there a row of poplars strung along the edge of a reed-grown dyke. Wheat, potatoes, beet, mustard and wheat again … A long village street with a grey and ancient church tower, a red-brick chapel, and the vicarage set in a little oasis of elm and horse-chestnut, and then once more dyke and windmill, wheat, mustard and grassland.

In the mid-1930s, Dorothy gave up writing detective novels. She turned to religious themes – a series of twelve plays on the life of Christ, *The Man Born to Be King*, which were broadcast to an enormous BBC radio audience in 1941. She also worked on translating the poetry of Dante.

Dorothy had an illegitimate son in 1924, and married Atherton Fleming in 1926: they lived at Witham, Essex, where he died in 1950. She died there on 18 December 1957. In 1998 an unfinished Peter Wimsey novel Dorothy had abandoned, *Thrones, Dominations*, as completed by Jill Paton Walsh, was published and was a best-seller.

The Second World War

In the Second World War, as in the First, the emphasis was very much on using every inch of Fenland to produce food: by 1940, 112,000 extra acres in the Fens were being cultivated. This had a lasting effect on the landscape, as noted by Christopher Taylor:

> [An] example of a minor technological improvement for specific purposes having wider social implications can be seen in the fenlands of eastern England. There, up to the last war, most roads were unsurfaced droveways, impossible for traffic for weeks at a time, which had to be regularly ploughed to remove the ruts. The result was the existence of a community that tended to be isolated from both the outside world and its near neighbours. During the war, however, when the pressures to improve the productivity of the fens were considerable and when, in a war economy, finance was unlimited, the War Agricultural Committees laid down hundreds of miles of concrete tracks along the droveways to improve access to the land. These tracks not only succeeded in their immediate purpose, but later on completely changed the life of the fenland people to a degree which is hard to appreciate now, only thirty years later.[119]

Before the war, the roads, being unpaved, were so muddy in winter as to be impassible at times. Winifred E. Long recalled how, when going for a walk as a child, she never used the road but always walked along the bank instead. This could have tragic consequences: the local baker was doing the same with his horse and cart one dark winter night when the horse slipped and fell into the river. The baker was unable to save his animal.[120]

The war involved upheaval for people of all nations, and Fenland was no exception. Even before the war, the Spanish Civil War had led to economic disaster, to which the people of the Fens responded: In February 1939, the 'Eastern Counties' food-ship sailed from Wisbech to Valencia, with tinned milk and meat, soap, groceries and sacks of potatoes for child victims. After the outbreak of the Second World War, many young evacuees came to Fenland. One was East London schoolboy Leslie Bently, who remembered: 'I attended Clenchwarton primary School – a two-room school house with gas lights, fire places and outside toilets that froze solid in winter.'

Evacuee children might disturb the local equilibrium, as Paul Mould, at school in Boston, recalled:

> We only had one evacuee in our class, Arthur Hollamby, and his brother Raymond was in my brother's class. By Christmas he was popular with the girls, because of his curly red hair, and with the boys, because of his prowess on the football field, so he received more than his share of cards. I came to know him quite well later in life. When he came home out of the forces, he brought back to Boston a beautiful wife, Inge, a German girl. They spent their early married years in a flat at the home of his best friend, Geoff Drummond, who lived for a time opposite our shop in High Street.[121]

Some Fenland children were themselves evacuees. One Wisbech couple, worried that the Germans might 'land on the marshes near our town' arranged for their daughter to join a group of child evacuees crossing the Atlantic, only to receive a phone call from Scotland early one morning: the ship had been torpedoed. The girl was picked up and taken back to Glasgow by a tanker: she came back to Wisbech, where she stayed for the rest of the war. [122]

As this story suggests, once again, there was a very real fear of invasion. In 1940, a Defence Area was created along the coast, covering Wisbech, March and Lynn: a motorcyclist who tried to rush a post was shot by the Home Guard. Pillboxes were erected as part of the defences, some still part of the Fenland landscape. Mike Osborne speaks of a line of pillboxes extending southwards through the Fens near the Lincolnshire/Cambridgeshire border, including an unusual version with two square-roofed chambers and a concrete platform between them for a machine gun: there is a good example at Holbeach. A smaller version had just one roofed chamber backed by the open platform: one can still be seen at Boston.[123]

There were relatively few air raids but many planes overhead. Local historian Trevor Bevis recalled:

> I remember well the town of March being rudely awakened in the small hours as the first droves of straining aircraft carried thousands of bombs to ill-fated Coventry. Half

an hour later the final waves of planes could be heard droning in a westerly direction. Three-quarters of an hour later the first wave of bombers had passed. March residents heard distant explosions, missiles raining upon Coventry, nearly 80 miles away. Most people left their beds and took to the streets to watch the western sky turn from blackness to glowing orange. Then, about 35 minutes later, the sound of racing aero engines filled the sky above March as the German planes sped home.[124]

The worst air raids in the region were naturally on the largest towns. King's Lynn suffered several times, a total of fifty-nine civilians being killed. About twenty airmen also died one night when the Duke's Head was hit when many men were celebrating the birthday of a colleague. The worst raid at Boston was 6 June 1941, in which seventeen people died, including Nancy Harris, aged 26, and her children Mary (7), William (4) and Sydney (3). There were other raids on Boston with one or two fatalities in 1942 and 1945. There a number of other air raids: one resident at Albany Road, Wisbech, was killed when a bomb was dropped by a lone raider on 11 November 1940 (Armistice Day!). Six people were killed at Spalding in May 1941, and Clara Billings died in another raid there in May 1942. Bicker, 9 miles from Boston, had a fortunate escape, now recorded in the church: twelve high-explosive bombs fell on the village but none of them exploded.

Because of the expectation of massive air raids, the blackout was introduced almost as soon as war broke out. In October 1939, a 19-year-old girl was sent to prison for a month by Wisbech magistrates for flashing a torch – this caused a local outcry, as people were normally simply fined for this offence, but she had apparently been 'defiant' when apprehended.

There were many planes flying the other way as well. Lincolnshire was known as 'bomber county' because of the number of bomber stations, but most were not in the Fens: bomber stations on the fringes of the Fens included Spilsby, East Kirkby and Coningsby. 'It was not uncommon to see the sky over Lincolnshire filled with Lancasters en route to form part of the 1,000 bomber sorties over Germany.' Training took place at Folkingham and Sutton Bridge, with ground stations at Holbeach range and Wainfleet range (both still open in 2000), and at Leverton.[125]

In 1943, men of the Royal Air Force were flying Lancaster bombers from Witchford (Ely), Scampton and Waterbeach. Fighters were flown from Snailwell, and a Pathfinder Force (to drop indicator bombs preliminary to air raids) operated from Warboys. On the weekend of 18 September 1944, during the airborne invasion of the Netherlands, Bevis recalled 'a massive air armada swept across the sky and filled it from horizon to horizon'. Holbeach Bank airman Kenneth Barnett died with six other crew members during a bombing raid over France on 1 July 1944, one of many Fenland heroes to make the ultimate sacrifice: his name was only added to the official memorial at Holbeach St Mark in 2004.

Sutton Bridge saw many Polish airmen train during the early years of the war. They were men who had managed to escape after Germany and Russia invaded Poland in September 1939. They came to Britain, which they referred to as 'Last Hope Island', to continue the struggle against Nazi Germany: the training course lasted between three and six weeks. Jeffrey Quill recalled two of them named Franciszek Gruszka and Wladyslaw Szulkowski: 'while we were having tea in the Mess at Sutton Bridge I had the chance to ask the two Poles about their escapes from their country, but their English was limited and they were obviously confused by the trauma of their recent lives, culminating in being trained to fly Spitfires in a foreign land and in a foreign tongue and then pitched into the strange environment of a Royal Air Force squadron. I wondered how they would ever understand anything over the R/T ... They spent hours poring over an English dictionary.' The Poles played a vital role in the Battle of Britain and many were killed, including Gruszka, killed in action on 18 August 1940. Szulkowski also died in action, on 27 March 1941. The all-Polish 303 Squadron undertook gunnery practice at Sutton Bridge firing range at the end of August 1940.[126]

Inevitably, there were several disasters. E.P. Brand recalled:

I remember three crashes, one plane loaded with bombs crashed on take-off from Wyton. The explosion was heard in Warboys where several people had their windows broken. Another plane crashed down on Dorrington's Farm at Wistow fen, while a third, flying low, hit the Warboys Knothole at the Warboys brick works, dropping bombs near the station ... As the plane was coming over the Fens from the East and flying low owing to engine trouble it went straight into a bank of clay ... I shall never forget the one at Dorrington's Farm, to which the Police Specials were called. We tried to save the lives of some of the crew, but the heat was terrific. We managed to get two out, but it was too late. It was an awful sight as their bodies were sizzling like a piece of bacon in a frying pan. This was one of the most awful jobs I have ever had to do in my life.[127]

The nature of the war meant that it was not necessary to serve abroad to be a hero – or to be a man. John Longbottom of the Home Guard died at Kirton Fen 23 September 1942; female deaths in the war include two buried in Spalding Cemetery – Florence Bowman, 21, who was in the WAAF, and Barbara Cannon, 19, who served in the ATS.

Three centuries earlier, Dutch prisoners of war had worked in the Fens: in the 1940s, it was the turn of the Germans and Italians. German camps included those at Moorby near Revesby; Fulney Park Camp, Spalding; and Sutton Bridge. Italian prisoners of war arrived after being captured in North Africa: 500 were sent to Ely, most set to work on local farms, often being moved from camp to land army hostels so they could be closer to their place of work. By 1943, as well as the Italian camp at Barton Field, Ely, there were others at, for example, Lakenheath, Feltwell Fen and Sawtry. Randell recalled:

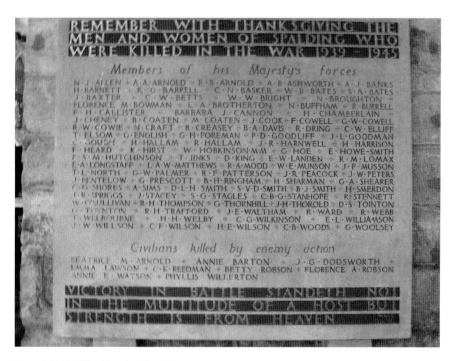

Memorial in Spalding Church to the soldiers and civilians killed in the Second World War.

A number of Italian prisoners of war were sent to work on farms round Waldersee or on the railway and for some time I had two of them helping me; they were good workers and we got on well together. They used to cook their macaroni on the stove in the hut, mixing it with olive oil, onions, lettuce, sage or apples. One day, after a heavy thunderstorm, they collected from the grass enough snails to fill a gallon tin, these they washed well, cooked, picked out from the shells, and then stewed with macaroni, oil, onions and sage. I must admit they smelt good, but though I was offered some I could not bring myself to eat them, although my mate had some and said they were delicious.[128]

Cyril Marsters recalled that:

Most of the [Italian] prisoners were smokers and, as cigarettes and tobacco were strictly rationed in their camp, they were always on the lookout for chances to obtain more. Some of the men, who had obviously been given access to a supply of osiers, made wicker baskets in their spare time. They would bring along samples of various shapes and sizes to try to obtain orders from the locals. Whether or not they were allowed to actually sell their baskets I'm not sure. In practice they would arrange to barter them for supplies of cigarettes and tobacco. It was in this way that I acquired a very useful bicycle basket for the front of my bike, by obtaining a packet of cigarettes in exchange for the basket.

One of the Italians – Berti Baldisserra – gave young Cyril an Italian prayer book.[129]

Rationing is perhaps the aspect of the war most remembered, especially sweets:

The shortage that affected children the most was, of course, sweets. The weekly ration was just 2oz, a small bar of chocolate or a bag of sweets ... The children from Staniland School supplemented their rations by buying liquorice wood from Dickinson's shop. I do not know where it came from but I never knew anyone else to sell it and today anyone would be considered mad to ever put it in their mouths but in the prevailing conditions we were only too pleased to put a handful in our pockets; no need for a bag. It looked like twigs off a tree but, when you started chewing, it turned yellow and tasted of liquorice. Small boys were walking down the street resembling the old fishermen, chewing on their Pigtail twist.[130]

There were occasional treats: in spring, the Ministry of Food announced:

> Fresh supplies of oranges will be available in the shops in Cambridge and district, including Newmarket, Ely, St Ives and part of Huntingdon, as from Monday next, April 6th, and will be reserved for a period of five days for issue at the rate of 1lb per head to children in possession of a green ration book ... After the five days, any surplus will be sold to other customers, but retailers are asked to give priority to children, schools, hospitals and invalids.

There were summer fruit-picking camps, from July to September, to gather the crops, including camps at Emneth, Terrington St John and Upwell.

Another aspect of the war remembered by many was recycling, as it is called today, then known as 'scavenging' – the organised collections of waste food such as potato peel, and of metals and waste paper. In Wisbech in 1940:

> The WVS appealed to the housewives to hand over their aluminium pans, and the aluminium rolled in. A lot of it was serviceable and virtually irreplaceable, perhaps for years. The whole was organised on the Market Place and, apart from the aluminium collection, there was an appeal for iron and waste paper. Started off by a cannon from the grammar school, relic of 1914–18, everything thing imaginable came. There were old swords and huge iron wheels, and one man rode a bicycle up to the heap and threw it on.

The Soham Disaster of 2 June 1944

On 2 June 1944, Ben Gimbert, an engine driver from March, was driving an ammunition train of about fifty trucks with unfused bombs through Soham. With him in the cab was his mate, Jim Nightall of Littleport. Gimbert suddenly saw a bright flame coming from the first truck. He knew that if the train blew up, thousands of people in Soham would be killed. As the wagon was immediately behind the engine, he was able to jump down and uncouple the rest of the train and get the truck into a cutting, where the effect of any explosion would be lessened. Gimbert called the Soham signalman, Frank 'Sailor' Bridges of Soham, in the nearby signal box, to stop the mail train, which was due to pass shortly. Almost immediately the bombs in the first truck exploded. The whole town rocked, and people sleeping as far away as Bury St Edmunds were awakened. A huge crater was made in the middle of the track into which the locomotive fell. A gasometer burst into flames and the buildings of Soham station disappeared. The Station Hotel, together with many roofs, windows and other parts of buildings in the town were blown away. Some 550 shops and houses were damaged. Rest centres were opened and 1,000 emergency meals served to the homeless. Bridges and Nightall were killed in the explosion, Gimbert badly injured: thirty-five people in the town were also hurt. American army bulldozers demolished the remains of the station-master's house, then with the track repaired, trains ran again the same evening; but it was nearly a week before Soham had its gas supply restored. It could have been so much worse: the actions of these three Fens heroes had saved many hundreds of lives.

Fenland Since the War

The Floods of 1947 and 1953

In March 1947, there was a crisis, caused by the thaw of a heavy fall of snow. The Barrier Bank between Over and Earith gave way on 17 March, followed by other breaches elsewhere. Two barges were swept away when the bank broke at Little Thetford, almost opposite the Fish and Duck Inn: more than 2,000 acres in Thetford and Stretham Fens were flooded. At Prickwillow, local men were helped by German prisoners, still held in camps although the war had ended two years before, and British troops in a successful attempt to prevent a breach. On the following day, the waters of the Ouse were pouring through the 50-yard gap at Over, into Over Fen and eventually into Hillrow Fen: 'Steadily and inexorably the flood advanced and by dusk much of what, in the morning, had been fertile fen, was a mass of grey water gleaming dully in the fading light. Houses, bungalows, farm buildings and stacks stood marooned and desolate.' On 22 March, a culvert gave way at Southery and within a few minutes, the water was tearing through a 30-yard chasm into Feltwell Fen.

On 24 March the first important step in saving the situation was taken. The gap at Over was closed in an army operation using amphibious track vehicles known as Neptunes: this enabled work to begin on repairing the bank. It was followed by the pumping of vast quantities of water from the various fens. A total of 37,000 acres were flooded in the South Level and the chief engineer of the Catchment Board said it was the greatest flood in living memory, and that it may well have been the greatest flood since the Fens were first drained. A

contemporary booklet drew an interesting parallel with a hero of an earlier millennium: 'The Fen folk, dour and undemonstrative, yet full of vigour and brave enterprise, will see to it that what vital food can be grown, will be grown this year on their re-claimed acres.' John Kisby recalled: 'We all worked desperately from dawn to dusk and the bank held. But we woke wearily in the morning to find that the bank had gone near the Fish & Duck. I believe some barges even got washed through the breach. All land from the Fish & Duck to Braham Dock was under water, and the railway embankment was washed away at one point leaving the rails suspended.' The spirit shown by these Fenmen in 1947 was compared with the heroism when, led by Hereward the Wake, their ancestors so heroically resisted the foreign invaders.'[131]

Many people will have seen films of forest fires and the animals desperately trying to escape. This happened in the Fens as well – when the bank burst at Over, vermin fled the oncoming waters and took refuge on the South Level Barrier bank beside the New Bedford River. They burrowed in, forming a network of holes that threatened to destroy the bank.[132]

In most floods, once the water has gone, it is simply question of drying everything out, but in the Fens flooding can have a drastic effect on the houses themselves, as Wentworth Day explained: 'A few days later many of the fen cottages, built on the soft and spongy soil, cracked and collapsed. Their roofs fell off, walls fell apart, and cottage furniture, representing the life work of many a humble family, was thrown into the flood.'[133]

The flood led to more powerful pumping engines, and to a revision and expansion of the Macdonald scheme. Before anything happened, there was another flood: a storm surge on the North Sea coast on 31 January 1953 led to the loss of many lives from Lincolnshire to Essex. In Boston, the river rose more than 6ft above the predicted level: the lower parts of the town were flooded to a depth of several feet. Fifteen people were drowned in King's Lynn.

South of the Wash, the Roman Bank once more fulfilled its vital role of keeping the sea out of the low-lying land behind it. However, more than 6,000 acres were flooded between Lynn and Denver when water spilled over the river embankments: the false rumour spread that the Denver Sluice had burst. One of the most serious breaches was at Magdalen. Thousands of acres were flooded at Watlington, Stow, Magdalen, Salters Lode and St Germans, and the area became the focus of a desperate effort to plug the breach. At Magdalen sandbags were filled on the spot and loaded into barges and a Dunkirk-style flotilla of little boats, to be taken out to the gap. There was exactly a fortnight before the next high tides

Sluice, Salter's Lode.

were due. In that time the breach had to be filled: civilian labour, national service-men and Cambridge students all played a vital part. The bank held.

These crises led to drastic solutions, in three stages:

1. A relief channel running beside the Ouse from Denver to near Lynn, 11 miles in length, was completed in 1959: admission of water from the Ouse into the new channel is controlled by the A.G. Wright sluice opened in the same year.
2. The channel of the Ouse between Denver Sluice and its junction with the River Cam, a distance of 18 miles, was completed in 1961; flood banks were also set back on a number of stretches of the river.
3. A cut-off channel 27½ miles long was dug from near Mildenhall to Denver. The channel intercepts the waters of the Lark, the Little Ouse and the Wissey, and conveys them, when necessary, into the relief channel and so on to the Wash: the work was completed in September 1964.

However, that was not the end. South-east England was crying out for water while there was an excess of it in Fenland. The solution: transfer water from the Fens to Essex. The work was done under the Ely Ouse–Essex Water Act of 1968, and was finished by April 1972. Water from the Ely Ouse can be turned

Outfall sluice, Long Sutton.

into the cut-off channel, flow to Blackdyke near Hockwold, and ultimately to reservoirs at Abberton and Hanningfield near Colchester and Chelmsford respectively, the latter about 90 miles from Denver Sluice. At last, the waters have been conquered, and schemes proposed by Vermuyden four centuries earlier have been put into full fruition. As Darby wrote, 'the nineteenth century had hoped to see "the destroyer by itself destroyed". The twentieth century now saw the destroyer tamed and made to serve a useful purpose.'[134]

Another new work was the bypass channel at Spalding, taking water from the River Welland around the town: opened in 1953, it is called the Coronation Channel. No boats are allowed on it apart from water taxis between Spalding town centre and Springfields shopping centre, so that it is become a haven for wildlife.

Floods became much rarer, but the forces of nature can never be completely tamed. There was further flooding in 1976, especially in Lynn. In December 2013, there were severe floods in Wisbech and Boston: in the latter town about 300 homes were under water and St Botolph's Church was flooded, causing £1 million worth of damage. The cause was a tidal surge, said to be the worst

Coronation Channel, Spalding, with water taxi.

since 1953. At Friskney, 500 acres of land were flooded, and 25 acres had to be given up, reverting from arable land to tidal marshes.

There had already been plans to build a flood barrier in Boston, a site near the Black Sluice pumping station being chosen so as not to interfere with shipping further downstream. It is to be completed by December 2019.

As elsewhere in Britain, the railway system shrank in the post-war period. The passenger service through Holbeach came to an end in 1959, and freight services stopped in 1965: the lines over Crosskeys Bridge were taken up and afterwards the bridge was used by road transport only. Within a decade, almost all the railway lines in Lincolnshire had gone, leaving trains running only from Sleaford to Boston and on to Skegness, and between Sleaford, Spalding and Peterborough. Even on these lines, most of the small stations were closed.

The presence of air bases led inevitably to some tragic accidents, including two major incidents in the 1970s. On 28 August 1976, an American military plane exploded in flames over Thorney during a thunderstorm, killing all eighteen crew and passengers, including one female member of the American armed forces. There were several witnesses, who reported that the plane was already in pieces as it hit the ground. David Taylor said at the time, 'My little nephew came running in and said that there were flames in the sky.' A memorial was erected on the site at Thorney Dyke, renewed in 2011. On 21 September 1979,

two Harrier jets from Wittering, apparently engaged in a mock dogfight, collided over Wisbech. One fell into a field, but the other crashed on the town leaving a crater in Ramnoth Road 50ft deep and 15ft wide. Three people in one house were killed instantly – William Trumpess (a former mayor of Wisbech), Robert Bowers (40) and his 2½-year-old son Jonathan. In the house next door, Jenny Shepherd and her 7-month-old daughter, Laura, had a lucky escape – Laura had to be pulled out of the rubble by a neighbour, Barbara Hurst.

Fenland was clearly an area with plenty of wind, as the windmills and pumps of previous ages demonstrated. Wind turbines of various sizes have been erected across the area. Large-scale energy development has also been introduced: the Sutton Bridge Power Station, powered by natural gas, was built in 1999. It cost £337 million to build and was said to supply 2 per cent of the electricity used in England and Wales.

As people's leisure time has increased, so has the demand for entertainment of all kinds. Fenland has a part, if not a large one, in the history of rock music. Keith Richards, writing in 2010, remembered his experiences playing with the Rolling Stones in Wisbech almost half a century before:

We were city boys, and this music is what's happening in the city. But you try playing Wisbech, in 1963, with Mick Jagger. You got a totally different reaction. All

Harvesting the wind.

of these hayseeds literally chewing on straw. The Wisbech Corn Exchange, out in the goddamn marshes. And a riot was started because the local yokels, the boys, couldn't stand the fact that all of their chicks were gawping and blowing themselves out about this bunch of fags, as far as they were concerned, from London. 'Eee by gum'. That was a very good riot, which we were lucky to escape from.

Richards' memory may not be perfect: one cannot imagine any Fenlander saying 'eee by gum'. In fact, just four years later, Fenland was leading the rock world with the Spalding Rock Festival held in a cow shed in August 1967. Featuring Jimi Hendrix, Pink Floyd, and Cream it was the first of its kind in Fenland, and the immediate ancestor of the great hippie festivals of Woodstock and the Isle of Wight! Pink Floyd were almost local to the Fens as they came from Cambridge, and have left an important permanent memento: the cover of their album *The Division Bell* features two giant 'Easter Island type' heads in a very flat field with dark Fenland soil – and with Ely Cathedral clearly visible in the distance. The photograph was created in a field in Stretham.

Fenland produced sporting heroes too, most notably Dave 'Boy' Green and Michael Lee. Green was born at Chatteris on 2 June 1953, and went to Cromwell School. He took up boxing in 1967, joining the Chatteris Amateur Boxing Club, where his trainer was Arthur Binder, who had taught Eric Boon, another famous local boxer. Green turned professional in 1974, won the British light-welterweight championship in 1976 and the European title in the same year. Green fought twice for the WBC world welterweight crown. On 14 June 1977, he fought Carlos Palomino at Wembley, losing to a knock-out from Palomino's left hook in the eleventh round, the first time that Green had ever been floored as a professional. On 31 March 1980 he tried again, fighting Sugar Ray Leonard in Maryland: he lost by a knock-out in the fourth round. His final bout was in November 1981, after which he retired at the age of 28. He later became chairman of Renoak Limited, a packaging company in Chatteris.

Michael Lee was born in Cambridge on 11 December 1958. He began his professional speedway career with Boston in 1975, moving to King's Lynn the following year. He was British champion in 1977 and 1978, and reached the pinnacle of his career in 1980 when he won the world speedway championship in Gothenburg: he won the world long track championship in the following year.

In 1983 he moved from King's Lynn to Poole. In 1984 he was banned for five years for allegedly dangerous riding, although the three other riders involved gave evidence that he had caused no danger. The sentence was later reduced to a year. After serving his ban, Lee returned to Lynn for two years but quit the sport after being fined for failing to show up to a match. He made a short comeback with Lynn in 1991, and in 2007 was convicted of growing cannabis for his own use. At the peak of their careers between 1970 and 1980 these two Fenland heroes were involved in some of British sports most exciting moments.

The region also produced a poet and a novelist of national importance. Elizabeth Jennings was born in Boston in 1926: she became a librarian and later a freelance writer. She is associated with the Movement, a loose grouping of poets determined to re-establish the value of skilled craftsmanship in poetry, but distinguished by her Roman Catholic faith. Her two collections *Recoveries* and *The Mind Has Mountains*, dealing with mental health issues, were very popular in the 1960s. To many people, the Fens are best described in literature by Graham Swift's *Waterland*, published in 1983 and made into a successful film: he describes Fenland as a 'landscape, which of all landscapes, most approximated to Nothing'.

With the growth of television and later forms of home entertainment, the cinema declined in Fenland, as elsewhere. The larger towns such as Boston, Lynn and Spalding had a cinema before the First World War. The 1930s were the boom years: Boston and Lynn had several picture houses, and even smaller towns including Holbeach and Long Sutton could boast a cinema. The second half of the century saw most of them disappear.

People were no longer satisfied with local village events. Alice Coe of Isleham thought this process had begun even before the Second World War: 'The radio put an end to lots of things that used to go on in the village. That and the war. The roads were built in the war – the Ely road and the Ruttersham road, and the Measham road across the fen there. They were all built, and we could get out then. And after the war, people moved in and got cars, so our own entertainments all died. That were a shame.' Given the lack of good public transport, Fenland today is very much a car-based society. The old and the young can very easily feel isolated, as 13-year-old Debbie Chilvers of Isleham noted in the 1970s: 'It's so boring in the village. There's nothing to do for people of my age. I wish there was a Disco on, about every month, like there is at Measham. But it's harder for the people of this village to get to Measham, because there's no buses or nothing.'[135]

The 1960s and '70s saw attempts at rationalisation of borders by Whitehall planners, perhaps only adding to confusion as to the county boundaries. In

1965, the counties of Ely and Cambridgeshire were merged to form the single county of Cambridgeshire and the Isle of Ely: the rural district of Thorney became part of a new county of Huntingdon and Peterborough. However, in 1974, Ely, Cambridgeshire, Huntingdon and Peterborough were merged into a single county – called Cambridgeshire! Just twenty-five years later, in 1998, the city of Peterborough was taken out of this county, becoming a unitary authority.

Reclamations were made at Holbeach and Moulton west of Holbeach air firing range in 1949–50 and 1956, and long, narrow strips of salt marsh have been reclaimed at Friskney and Wainfleet, most recently in 1976–78. The most dramatic plan in this area was for a straight 15-mile-long 'Wash Speedway' between high and low water marks from Gibraltar Point to Clay Hole at the mouth of the Witham. The race track would be 200 yards wide, with a grandstand 4 miles long and parking for 50,000 cars. It would also protect 10,277 acres of foreshore. Despite the support of Sir Alan Cobham and Sir Malcolm Campbell the scheme came to nothing.[136]

In 1965 the Binnie Report proposed a barrage to cut off about half of the area of the Wash and incorporate high-level freshwater reservoirs.

The name 'Fen Tiger' was used with pride in the later twentieth century, with reference to any sporting team or individual from the Fens – footballers, speedway riders and boxers. It was also used as the nickname for a giant cat said to be found in Fenland, similar to many similar sightings in the wilder parts of Britain. Sightings of the creature include those at Cottenham in 1982 and again in 1994, where it was filmed by William Rooker. It was seen at Manea in 2008, in which year also the footprints of a giant cat-like creature were seen at Chatteris. The animal (if it/they exist at all) is clearly not a tiger, despite the nickname, but something more like an ocelot.

Climate change has a direct effect on a landscape as fragile as Fenland: there is an increased risk of inundation by either fresh or salt water. The Middle Level Commissioners are currently building Europe's second-largest pump to enable the Fens to be kept as it is. Now around 400 miles of rivers and artificial waterways controlled by pumps maintain the fine line between flooding and fertility keeping the Fens in their current state of first-class agricultural land. It may all be too late: as Francis Pryor concluded, 'Before the end of the present century large areas of the Fens will have to be abandoned to the sea. And that's an end to the matter.'[137]

However, the attempt *is* being made. The National Trust site of Wicken Fen near Ely is an attempt to preserve the old Fenland, and today provides a habitat

for fen plants, birds and insects, attracting marsh harriers and reed warblers, and large numbers of people with binoculars. The sedge that is grown here is again harvested and sold for thatching. In October 2001, the National Trust acquired Burwell Fen Farm, adding a further 415 acres to the Wicken Fen reserve: this cost £1.7 million, the bulk provided by a grant of £933,500 from the Heritage Lottery Fund. It is hoped in the long term to increase the reserve to 10,000 acres providing a 'green lung' out of Cambridge – and an alternative habitat if rises in sea level swamp the nature reserves along the North Sea Coast. The RSPB also have several reserves in the Fens, at Lakenheath – where the crane is being reintroduced after an absence of four centuries – at Needingworth Quarry and (in partnership with other bodies) at the Nene Washes. The Lincolnshire Wildlife Trust owns 45 hectares at Baston and Thurlby Fens, the last remaining area of peat in south Lincolnshire. In the extreme north of the Fens, wetland is being restored along 15km of the River Witham.

The only surviving windpump of the many hundreds that once existed is that at Wicken Fen. This originally stood in Norman's Dyke and served the turf diggings on Adventurers Fen. It was erected in 1908 by Hunt of Soham as an iron-framed mill, and was clad in weatherboarding in 1910. It has a 13ft diameter scoop wheel. It was operated until 1938. 'In 1955 it was decided to move the mill about a mile away to the National Trust nature reserve at Wicken Fen where it could be used to raise the water level in the sedge fen, a reversal of its previous drainage role. With considerable ingenuity and care the original iron frame was dismantled and re-erected at the new site, but the woodwork was completely replaced. New sails were fitted and the renovation of the mill was completed in September 1956.'[138]

Another exciting conservation project is the Great Fen project, which aims to create a 3,700-hectare wetland between Peterborough and Huntingdon to safeguard two National Nature Reserves, Holme Fen and Woodwalton Fen: the latter currently helps protect surrounding farmland by storing occasional flood water, and showing that agriculture and conservation *can* work to the mutual benefit of both. The project represents a partnership between English Nature, Wildlife Trust for Cambridgeshire, Huntingdonshire District Council and the Environment Agency. The project began in 2001, a collaboration of five partners addressing conservation problems. Some people see it as a reversal of the efforts of drainers.

Such conservation efforts bring in tourists, also attracted by the area's unique beauty. As Professor David Bellamy, Honorary President of Fens Tourism, puts it: 'How can you not be instantly drawn to the breathtaking views? This is the

Peckover House.

land of sunsets and sunrises, and when the odd storm does decide to rear its ugly head, take a look at the colours it creates – simply natural and beautiful.'

With such enormous skies, Fenland is inevitably a paradise for UFO spotters. They were many sightings in 2008, for example. In February, Graham Chapman of Walpole Highway saw lights over several nights: 'From the ground all you could see was a pulsating light … when I looked at the light with my binoculars I could see a red and blue flashing light.' Reg Wenn commented that he had seen a group of strange lights over his Chatteris home for fifteen years: 'It has alternating orange, green and red lights at the bottom and bright lights above, like a cluster of stars.' There were many reports of strange lights over the Fens in November and December, witnesses contacting the *Fenland Citizen* from Wisbech, March, Wimblington and Chatteris.

Tourists are brought in by nostalgia, and this is an increasing industry in Fenland. Peckover House in Wisbech is one of the most popular National Trust properties in the area. Ayscoughfee Hall in Spalding is a major museum,

and Fydell House in Boston, built in 1702 and the property of the Boston Preservation Trust since 1935, is well worth a visit if it is open: the gardens are a delight. These are properties formerly owned by the wealthy, but daily life in Fenland is not neglected with several windmills and steam pumping stations open to the public. The Chain Bridge Forge in Spalding opened in 2012 as a 'living museum' celebrating the skills of the blacksmith, while the Bubblecar Museum at Langrick near Boston celebrates 1950s and '60s nostalgia well beyond the bubblecar itself.

The waterways, once key elements in the transport system of the Fens, are being successfully developed for leisure traffic, as anyone looking out of the train window at Ely can see. It is intended to develop a Fen Waterways Link, designed to connect Lincoln through Boston and Spalding to Peterborough and to Ely and Cambridge. The Link, which began with the opening of Boston Lock in 2009, will open up 145 miles of existing waterway and create 50 miles of new: it is the largest water enhancement plan in Europe. There is no better way to appreciate Fenland than by boat.

Above all, it is the landscape of the Fens that appeals. Fenland's residents already know its unique qualities: they are attracting the incomer in increasing numbers. Long may it continue. And always there are those skies:

They have a beauty of their own, these great fens, even now, when they are dyked and drained, tilled and fenced – a beauty as of the sea, of boundless expanse and freedom ... Overhead the arch of heaven spread[s] more ample than elsewhere, as over the open sea; and that vastness ... gives such cloudlands, such sunrises, such sunsets, as can be seen nowhere else within these isles.[139]

NOTES

1 Anonymous ballad.
2 H.V. Morton, *The Land of the Vikings* (1928), p.76.
3 *Eastern Daily Press*, 26 September 2012.
4 Francis Pryor, *Flag Fen: Life and Death of a Prehistoric Landscape (2005)*, p.147.
5 Helen Clarke, *East Anglia* (1971), pp.68–69.
6 Oliver Rackham, *The History of the Countryside* (1986), p.383.
7 Tim Malim, *Stonea and the Roman Fens* (2005), pp.103–107.
8 Malim, *op. cit.*, p.131.
9 *The Times*, 21 November 1861.
10 Malim, *op, cit.*, pp.142–149.
11 Malim, *op. cit.*, p.173.
12 Peter Hunter Blair, *Roman Britain and Early England* (1966 edition), pp.120–121.
13 Hunter Blair, *op. cit.*, pp.182–183.
14 Margaret Gelling, *Place-Names in the Landscape* (1984), p.126.
15 Gelling, *op. cit.*, p.24.
16 Morton *op. cit.,* p.76.
17 Michael Drayton, *Polyolbion*, 1622.
18 C.E. Hennels, 'With the Fenland catchers', *East Anglian Magazine*, vol. 17 (1957–58), p.477.
19 TNA, Assize Roll 529. Lincs, cited in H.C. Darby, *The Medieval Fenland* (1940), p.20.
20 Frank Meeres, *Not of this World; Norfolk's Monastic Houses* (2001), p.86.
21 Michael Drayton, 'Lincolnshire's Holland speaks of her waterfowl'.
22 Francis Willoughby, *Ornithology*, originally published in 1676.
23 J. Wentworth Day, *A History of the Fens* (1954), p.93.
24 Charles Lucas, *The Fenman's World* (1930) p.52.
25 Simon Pawley, 'Maritime Trade and Fishing in the Middle Ages', in Stewart and Nicholas Bennett, editors, *A Historical Atlas of Lincolnshire* (1993), p.56.
26 Charles Lucas, *The Fenman's World* (1930), pp.23–24.
27 J.R. Ravensdale, *Liable to Floods* (1974), *passim.*
28 W. Martin Lane, 'The last of the Fen Peat Diggers', *East Anglian Magazine* October 1961, pp.683–686.
29 Mary Chamberlain, *Fenwomen* (first published 1975, Full Circle edition undated), p.41.

30 George Crabbe, 'East Anglian Fen'.

31 Nikolaus Pevsner and John Harris, *Lincolnshire* (1989), p.22, Simon Jenkins, *England's Thousand Best Churches* (2000 edition) *passim.*

32 Rodney W. Ambler, 'Markets and Fairs, 1086–1792', in Stewart and Nicholas Bennett, editors, *op. cit.* p.54; Frank Meeres, *The Story of Norwich* (2011), p.43.

33 M.T. Clanchy, *From Memory to Written Record* (1993 edition), pp.101–102,158, 320.

34 Richard Holt, *The Mills of Medieval England* (1988) *passim.*

35 William A Hinnebusch, *The Early English Friars Preachers* (1951), p.195.

36 Clanchy, *op. cit.*, pp.181-2.

37 Alec Clifton-Taylor, *The Cathedrals of England* (1967), p.180.

38 John Harvey, *The English Cathedral* (1956 edition), pp.116–117.

39 H.E. Hallam, *Settlement and Society* (1965), pp 221–222.

40 E.D. Jones, 'Summary execution at Spalding Priory 1250–1500', *Journal of Legal History*, vol. 16, no. 2 (1995), pp.189–198.

41 John Dyer.

42 *Drayning of Fennes*, 1629, spelling modernised: hars are mists.

43 Mrs Alfred Berlin, *Sunrise-land* (1894), p.250.

44 Joan Thirsk, *The Rural Economy of England* (1984), pp.140–141).

45 Christopher Taylor, 'Post-medieval drainage of marsh and fens', in Hadrian Cook and Tom Williamson, editors, *Water Management in the English Landscape* (1999), p.147).

46 Joan Thirsk, *op. cit.*, p.141.

47 Eric Kerridge, *The Agricultural Revolution* (1967) pp.230–231, I have modernised the spelling.

48 R.L. Hills, *Machines, Mills and Uncountable Costly Necessities*, (1967) pp.9–11, citing Dodson (1665).

49 B.A. Holderness, *The Agrarian History of England and Wales* vol. VI (1984), pp.204–205.

50 Cobbett quoted in F.V. Morley, *Travels in East Anglia* (1923) p.215; Mrs Alfred Berlin, *Sunrise-land* (1894) pp.249–250.

51 E.A. Labrum, *Civil Engineering Heritage – Eastern and Central England* (1994), pp.89–91.

52 John Clare.

53 Hills *op. cit.*, p.204.

54 Christopher Taylor, *Village and Farmstead* (1984 edition), p.207.

55 Eric Kerridge, *The Agricultural Revolution* (1967), p.237.

56 *Lincolnshire Chronicle*, 1887.

57 Kerridge, *op. cit.*, pp.234–235.

58 *Calendar of Mariners Apprenticeships enrolled at King's Lynn 1740–61* (typescript). There is a copy of this at the Norfolk Record Office.

59 Gregorio Leti, *Teatro Britannico* i, 316–317 (1683).

60   E. Carus-Wilson, 'The medieval trade of the ports of the Wash' in *Medieval Archaeology* 6–7, p.189; R.W.K. Hilton, *The Eastland Trade and the Common Weal in the Seventeenth Century*, p.10.

61   Alan Metters, *The Lynn Port Books 1610–1614,* Norfolk Record Society vol. 73 (2009), *passim.*

62   Jean Ingelow, 'The High Tide on the coast of Lincolnshire (1571)'.

63   Norfolk Record Office (hereafter NRO), WLP 17/4/89.

64   Labrum, *op. cit.* p.65; *Lincolnshire History and Archaeology* vol. 43 (2008), p.80.

65   R.C. Wheeler, 'Sir Joseph Banks and the draining of the East, West and Wildmore Fens', in *Lincolnshire History and Archaeology* vol. 42, (2007), p.12.

66   Philip Larkin, 'The Whitsun Weddings'.

67   J.A. Clarke, *Fenland Sketches* (1852), p.251.

68   Peter Charnley, *Old Dykes I Have Known* (undated), p.73.

69   Labrum, *op. cit.,* pp.85–6.

70   *Fenland Notes and Queries* 1893; NRO, BL C 52/1/28.

71   Charnley, *op. cit.*, p.60.

72   NRO, WLP 17/4/89.

73   Neil Wright, *Spalding an Industrial History* (1973) p.29; idem *Lincolnshire Towns and Industry 1700–1914* (1982), p.52.

74   NRO, MC 257/59/19.

75   Jonathan Bate, *John Clare, A Biography* (2004 edition), p.68.

76   Jean Ingelow, *op. cit.*

77   Frances Cornford, 'Cambridgeshire'.

78   NRO, C/S3/43.

79   C.S. Orwin and E.H. Whetham, *History of British Agriculture 1846–1914* (1971 edition), p.353.

80   For a summary of population changes in Lincolnshire, with excellent maps, see Bennett and Bennett, editors, *op. cit.*, pp.86–89.

81   Arthur Randell, *Sixty Years a Fenman* (1966), pp.6–7.

82   Norman Wymer, *Wheatsheaf and Willow*, 1949, p.97.

83   NRO, FX 357/1.

84   D.I. Gordon, *A Regional History of the Railways of Great Britain – the Eastern Counties* (1977 edition), p.222.

85   Labrum, *op. cit.*, pp.86–87.

86   Charnley, *op. cit.*, p.69.

87   Elizabeth Jennings, 'A Class-Room'.

88   William A. Dutt, *Highways and Byways in East Anglia* (1904), pp.299–300.

89   A.K. Astbury, *The Black Fens* 1957, p.43.

90   W. Wells, 'The Drainage of Whittlesea Mere', *Journ. R. Agric. Soc.* (1st Ser.), xxi (1860), p.134 et seq.

91   Dutt, *op. cit.*, pp.300–301.

92   Alan Bloom, *The Skaters of the Fens* (1958), *passim.*

93   Randell, *op. cit.*, p.8.

94   J. Wentworth Day, *op. cit.*, p.91.

95   Sylvia Plath, 'Winter landscape, with rocks'.

96   Tom Williamson and Susanna Wade-Martins, *The Countryside of East Anglia: Changing Landscapes 1870–1950* (2008), pp.108–110.

97   *Daily Mail*, 28 August 1912.

98   Williamson *ibid.*, p.56.

99   *Within Living Memory*, p.137.

100 T.M. and M.C. Hughes, *Geography of Cambridgeshire* (1909) *passim*; John R. Dawbarn, in *East Anglian Magazine*, 11, 1952, p.386; Neil Wright 'Site of woad mill in Tattershall Road Boston' in *Lincolnshire History and Archaeology* 39, 2004, pp.5–9.

101 R.C. Dobbs, *Bulbs in Britain, a Century of Growing* (1983), p.3.

102 E.P. Brand, *A Fenman Remembers* (1977), *passim*.

103 Sybil Marshall, *Fenland Chronicle* (1967), pp.172–173; Winifred E. Long, 'The Changing Face of Fenland' in *East Anglian Magazine*, 11, 1952, pp.600–603.

104 Arthur Randell, *Fenland Railwayman* 1968, pp.6–8.

105 Short pp.219-2; Mary Chamberlain, *Fenwomen: a Portrait of a Woman in an English Village* (first published 1975, Full Circle edition undated), *passim*.

106 Arthur Randell *Sixty Years a Fenman* (1966), pp.7–10.

107 Arthur Randell *Fenman*, p.43.

108 Diaries of Edward Lee Hicks, Bishop of Lincoln *Lincolnshire Record Society* vol. 82 (1993), p.233.

109 NRO, FX 357/1.

110 *Victoria County History of Huntingdonshire* vol. 3, quoting a report in *Nature* 6 October 1934.

111 Charles Lucas, *The Fenman's World* (1930), p.10.

112 Gordon *op. cit.*, p.222.

113 Cyril Marsters, *Boys on a Branch: A King's Lynn and Isle of Ely Boyhood* (2005), pp.79–83.

114 A.K. Astbury, *The Black Fens* (1970 edition), pp.67–68.

115 E.P. Brand, *A Fenman Remembers* (1977), *passim*.

116 *Fenland Railwayman*, pp.31–32.

117 Marsters *op. cit.*, pp.61–68.

118 *Fenland Railwayman*, p.39.

119 Christopher Taylor, *Roads and Tracks of Britain* (1979), p.181.

120 Winifred E. Long, 'The Changing Face of Fenland' in *East Anglian Magazine*, 11, 1952, pp.600–603.

121 Paul Mould, *Wartime Schooldays in Boston* (1986), pp.34–35.

122 Norfolk Federation of Women's Institutes, *Norfolk within Living Memory* (1995), pp.150–151.

123 Mike Osborne, *Pillboxes of Britain and N. Ireland*, (2008) *passim*.

124 Trevor Bevis, *From Out of the Sky – March in World War Two* (1978).

125 Terry Hancock, 'The RAF in Lincolnshire' in Bennett and Bennett, editors, *op. cit.*, p.128.

126 Robert Gretzyngier, *Poles in Defence of Britain* (2001), p.5, 28, 45.

127 Brand *op. cit.*, p.88.

128 *Fenland Railwayman*, pp.73–74.

129 Marsters *op. cit.*, pp.94–104.

130 Mould, *op. cit.*, p.21.

131 Anonymous, *The Battle of the Banks*, p.28.

132 Astbury, *op. cit.*, p.69.

133 J. Wentworth Day, *A History of the Fens* (1954), pp.253–254.

134 H.C. Darby, *The Changing Fenland*, p.226.

135 Mary Chamberlain, *op cit.*, p.53, 114.

136 Dennis Mills, ed., *Twentieth Century Lincolnshire* (1989), pp.167–169.

137 Pryor, *op. cit.*

138 Labrum, *op. cit.*, p.107.

139 Charles Kingsley, *Hereward the Wake*.

BIBLIOGRAPHY

The books by Richard Gurnham and Paul Richards describe the two urban centres within the Fens and could be seen as a trilogy together with this book. The other books amplify the themes of rural Fenland discussed in this book.

Astbury, A. K., *The Black Fens* (1970)

Chamberlain, Mary, *Fenwomen* (1975)

Charnley, Peter, *Old Dykes I Have Known*

Clarke, J. A., *Fenland Studies* (1852)

Darby, H. C., *The Medieval Fenland* (1940)

Darby, H. C., *The Draining of the Fens* (1956)

Gurnham, Richard, *The Story of Boston* (2014)

Hills, R. L., *Machines, Mills and Uncountable Costly Necessities* (1967)

Lucas, Charles, *The Fenman's World* (1930)

Marshall, Sybil, *Fenland Chronicle* (1967)

Marsters, Cyril, *Boys on a Branch: a King's Lynn and Isle of Ely Boyhood* (2005)

Richards, Paul, *King's Lynn* (2006)

Randell, Arthur, *Fenland Railwayman* (1968)

Ravensdale, J. R., *Liable to Floods* (1974)

Swift, Graham, *Waterland* (1983)

Wheeler, W. H., *A History of the Fens of South Lincolnshire* (1868)

INDEX